TALKING HORSE

◆

A TALKING HORSE   *First Draft*

Abramowitz wonders.

Whether Am I a man in a horse, or just a horse that talks—whoever deserves that fate? If the first, then Jonah had it better in his Big Fish; *we weren't* at least lots more room—also he knew where he was and how he got (in) there. After three days and nights the Fish stopped at Ninevah and Jonah got off. But Abramowitz is no *But not Abramowitz; no prophet.* Prophet. On the contrary, he works in a circus sideshow—recently advanced to a ring inside the main tent—with his deaf-mute master, Goldberg—may the Almighty punish him for his sins. All I know is I've been trapped here for a long time and still don't understand the nature of my fate; in short, if I'm Abramowitz, a horse, or a horse including Abramowitz. [Maybe it's a punishment for something I said or thought, or did, or didn't do, in my past life.]

Yet sometimes when Abramowitz was standing in his narrow stall chewing in his bag of yellow oats, he had thoughts, far-away memories, they seemed, of young horses racing in green fields. So who's to say what's the truth?

I've asked Goldberg, who talks to me rarely in private, and usually with his bull whip—*slashing cane* there's oats and once in a while a joke to make me relax, but usually there's pain—and sometimes *how add these* he taps out a Morse Code message on the top of my skull with his big knuckle—crack crack crack—when he wants to tell me what to do next, or how many lashes for this last mistake [I made]; *mg* but his first message I remember was NO QUESTIONS. UNDERSTOOD? I shook my head and a little bell jingled under the forelock. [It was the first time I knew it was there.]

To weaken Abramowitz like this. Flashback?

TALK, he knocked on my head.

I answered, "Yes." What else could I say?

My voice [must have] surprised me when it first [came through a tunnel [the size] of a horse's neck; but I could be wrong. Goldberg is a deaf mute; he reads my lips. Once when he was drunk and verging towards sentimental he tapped to me that I used to carry goods on my back to fairs and markets before we joined the circus, but I don't remember that or even when we joined the circus; [I *thought?* figured I was born there.]

"On a rainy, snowy, crappy night," Goldberg tapped out on my skull.

Facsimile of the first page of Malamud's annotated first draft of "Talking Horse."
Reproduced with permission from the Collections of the Library of Congress.

TALKING HORSE

◆

Bernard Malamud on Life and Work

EDITED BY

Alan Cheuse and Nicholas Delbanco

COLUMBIA UNIVERSITY PRESS *New York*

Columbia University Press

New York   Chichester, West Sussex

Copyright © 1996 Alan Cheuse and Nicholas Delbanco

All rights reserved

Library of Congress Cataloging-in-Publication Data

Malamud, Bernard.

    Talking horse : Bernard Malamud on life and work / edited by Alan Cheuse and Nicholas Delbanco.

       p. cm.

    ISBN 0–231–10184–8

    1. Malamud, Bernard. 2. American fiction—History and criticism—Theory, etc. 3. Jewish fiction—History and criticism—Theory, etc. 4. Novelists, American—20th century—Biography. 5. Fiction—Authorship. 6. Jews in literature. I. Cheuse, Alan.
II. Delbanco, Nicholas. III. Title.

PS3563.A4Z475   1996

813'.54—dc20   95–25957

For Ann Malamud

◆

Home is where the book is.

—B. MALAMUD, *The Tenants*

CONTENTS

◆

ACKNOWLEDGMENTS

◆

First, and foremost, we are grateful to the members of the Malamud family: Ann Malamud, Paul Malamud, and Janna Malamud Smith. Without their encouragement, this book would not exist. We would also like to thank the literary executors of Bernard Malamud's estate—Robert Giroux, Timothy Seldes, Daniel Stern—for their full and free permission of access to the files. In his additional capacities as agent for the Malamud estate and as agent for this book, Timothy Seldes in particular has been indispensable.

Alice Birney and the staff of the Manuscript Room at the Library of Congress were helpful and expeditious throughout this lengthy process, and Glenn Horowitz, Bookseller, also provided his kind expertise. We are grateful to Bernard Malamud's publishers, Farrar, Straus & Giroux— and especially to Roger Straus—for permission to quote at length from the author's work. The Office of the Vice President for Research at the University of Michigan provided welcome funding assistance, and we are grateful to Margaret Price for her meticulous editorial labor. The Publisher for the Humanities at Columbia University Press, Jennifer Crewe, helped and advised us throughout. Finally, our wives—Kristin O'Shee and Elena Delbanco—supported as well as tolerated our collaborative enterprise for the past four years. Thank you, thank you all.

◆

The achievement of Bernard Malamud is well known and widely recognized. He was and is a master of American prose. Few writers have had as respectful an audience in their lifetimes; few writers seem more likely to endure. There are conferences in his honor, a prestigious award in his name, even "The Bernard Malamud Society" (founded in 1991), and a newsletter to which his adepts subscribe. His fiction thrives in paperback and translation, on bookstore and library shelves; the critical bibliography grows apace.

What follows is a collection of prose that should remind those who need the reminding of what our late colleague accomplished. For the first time since his death in 1986, his family and executors have given unimpeded access to thousands of pages of notebooks, essays, unpublished manuscripts, lecture material, and letters. In solitude, for many decades, and with no view to publication, Malamud engaged the subject of prose fiction with an ambition tempered by modesty and a seriousness leavened by wit. And *Talking Horse* should reaffirm, if such affirmation be needed, the size and special nature of this writer's gift.

One aspect of the career, however, seems to us ill understood. Malamud was not some sort of instinctual fabulist with no need to "talk shop." In his lifetime he published prose fiction—those short stories and novels for which he grew famous—and nearly nothing else. Yet his books did not spring full-blown out of the surrounding air. His notebooks, letters, and his few published ruminations on the art of writing attest to a thoroughly self-conscious and disciplined artist—a picture at important odds with the widespread public notion of the author as a "natural." Moreover, and since he remained so resolutely private about the construction of his finished work, even the most devoted of his readers have little idea of how much he wrote about the enterprise of art.

"There's no one way," as he remarks. "There's so much drivel about this subject." Yet in little and large ways over the years he addressed himself unstintingly to the preservation and instruction of the artistic self. While there are writers who may fairly be described as indifferent caretakers of their talent, Malamud proved conscientious in the extreme. And this idea of preservation is central to our present project; *Talking Horse*, both in its component parts and its entirety, shows the extent to which he knew himself custodial—as he put it in a lecture in 1984, at the age of seventy—of his "Long Work, Short Life."

It may be useful here to summarize, briefly, both the life and work. Bernard Malamud was born in the Gravesend section of Brooklyn on April 26, 1914, the son of an immigrant shopkeeper, Max Malamud, and his theatrically talented wife, Bertha Fidelman. Although the New York boroughs in this time hosted many an enclave thick with Jews, Gravesend was not one of them. Cross the East River and head north toward Harlem and you would find the world of Henry Roth, kids climbing hills in Mount Morris Park or diving off rocks into the cooling Hudson. In this section of Brooklyn, however, Malamud's father's grocery store stood like a small Jewish island in a Gentile sea.

"My parents worked late," he explained in one of his rare autobiographical revelations, "and I was allowed to stay out late and wander in the neighborhood. We skated, sledded, climbed trees, and played running games." An occasional trip to Coney Island offered an expansive vista and alternative horizon: "The ocean, especially at night, moved me". . . .

So did literature. His formal education commenced at Erasmus Hall High School, where his compositions received high grades and his first stories and sketches appeared in the high school magazine. Crossing the river to attend classes at City College of New York, he received his bachelor's degree at the age of twenty-two in 1936. Less a late bloomer than slow starter, he honed his prose assiduously while teaching high school at Erasmus Hall and in Harlem; at Columbia University Malamud produced an M.A. thesis, "The Reception of Thomas Hardy's Poetry in

America." Ann de Chiara (an Italian-American from New Rochelle, New York) and he were married in 1945 and, two years later, their son Paul was born. In 1952—the year of *The Natural*—their daughter Janna arrived.

For twelve years (1949–1961) he taught at Oregon State College (now Oregon State University) at Corvallis; thereafter he served on the faculty of Bennington College in Bennington, Vermont. For two years (1966–1968) he taught at Harvard College, but this most urban of authors responded most strongly to landscape; *A New Life* and *Dubin's Lives* celebrate, respectively, Oregon and Vermont. And the man who seemed the picture of the sedentary writer—always at his desk—also loved to move about. The Malamuds traveled a good deal—in Europe, Israel, and the Soviet Union—and settled for brief periods in Rome, London, Cambridge, and Palo Alto. In his last years he divided his time between the clapboard "country" house in New England and an apartment on Manhattan's Upper West Side.

"One day I began to write seriously: my writing had begun to impress me. Years of all sorts had gone by." The writing impressed others too. From his first commercial publication (short stories in *The Partisan Review*, *Harper's Bazaar*, and *Commentary*) in 1950 through *The Assistant* (1957), *The Magic Barrel* (1958), and *A New Life* (1961), Malamud acquired a steadily expanding readership. He alternated a collection of stories with a novel, turn by turn; his honors would come to include the Rosenthal Foundation Award of the National Institute of Arts and Letters, the Pulitzer Prize and, twice, the National Book Award. By *Idiot's First* (1963) and *The Fixer* (1966), his reputation had grown worldwide; he received the Jewish Heritage Award, the Governor's Award from the Vermont Council on the Arts, the Brandeis Creative Arts Award, and—for *The Stories of Bernard Malamud* (1983)—the American Academy-Institute Gold Medal for Fiction. His other titles consist of the short-story collection *Pictures of Fidelman: An Exhibition* (1969), *The Tenants* (1971), *Rembrandt's Hat* (1973), *Dubin's Lives* (1979), and *God's Grace* (1982). He chose and named *The Stories of Bernard Malamud* carefully, calling them neither "Selected" nor "Collected," and in the preface to that volume averred: "Working alone to create stories, despite serious inconveniences, is not a bad way to live our human loneliness." *The People and Uncollected Stories* (a novel-in-progress, together with stories chosen by the author's longtime editor Robert Giroux) appeared as an *opus posthumous* in 1989.

A resolutely private person, Malamud left neither scandal nor biographers behind. In 1970 he explained this reticence by letter to a Library of Congress official:

> I'm still writing and expect to be writing for the next ten to fifteen years. I think it hurts a writer to have his secrets known—his method of working disclosed while he is still active. It would bother me; so much of writing is a fragile thing, so much depends on one's ability to maintain illusion. I don't want the privacy of that invaded in any way; I don't want people to know now—and write about—how I do things.

Yet the "Malamud Finding" at the Library of Congress—where the bulk of his papers reside—offers a detailed and meticulous accounting of the writer's life. We mean by this his life in art: draft after draft of the stories and novels, research notes, clippings, speeches, a reader's journal, lesson plans, and responses to questions abound. He was scrupulous as to procedure, systematic in his methodology, and retentive of his "by-blows"; in the age of the computer and the daily discard of revision it's improbable we'll find again so comprehensive a road map of one mind's terrain.

Story after story and chapter after chapter represent this process of revision, a series of stages—sometimes as many as eighteen drafts—from holograph to galley proofs wherein the prose gets reworked. Malamud hand-wrote the *third* draft of *The Assistant*, for example, after his wife had typed a second draft from the handwritten first. Outline after outline and query after query provide a kind of "lesson plan," as though the habits of the high-school teacher stayed deeply ingrained in the professional author; he became his own instructor in the discipline of art.

Here (from a talk Malamud gave at Harvard's Kirkland House in December 1966) is a description of his method of composition:

> The major advantage is that an outline prefigures form. If you can get form into an outline, you can prefigure the form that you need in your book, it does give you a sense of the whole. It divides the work. The labor may appeal to you simply because the work can't be divided into chapters and sections as less formidable when you consider it piece by piece. And let's face it, working on an outline over and over again could lead the story to grow. And there are some people who won't even begin writing until they've done a

number of outlines over a certain period of time. I tend to be that way. I tend to have an idea for a book and then do a cursory outline of it, or as large or detailed outline of it as I can. Then I put it away. After several months I come back to it. I look it over and work it over and try to get something more out of it. When I say something more, I mean something more in terms of possibility in terms of form, in terms of excitement for myself as I look it over. If I am satisfied, then I may begin the book. But if I still feel that something is lacking, I may rewrite the outline right then two or three more times until I get something again that looks like form. If that doesn't work, I may put it aside for a while again and then come back to it hoping that somewhere along the line in between I've got some ideas that have bolstered some of the sections, that connect them better, that give me riper ideas, richer ideas. And I try that. And then finally when I have something that looks like a good kick-off point, because an outline, please note, is not a straitjacket, it is a take-off point, it is the equivalent of a scientific hypothesis, you are really saying to yourself, On the basis of this, I think I can write a book. And this is what you're betting on and this is what you carry on from.

Henry James went out to dinner three hundred times a season and kept his notebooks assiduously; why should a chance remark at table have engendered *Portrait of a Lady*, and the next remark be merely gossip to his ear? Tolstoy read the paper each morning; why should an article about a woman and a train have engendered *Anna Karenina* and the adjacent article about a man and carriage, say, have caused him, yawning, to turn the page? The world is full of instances, of stimuli; the question for the writer is more properly perhaps: what triggers a response? How may one recognize a subject or, in Malamud's fine phrase, learn "what one's fiction wants him to say."

For once he *did* respond to or recognize a subject he left very little to chance. He filled notebook and journal with citations and quotations and articles and buttressing data; if his character went walking, he listed the flowers by season; if he read about the Nez Perces, he listed—for possible use in his character's sojourn in the region—authentic tribal names. As suggested above, the image of this writer as a "natural," a kind of Mickey Mantle if not Roy Hobbs of prose fiction—whose swing was smooth, whose stride had no hitch—is almost entirely wrong. The author of *The Natural* was in fact ceaselessly self-tutored, and the "Malamud finding" provides a major demonstration of the value of such tutelage: a focused inquiry not so much upon the teller as the tale.

Often such labor seemed grievous, its pleasure transmuted to pain. The hero of the novel for which he's now most famous does not hit a home run (as in the movie version of that baseball book, where Robert Redford explodes the grandstand night-lights into fireworks) but rather implodes and strikes out. Thomas Edison remarked that "Genius is one percent inspiration and ninety-nine percent perspiration," and that proportion holds equally true for one of the paired protagonists of Malamud's urban parable, *The Tenants*. Here "Lesser" describes his failed work.

Although he had sat at his desk for hours, that day for the first time in more than a year Lesser had been unable to write a single sentence. It was as though the book had asked him to say more than he knew; he could not meet its merciless demands. Each word weighed like a rock. If you've been writing a book for ten years time adds time to each word; they weigh like rocks—the weight of waiting for the end, to become the book. Though he struggled to go on, every thought, every decision, was impossible. Lesser felt depression settle on his head like a sick crow. When he couldn't write he doubted the self; this expressed itself in reservations about the quality of his talent—was it really talent, not an illusion he had dreamed up to keep himself writing? And when he doubted the self he couldn't write. Sitting at his desk in the bright morning light, scanning yesterday's pages, he had felt about to throw up: language, form, his plan and purpose. He felt sick to death of the endless, uncompleted, beastly book, the discipline of writing, the overdedicated, ultimately limited, writer's life. It needn't be so but was for Lesser. What have I done to myself? So much I no longer see or feel except in language. Life once removed. So against the will he had taken the morning off and gone for a walk in the February sun. Lesser tried to put his thoughts out of mind as he walked. He named his unhappiness "depression," and let it go at that; for though he presently resisted everything concerned with writing he could not forget he wanted more than anything else to write a fine book.

Again:

Sometimes the writing goes really badly. It is painful when images meant to marry repel each other, when reflections, ideas, won't coalesce. When he forgets what he meant to write and hasn't written. When he forgets words or words forget him. He types wither for either all the time. Lesser sometimes feels despair's shovel digging. He writes against cliffs of resistance. Fear, they say, of completing the book? Once it's done what's there to finish? Fear of the ultimate confession? Why? If I can start another book after this. Confess once more. What's the distant dark mountain in my mind when I write? It won't fade from inscape, sink, evanesce; or volatilize into light. It won't become diaphanous, radiance, fire, Moses himself climbing down the burning rock, Ten lit Commandments tucked under his arm. The writer wants his pen to turn stone into sunlight, language into fire. It's an extraordinary thing to want by a man his size and shape, given all he hasn't got. Lesser lives on his nerve.

His published work should indicate how closely and how often Malamud described the process of prose fiction. Many of his characters live in the workaday world—as grocers' assistants and baseball players, teachers and inmates and castaways and cowboys—yet it's notable how many of them also work in the world of art. He wrote of what he knew. This is an aspect of the oeuvre insufficiently noted by critics: many of his characters are writers, painters, cellists—and towards the end of his creative life explicitly such figures as Alma Werfel Mahler and Virginia Woolf. Fidelman in the series of short stories that comprise his "pictures," Lesser and Willy Shakespeare sweating over pages in *The Tenants*, Dubin composing his "Lives" in his study and on long solitary walks— all these discourse on the nature of imagination, its pleasures and travails. Like their progenitor, they work at the artist's trade.

Malamud was in this regard a modernist; his prose seems in no small part self-referential and focused on the making of the artifact itself. He did not share or emulate the strategies of "metafiction," the aesthetics of Barth, Barthelme, Gass, Hawkes et al., but in important ways his characters face inward at their labor. The figures of "Rembrandt's Hat" or "The Model"—to take just two examples—represent as well as ruminate on the nexus established between art and life. That nexus bears close scrutiny and was often "magical" or "fabulous" in its conjunction of the actual and imagined world, as well as the realistic and the self-reflexive strategy of narration. It is why we've named this volume for the last piece he chose in *The Stories of Bernard Malamud*, "Talking Horse."

He bestowed his mother's maiden name, for instance, on the protagonist of his linked tales: *Pictures of Fidelman: An Exhibition.* Here we have the same self-deprecating intensity of effort, the same distance between intention and execution as that which bedeviled Harry Lesser; the genre has shifted from writing to painting, but the harsh imperatives of work remain the same:

> The copyist throws himself into his work with passion. He has swallowed lightning and hopes it will strike whatever he touches. Yet he has nagging doubts he can do the job right and fears he will never escape alive from the Hotel du Ville. He tries at once to paint the Titian directly on canvas but hurriedly scrapes it clean when he sees what a garish mess he has made. The Venus is insanely disproportionate and the maids in the background foreshortened into dwarfs. He then takes Angelo's advice and makes several drawings on paper to master the composition before committing it again to canvas.
>
> Angelo and Scarpio come up every night and shake their heads over the drawings.
>
> "Not even close," says the padrone.
>
> "Far from it," says Scarpio.
>
> "I'm trying," Fidelman says, anguished.
>
> "Try harder," Angelo answers grimly.

Were there a motto for Malamud's performance as author-teacher, and a single instruction he gave to his students, it resides in the exchange above. *"I'm trying,"* says the anguished apprentice; *"Try harder,"* the master insists. From the "passion" of one who "has swallowed lightning" to the artist plagued by "nagging doubts . . . and fears" we may limn the writer's terrain. And for the Franklin Library, in "A special message to the members of The First Edition Society," he offered his readers an extract from "a careless notebook into which I've looked lately." Although he's writing about *Dubin's Lives*, these lapidary assertions are characteristic Malamudiana—a compound of folk-wisdom, the offhand epigram and laborious *bon mot*.

> One thing about my book that bothers me is that it is reasonable—it lacks madness.
>
> Simplicity is at its potential best coming from one endowed to be more than simple.
>
> So much writing goes on without the right thought.
>
> One must transcend the autobiographical detail by inventing it after it is remembered.
>
> If it is winter in the book spring surprises me when I look up.
>
> At a time of peril one wants to write of peril.

Through story a child learns he has a future.
Every sentence one puts down reduces his thought by one hundred sentences.
How do you make a mystery? Formed, it runs to plot. Unformed, it may
haunt language or live in idea or mood.

Like any good biographer, the eponymous hero of *Dubin's Lives* is
selective—ready to jettison detail—and retentive at the same time. This
held true for his progenitor as well. For every project brought to fruition
there was something he abandoned or deferred. Malamud made extensive notes; he copied out passages verbatim (from critics and source-
books and articles) whether to endorse them or to disagree. Although he
did give interviews (more than twenty-five *Conversations with Bernard
Malamud* have been usefully collected by Lawrence Lasher—University
Press of Mississippi, 1991) he was chary of the essay and the book
review, those secondary staples of the writer's craft. And when he did
compose a speech he left behind multiple versions. Again, from his
remarks at Harvard (Kirkland House, December 1966):

So rewriting is often the best part of writing. The fear of failure is probably
gone because you have it down, it's there. There are fewer chances to take. A
greater effort, in a sense, can be concentrated on style. All I can say about
rewriting is that one ought to rewrite up to the point where he's satisfied,
remembering that a work of art is never completed, it's abandoned. One
must always learn in rewriting to shape the work as if one were squeezing
the best out of it. Rewriting is a form of having a second chance to distill
something or to think over something and there are some writers who find
that their most imaginative ideas come to them as afterthoughts.

A thing worth saying was worth the saying well.

From behind his book, held to his face, he [Dubin] reflected on his silence.
He had nothing to say because he hadn't said it when it was his to say. What
you don't say grows into not saying. A locked house is full of locked rooms.

The bulk of the "Malamud Finding," as well as of our editorial com-
pilation, may be described as a man talking to himself—with a view,
soon, of talking to others. For the house was not locked and the "not saying" provisional; if asked he would answer at length. Mailer, Barth,
Updike, Roth, Hawkes, Bellow, Ellison (to name only a few of the
authors he named) seem like interlocutors, as though the notebook's pri-

vate monologue were part of a public if unspoken dialogue—with a topic on the table and an assumption of shared interest in matters of the trade. Such conversations were rarely casual; Malamud was nothing if not thorough and, as it were, *prepared*.

So our problem was that of exclusion—how to choose, from the thousands of pages, the few hundred we would select. Perhaps no American author since Henry James has devoted himself in such a sustained fashion to the theory and the practice of the writing life. The notion of "a momentary stay against confusion" seems somehow apposite here; he had an abiding need to order and contain his thoughts, a distaste for uncertainty. At the poker or the dinner table this same insistence on order obtained; Malamud saved daring for the prose itself. To see him arrive at a faculty meeting with pages of a penned statement in hand, to watch him check his text or pause to fortify himself with water before venturing, dry-mouthed, to speak was to gain some sense of how seriously he took his role as citizen and how much all this cost.

But precisely because of the effort entailed he did not engage in it often. Not for this writer the talk-show or panel or whirlwind publicity tour. Not for him the sweeping assertion or improvised response. He was, in effect, less secretive than guarded; he espoused the notion that an artist has a fund of psychic capital that might be expended carelessly and must be invested with care. Time after time he took Bartleby's position, "I prefer not to," when asked to go public and discourse on his work. This self-protective caution had its roots in character, but it did not feel obsessive and was not absolute. By comparison with such extreme privacies as those of J. D. Salinger or Thomas Pynchon, for example, Malamud seemed positively forthcoming and—once determined on disclosure—he was courteous, not curt. So it is in the spirit and not in contravention of his method that we have collected these pages; he did choose to have them preserved. And his 1970 caveat ("I think it hurts a writer to have his secrets known—his method of working disclosed while he is still active") no longer, alas, carries weight.

One hallmark of his work, of course, is the seeming-seamless blend of fact and fantasy—a mixture that obtains in ballpark and island and tenement equally. The imagination is allegorical, parabolic; there's an insistent linkage of morality and art. Novelist Herbert Gold, writing of Malamud's tortured souls, called up associations with Dostoevsky, "if we can imagine Dostoevsky tempered by Chagall's lyric nostalgia for a lost Jewish past." That's the Malamud who has one foot in the Old Country.

But the other foot was equally firmly planted in the New World. The personal amalgam stands out more distinctly than that of other writers in his generation, harking back to our home-grown masters (Hawthorne comes insistently to mind, in a story such as "Angel Levine" about black Jews from heaven) and yet forging from the disparate modes of naturalism and magic realism a texture all its own.

This is apparent by the time of his first novel. Malamud's characters are salt of the earth U.S. of A., his plot of "foreign extraction." Thoroughly American in its attention to the sport of baseball, yet "old World" in its underlying fealty to antique myths (from the Grail quest back to the scenarios of vegetation kings and human sacrifice), *The Natural* is thus a mix of Wonder Bread and dark European rye. What also links this early text to the later canon is Malamud's attention to sentence-making and the irony attendant on the meaning of each sentence.

For example, at one point in the successful season of the main character, the "natural" Roy Hobbs, we hear that "he blazed away for her with his golden bat. It was not really golden, it was white, but in the sun it sometimes flashed gold and some of the opposing pitchers complained it shone in their eyes." The cadence of such a construction yields irony, and it also reveals a gift for making wholly English constructions with the bite and flash of inflected speech. In the opening pages of *The Assistant*, we witness Jewish immigrant Morris Bober opening his poor grocery store of a chilly November morning. He has barely finished adding up the first sales of the day (three cents for a roll, and a sale on credit for two dollars) when, Malamud tells us, he looks down the store as if through a long dark tunnel. "The grocer sighed and waited. Waiting he did poorly. When times were bad times was bad. It died as he waited, stinking in his nose."

In the terseness of its irony, Malamud's syntax embraces both the naturalness of fiction and our awareness of its artificiality. Take the case of S. Levin, formerly a drunkard, whose tale of recuperation and reconstitution of self Malamud dramatizes in his third novel, *A New Life*. Having bungled his entry into college teaching by behaving like an honorable man in his department and, in his free time, getting entangled in an affair with the wife of his Department Chair, Levin seems at the end poised to leave: "Flight flew in him," Malamud writes. "He wasn't fleeing yet fled, unable to determine whom he was running from, himself or her. He blamed the flight, paradoxically a pursuit of feeling, on the fact that too much had happened in too short a time."

Close analysis of prose style is, however, not the editors' present intention. Nor is a sustained discussion of the fiction's substance within this volume's scope. *Talking Horse* has been conceived of as an instruction manual for students of this author in particular and, more generally, for anyone who takes an interest in the writer's trade. This is a collective effort, really, an attestation to and demonstration of how very vivid the legacy remains. We have had the unstinting cooperation of the Malamud family, his literary executors and his publishers, as well as personnel at the Library of Congress; we are grateful to them all.

The book has three major components: (1) Those speeches, introductions, and interviews that appeared during Malamud's lifetime but have not been gathered together; (2) those speeches, lesson plans, and essays that he did not usher into print; and (3) a series of unpublished notes and responses and *apercus* as to the nature of prose fiction. The contents of these sections have clustered together, as it were, by contextual affinity and do not follow the logic of chronology; his were lifelong subjects—variations on a theme. Each of the sections that follow has headnotes, but ours is neither a variorum edition nor a close scholarly inquiry into the whole, and much work remains to be done.

Many of these entries are undated; some are handwritten, indistinct. Where unintelligible, we have left a sentence out—and this decision, taken four or five times in the manuscript, is signaled by ellipses. But we have altered nothing beyond orthography, and spelling errors are rare. As teacher, student, colleague, friend, the dead writer quickens for us on every page; the voice is unimpeded and it should be heard.

For years before his death the Malamuds left Bennington during the harsh, grim winter and went south to their home in Manhattan. Often Bern would call or write to those of us who stayed behind and ask a favor—a note or draft or book or letter was in his study in Vermont and now was needed; would it be too much trouble to collect and send it on down? The room where he worked was protected but not, as it were, out of bounds; he left us each a key. And what was astonishing, always, was the precision of his files: if he informed us where a book resided (which corner of which shelf) or a document could be located (which drawer of which cabinet), it came always precisely to hand. It's therefore doubly a pleasure to resume the old habit of hunting through files—to find, as it were, the needed passage and render it available once more.

TALKING HORSE

◆

Part 1

THE MAN AND HIS WORK

◆

♦

EDITOR'S NOTE

I first met Bernard Malamud in
1966. An ambitious boy of twenty-three, I had a novel about to appear
and the self-confident conviction that I could and should replace him
while he took a leave of absence from his teaching job. My editor
informed me that the writer was leaving Bennington College for what
turned out to be a two-year stint in Cambridge, Massachusetts; his position would have to be filled. I applied and drifted into town and was
hired—astonishingly, I still believe—by elders who saw something in
this junior they might shape. By the time the Malamuds returned, I was
happily ensconced as their near neighbor in Vermont; over the years we
grew close.

The relation was avuncular; though Bennington's faculty is
unranked, Malamud was much my senior colleague. It was and is a small
school and town, and the Language and Literature Division seemed very
small indeed. With no hint of condescension he described me as his pro-
tegé; I asked for and took his advice. We attended committee meetings
and movies and concerts and readings and poker games together; we
shared meals and walks. When I married, in 1970, the Malamuds came
to the wedding; my wife Elena and I were part of that party described in
the introduction to the *Paris Review* interview hereafter. The families
grew close. Our daybook bulks large with collective occasions: cocktails,
picnics, weddings, and funerals shared. In times of celebration or trouble—when our daughters were born or had birthdays, during the years
I served as director of the Bennington Writing Workshops, at cere-

monies in his honor or when in failing health Bern needed a hand with a suitcase or car—we saw each other often.

In the fall of 1985 the Delbancos moved to Michigan; the Malamuds came to Ann Arbor to make sure we were properly settled. On January 22, 1986, he gave the annual Hopwood Reading here; it was, to my knowledge, his last public appearance. At his death on March 18, it seemed to me and to my wife and children that we had lost a relative. The loss endures.

This unit has three entries, each previously available in print. First, the brief introduction he composed for his carefully selected, *The Stories of Bernard Malamud*. Next, the extensive interview conducted by the writer Daniel Stern and published in *Writers At Work*, volume 6. Of the many interviews he published in his lifetime, it seems to us the one by which the writer was engaged most fully. And Malamud's single most ambitious self-examination was a lecture prepared and delivered in honor of his longtime Bennington College colleague, the poet Ben Belitt. Titled "Long Work, Short Life," it too deserves full inclusion. Composed in 1984, this memoir may serve as a kind of précis for the autobiography he never produced; though written and revised with care it evokes the author at his conversational ease. Together, these pages comprise reminiscence: as close as we will likely come to the feel and flavor of the life in print. —*Nicholas Delbanco*

1

INTRODUCTION TO *The Stories*
of Bernard Malamud, 1983

◆

One day I began to write seriously: my writing had begun to impress me. Years of all sorts had gone by. The annunciation had long since tolled and the response was slow awakening. Much remained to do and become, if there was time. Some are born whole; others must seek this blessed state in a struggle to achieve order. That is no loss to speak of; ultimately such seeking becomes the subject matter of fiction. Observing, reading, thinking, one invents himself. A familiar voice asks: Who am I, and how can I say what I have to? He reads his sentences to see if the words answer the question. Thus the writer may tell his fortune. His imagination impels him to speak in several tongues though one is sufficient. At this point he, or she, may begin to write a story, a daring endeavor.

My early stories appeared in the nineteen-forties in noncommercial magazines, meaning I didn't get paid for them but was happy to have them published. "The Cost of Living" was the first story I sold. Diarmuid Russell, my agent, sent it to Pearl Kazin at *Harper's Bazaar* in 1949, the year my wife and I left New York for Oregon. About three years later and a few stories in print, Catharine Carver of the *Partisan Review*, to my surprise, wanted "The Magic Barrel," a story I had asked her to read. I had written it in a carrel in the basement of the library at Oregon State, where I was allowed to teach freshman composition but not literature because I was nakedly without a Ph.D. Later, they permitted me to offer a night workshop in the short story to townspeople who, for one reason or another, wanted to take a writing class;

I earned about a hundred dollars a term and got more pleasure than I had expected.

New York had lost much of its charm during World War II, and my wife and I and our infant son took off for the Pacific Northwest when I was offered a job in Corvallis, Oregon. Once there, it was a while before I had my bearings. I was overwhelmed by the beauty of Oregon—its vast skies, forests, coastal beaches—and the new life it offered, which I lived as best I could as I reflected on the old. My almost daily writing—I taught three days a week and wrote the other four—helped me make reasonable choices: what to zero in on and what to omit. On the whole I was learning much about America and holding fast to the discipline of the writing life.

Yet, almost without understanding why, I was thinking about my father's immigrant life (how he earned his meager living and what he paid for it) and about my mother's (diminished by fear and suffering) as perhaps matter for my fiction. In other words, I had them in mind as I invented the characters who became their fictional counterparts. I didn't much worry about what I was asked to teach at the college so long as I had plenty of time to work. My wife, wheeling a stroller, handed me sandwiches at lunchtime through the window of the Quonset hut I wrote and taught in until I gave up writing on Sundays.

It was a while before I was at ease in the new culture—longer for my New Rochelle-born wife. At first I felt displaced—one foot in a bucket—though unafraid of—certainly enjoying—new experience. Yet too much was tiresome. Oregon State, a former land-grant college, had barely covered its cow tracks: Liberal Arts was called the "Lower Division," to no one's embarrassment. But the writing held me steady as I reacted to a more surprising world than the one I had left in Brooklyn when my wife enticed me across the bridge into Manhattan. I was enjoying our young family—my son was four when my Western daughter was born. We were making friends, some of whom became lifelong friends, and were happy we had adventured forth.

At this time I was sharing an office with a colleague who often wished aloud that he were a Jew. I understood the sentiment. I was glad I was, although my father had his doubts about that. He had sat in mourning when I married my gentile wife, but I had thought it through and felt I knew what I was doing. After the birth of our son my father came gently to greet my wife and touch his grandchild. I thought of him as I began *The Assistant* and felt I would often be writing about Jews, in celebration and expiation, though perhaps that was having it both ways.

I wanted it both ways. I conceived of myself as a cosmopolitan man enjoying his freedom.

Before we expected it we were on our way abroad with the happy prospect of a year in Rome. *Partisan Review* had recommended me for a Rockefeller Grant; and the college, somewhat reluctantly, kicked in with my first sabbatical leave. Back in New York City, in 1956, I said hello to Philip Rahv, who gazed at my innocence and thought it was a good idea that I go abroad. We looked up Edna and William Phillips in Paris and afterwards moved into their hotel, the Lutèce, in Montparnasse. In Rome we met Ralph and Fanny Ellison, who were at the American Academy.

Before meeting Ralph I had talked to Saul Bellow one night in Eugene, Oregon, at a lecture he gave. In 1952, after *The Natural* had appeared in a burst of imagination, I called on him at his apartment in Queens. He was about to publish *Augie March*.

That was in 1952. In 1956, after I had written *The Assistant*, Diarmuid Russell submitted it to Robert Giroux, who had bought *The Natural* for Harcourt, Brace. *The Assistant* had been to Harcourt before Giroux read it for Farrar, Straus, where he was now editor in chief. He cabled his acceptance as I sailed the high seas.

Almost from the beginning of my career as a writer I have more or less alternated between writing novels and periods of work on short stories. I like the change of pace and form. I've enjoyed working in both forms—prose makes specific demands—although I confess having been longer in love with short fiction. If one begins early in life to make up and tell stories he has a better chance to be heard out if he keeps them short. *"Vus boks du mir a chinik?"* ("What tune are you banging on your pot?") my father once asked me when I went into a long tale about my mother's cousin.

Writing the short story, if one has that gift, is a good way to begin writing seriously. It demands form as it teaches it, although I've met some who would rather not be taught. They say that the demands of form interfere with their freedom to express themselves. But no good writer writes only as he pleases. He writes for a purpose, an idea, an effect; he writes to make himself understood and felt. I'm for freedom of thought, but one must recognize that it doesn't necessarily lead to art. Free thought may come close to self-deceit. One pays for free thought in the wrong cause if it intrudes, interferes with the logic of language and construction—if it falls like a hammer blow on the head as one is attempting to work out his fiction. Standards diluted at the start may exact a mean toll. Not many "make it" as serious writers of fiction, especially those who think of form as a catchword. Elitism in a just cause has its merits. Some in art have, by definition, to be best. There are standards in literature that a would-be writer must become familiar with—must uphold: as in the work of the finest writers of the past. The best endures in the accomplishment of the masters. One will be convinced, if one reads conscientiously and widely, that form as ultimate necessity is the basis of literature.

Soon I began to teach what Randall Jarrell called "imaginative writing," and most college catalogues—when these courses became popular after World War II—list as Creative Writing and teach too much of. I had gone into teaching with certain doubts—although I felt I could teach effectively—in order to support my family and get on with my writing. But being a teacher never interfered with my best concerns as a writer. I wrote steadily and happily, although it took Diarmuid Russell at least three years to sell a story. I had come to him via Maxim Lieber, who had never succeeded in selling any of my early work. "Here are some of your chickens coming home to roost" was his cheery word when he returned two or three stories. Afterwards, for one reason or another, he disappeared into Mexico, and when I last heard of him, was alive in Poland.

The doubts I speak of went with the job, for not everybody who joined my classes was a talented writer. Too many were in who should have been out. I had to teach anybody who wanted to be in my classes, though that changed when I began to teach at Bennington, where nobody frowned if I taught only six or eight people. Talent is always in short supply, although I had a handful of good writing students whom I enjoyed teaching and learning from. In essence one doesn't teach writing; he encourages talented people whom he may be able to do something for. I feel that writing courses are of limited value, although they do induce some students to read fiction with care. On the whole I think such courses are overdone and overvalued. A year of them, at the most, can be helpful. After that, "creative writing" must yield to independent work with some serious self-exploration going on, or the young writer will never come up with a meaningful subject matter and theme to organize his thinking around, and thus begin to provide himself with material for the long pull of a serious career. The more a writer does for himself, the better off he is. He mustn't be satisfied merely with learning tricks of the trade. Writing teaches the writer. Learning the art of the (human) sentence can keep him gainfully employed most, if not all, of his writing life.

Some writers don't need the short story to launch them into fiction, but I think it is a loss not to attempt to find out whether one can write them. I love the pleasures of the short story. One of them is the fast payoff. Whatever happens happens quickly. The writer mounts his personal Pegasus, even if it is an absentminded nag who never made it on the race track; an ascension occurs and the ride begins. The scenery often surprises, and so do some of the people one meets. Somewhere I've said that a short story packs a self in a few pages predicating a lifetime. The drama is tense, happens fast, and is more often than not outlandish. In a few pages a good story portrays the complexity of a life while producing the surprise and effect of knowledge—not a bad payoff.

Then the writer is into the story for more than the ride. He stays with it as the terrain opens and events occur; he takes pleasure in the evolving fiction and tries to foresee its just resolution. As soon as his characters sense his confidence they show him their tricks. Before he knows it he becomes a figure in a circus with a boom-boom band. This puts him in high spirits and good form. If he's lucky, serious things may seem funny.

Much occurs in the writing that isn't expected, including some types you meet and become attached to. Before you know it you've collected two or three strangers swearing eternal love and friendship before they begin to make demands that divide and multiply. García Márquez will start a fiction with someone pushing a dream around, or running from one, and before you know it he has peopled a small country. Working alone to create stories, despite serious inconveniences, is not a bad way to live our human loneliness.

And let me say this: literature, since it values man by describing him, tends toward morality in the same way that Robert Frost's poem is "a momentary stay against confusion." Art celebrates life and gives us our measure.

I've lived long among those I've invented.

"Good morning, Professor. Are you by any chance looking for a bride, I offer only the best quality."

"I've got one, Salzman, but if she should come up with other plans I'll let you know. In the meantime, I'm hard at work on a new story."

"So enjoy," said Salzman.

2

◆

Bernard Malamud lives in a white clapboard house in Bennington, Vermont. Spacious and comfortable, it sits on a gentle downward slope, behind it the rise of the Green Mountains. To this house on April 26, 1974, came friends, family, colleagues, and the children of friends—to celebrate Malamud's sixtieth birthday. It was a sunny weekend, the weather and ambience benign, friendly.

There were about a half-dozen young people taking their rest in sleeping bags in various bedrooms and in a home volunteered by a friend and neighbor. Three of them, from nearby universities, were children of friends on the faculty of Oregon State University more than a dozen years ago.

On Saturday night there was a birthday party, with champagne, birthday cake, and dancing. At the end of the evening the young people drummed up a show of slides: scenes of past travels; in particular, scenes of Corvallis, Oregon, where Malamud had lived and taught for twelve years before returning East.

Bernard Malamud is a slender man with a graying mustache and inquisitive brown eyes that search and hide a little at the same time. He is a quiet man who listens a lot, and responds freely. His wife, Ann, an attractive, articulate woman of Italian descent, had planned the party, assisted by the young people from Oregon and the Malamuds' son, Paul, and daughter, Janna.

The taping of the interview began late Friday morning, on the back porch, which overlooks a long, descending sweep of lawn and, in the distance, the encircling mountains. It was continued later in the book-filled study where Malamud writes. (He also writes in his office at Bennington College.) At first he was conscious of the tape recorder, but grew less so as the session—and the weekend—continued. He has a quick laugh and found it easy to discourse on the questions asked. An ironic humor would seem to be his mother tongue.

DANIEL STERN (INTERVIEWER): Why sixty? I understand that when the *Paris Review* asked you to do an interview after the publication of *The Fixer*, you suggested doing it when you hit sixty?

MALAMUD: Right. It's a respectable round number, and when it becomes your age you look at it with both eyes. It's a good time to see from. In the past I sometimes resisted interviews because I had no desire to talk about myself in relation to my fiction. There are people who always want to make you a character in your stories and want you to confirm it. Of course there's some truth to it: every character you invent takes his essence from you; therefore you're in them as Flaubert was in Emma—but, peace to him, you are not those you imagine. They are your fictions. And I don't like questions of explication: What did I mean by this or that? I want the books to speak for themselves. You can read? All right, tell me what my books mean. Astonish me.

INTERVIEWER: What about a little personal history? There's been little written about your life.

MALAMUD: That's how I wanted it—I like privacy, and as much as possible to stay out of my books. I know that's disadvantageous to certain legitimate kinds of criticism of literature, but my needs come first. Still, I have here and there talked a little about my life: my father was a grocer; my mother, who helped him, after a long illness, died young. I had a younger brother who lived a hard and lonely life and died in his fifties. My mother and father were gentle, honest, kindly people, and who they were and their affection for me to some degree made up for the cultural deprivation I felt as a child. They weren't educated, but their values were stable. Though my father always managed to make a living, they were comparatively poor, especially in the Depression, and yet I never heard a word in praise of the buck. On the other hand, there were no books that I remember in the house, no records, music, pictures on the wall. On Sundays I listened to somebody's piano through the window. At nine I caught pneumonia, and when I was convalescing my father bought me *The Book of Knowledge*, twenty volumes where there had been none. That was, considering the circumstances, an act of great generosity. When I was in high school he bought a radio. As a kid, for entertainment I turned to the movies and dime novels. Maybe *The Natural* derives from Frank Merriwell as well as the adventures of the Brooklyn Dodgers in Ebbets Field. Anyway, my parents stayed close to the store. Once in a while, on Jewish holidays, we went visiting, or saw a Jewish play—Sholem Aleichem, Peretz, and others. My mother's brother, Charles Fidelman, and their cousin, Isidore Cashier, were in the Yiddish theater.

Around the neighborhood the kids played chase-the-white-horse, ringolevio, buck-buck, punchball, and one o'cat. Occasionally we stole tomatoes from the Italian dirt farmers, gypped the El to ride to Coney Island, smoked in cellars, and played blackjack. I wore sneakers every summer. My education at home derived mostly from the presence and example of good, feelingful, hardworking people. They were worriers, with other faults I wasn't much conscious of until I recognized them in myself. I learned from books, in the public schools. I had some fine teachers in grammar school, Erasmus Hall High School, and later in City College, in New York. I took to literature and early wanted to be a writer.

DS: How early?

MALAMUD: At eight or nine I was writing little stories in school and feeling the glow. To any one of my friends who'd listen I'd recapitulate at tedious length the story of the last movie I'd seen. The movies tickled my imagination. As a writer I learned from Charlie Chaplin.

DS: What in particular?

MALAMUD: Let's say the rhythm, the snap of comedy; the reserved comic presence—that beautiful distancing; the funny with sad; the surprise of surprise.

DS: Please go on about your life.

MALAMUD: Schools meant a lot to me, those I went to and taught at. You learn what you teach and you learn from those you teach. In 1942 I met my wife, and we were married in 1945. We have two children and have lived in Oregon, Rome, Bennington, Cambridge, London, New York, and have traveled a fair amount. In sum, once I was twenty and not so young, now I'm sixty inclined on the young side.

DS: Which means?

MALAMUD: Largely, the life of imagination, and doing pretty much what I set out to do. I made my mistakes, took my lumps, learned. I resisted my ignorance, limitations, obsessions. I'm freer than I was. I'd rather write it than talk. I love the privileges of form.

DS: You've taught during the time you were a professional writer?

MALAMUD: Thirty-five years—

DS: There are some who say teaching doesn't do the writer much good; in fact it restricts life and homogenizes experience. Isn't a writer better off on the staff of the *New Yorker*, or working for the BBC? Faulkner fed a furnace and wrote for the movies.

MALAMUD: Doesn't it depend on the writer? People experience similar things differently. Sometimes I've regretted the time I've given to teaching, but not teaching itself. And a community of serious readers is a miraculous thing. Some of the most extraordinary people I've met were students of mine, or colleagues. Still, I ought to say I teach only a single class of prose fiction, one term a year. I've taught since I was twenty-five, and though I need more time for reading and writing, I also want to keep on doing what I can do well and enjoy doing.

DS: Do you teach literature?

MALAMUD: If you teach prose fiction, you are teaching literature. You teach those who want to write to read fiction, even their own work, with greater understanding. Sometimes they're surprised to find out how much they've said or not said that they didn't know they had.

DS: Can one, indeed, teach writing?

MALAMUD: You teach writers—assuming a talent. At the beginning young writers pour it out without much knowing the nature of their talent. What you try to do is hold a mirror up to their fiction so, in a sense, they can see what they're showing. Not all who come forth are fully armed. Some are gifted in narrative, some shun it. Some show a richness of metaphor, some have to dig for it. Some writers think language is all they need; they mistake it for subject matter. Some rely on whimsy. Some on gut feeling. Some of them don't make the effort to create a significant form. They do automatic writing and think they're probing themselves. The odd thing is, most young writers write traditional narrative until you introduce them to the experimental writers—not for experiment's sake, but to try something for size. Let the writer attempt whatever he can. There's no telling where he will come out stronger than before. Art is in life, but the realm is endless.

DS: Experiment at the beginning?

MALAMUD: Sometimes a new technique excites a flood of fictional ideas. Some, after experimenting, realize their strength is in traditional modes. Some, after trying several things, may give up the thought of writing fiction—not a bad thing. Writing—the problems, the commitment, the effort, scares them. Some may decide to try poetry or criticism. Some turn to painting—why not? I have no kick against those who use writing, or another art, to test themselves, to find themselves. Sometimes I have to tell them their talents are thin—not to waste their lives writing third-rate fiction.

DS: Fidelman as a painter? The doubtful talent?

MALAMUD: Yes. Among other things, it is a book about finding a vocation. Forgive the soft impeachment.

DS: In *Fidelman* and *The Tenants* you deal with artists who can't produce, or produce badly. Why does the subject interest you so much? Have you ever been blocked?

MALAMUD: Never. Even in anxiety I've written, though anxiety, because it is monochromatic, may limit effects. I like the drama of nonproductivity, especially where there may be talent. It's an interesting ambiguity: the force of the creative versus the paralysis caused by the insults, the confusions of life.

DS: What about work habits? Some writers, especially at the beginning, have problems settling how to do it.

MALAMUD: There's no one way—there's so much drivel about this subject. You're who you are, not Fitzgerald or Thomas Wolfe. You write by sitting down and writing. There's no particular time or place—you suit yourself, your nature. How one works, assuming he's disciplined, doesn't matter. If he or she is not disciplined, no sympathetic magic will help. The trick is to make time—not steal it—and produce the fiction. If the stories come, you get them written, you're on the right track. Eventually everyone learns his or her own best way. The real mystery to crack is you.

DS: What about the number of drafts? Some writers write only one.

MALAMUD: They're cheating themselves. First drafts are for learning what your novel or story is about. Revision is working with that knowledge to enlarge and enhance an idea, to re-form it. D. H. Lawrence, for instance, did seven or eight drafts of *The Rainbow*. The first draft of a book is the most uncertain—where you need guts, the ability to accept the imperfect until it is better. Revision is one of the true pleasures of writing. "The men and things of today are wont to lie fairer and truer in tomorrow's memory," Thoreau said.

DS: Do you teach your own writing?

MALAMUD: No, I teach what I know about writing.

DS: What specific piece of advice would you give to young writers?

MALAMUD: Write your heart out.

DS: Anything else?

MALAMUD: Watch out for self-deceit in fiction. Write truthfully but with cunning.

DS: Anything special to more experienced types?

MALAMUD: To any writer: teach yourself to work in uncertainty. Many writers are anxious when they begin, or try something new. Even Matisse painted some of his fauvist pictures in anxiety. Maybe that helped him to simplify. Character, discipline, negative capability count. Write, complete, revise. If it doesn't work, begin something else.

DS: And if it doesn't work twenty or thirty times?

MALAMUD: You live your life as best you can.

DS: I've heard you talk about the importance of subject matter?

MALAMUD: It's always a problem. Very young writers who don't know themselves obviously often don't know what they have to say. Sometimes by staying with it they write themselves into a fairly rich vein. Some, by the time they find what they're capable of writing about, no longer want to write. Some go through psychoanalysis or a job in a paint factory and begin to write again. One hopes they then have something worth saying. Nothing is guaranteed. Some writers have problems with subject matter not in their first book, which may mine old childhood experience, or an obsession, or fantasy, or the story they've carried in their minds and imagination to this point, but after that—after this first yield—often they run into trouble with their next few books. Especially if the first book is unfortunately a best seller. And some writers run into difficulties at the end, particularly if they exclude important areas of personal experience from their writing. Hemingway would not touch his family beyond glimpses in short stories, mostly the Nick Adams pieces. He once wrote his brother that their mother was a bitch and father a suicide—who'd want to read about them? Obviously not all his experience is available to a writer for purposes of fiction, but I feel that if Hemingway had tried during his last five years, let's say, to write about his father rather than the bulls once more, or the big fish, he mightn't have committed suicide. Mailer, after *The Naked and the Dead*, ran into trouble he couldn't resolve until he invented his mirror-image, Aquarius, Prisoner of Sex, Doppelgänger, without whom he can't write. After he had invented "Norman Mailer" he produced *The Armies of the Night*, a beautiful feat of prestidigitation, if not fiction. He has still to write, Richard Poirier says, his *Moby Dick*. To write a good big novel he will have to invent other selves, richly felt selves. Roth, since *Portnoy*, has been hunting for a fruitful subject. He's tried various strategies to defeat the obsession of the hated wife he almost never ceases to write about. He'll have at last to bury her to come up with a new comedy.

DS: What about yourself?

MALAMUD: I say the same thing in different worlds.

DS: Anything else to say to writers—basic stuff?

MALAMUD: Take chances. "Dare to do," Eudora Welty says. She's right. One drags around a bag of fears he has to throw to the winds every so often if he expects to take off in his writing. I'm glad Virginia Woolf did *Orlando*, though it isn't my favorite of her books, and in essence she was avoiding a subject. Still, you don't have to tell everything you know. I like Updike's *Centaur*, Bellow's *Henderson*. Genius, after it has got itself together, may give out with a *Ulysses* or *Remembrance of Things Past*. One doesn't have to imitate the devices of Joyce or Proust, but if you're not a genius, imitate the daring. If you are a genius, assert yourself, in art and humanity.

DS: Humanity? Are you suggesting art is moral?

MALAMUD: It tends toward morality. It values life. Even when it doesn't, it tends to. My former colleague, Stanley Edgar Hyman, used to say that even the act of creating a form is a moral act. That leaves out something, but I understand and like what he was driving at. It's close to Frost's definition of a poem as "a momentary stay against confusion." Morality begins with an awareness of the sanctity of one's life, hence the lives of others—even Hitler's, to begin with—the sheer privilege of being, in this miraculous cosmos, and trying to figure out why. Art, in essence, celebrates life and gives us our measure.

DS: It changes the world?

MALAMUD: It changes me. It affirms me.

DS: Really?

MALAMUD: *(laughs)* It helps.

DS: Let's get to your books. In *The Natural*, why the baseball-mythology combination?

MALAMUD: Baseball flat is baseball flat. I had to do something else to enrich the subject. I love metaphor. It provides two loaves where there seems to be one. Sometimes it throws in a load of fish. The mythological analogy is a system of metaphor. It enriches the vision without resorting to montage. This guy gets up with his baseball bat and all at once he is, through the ages, a knight—somewhat battered—with a lance; not to mention a guy with a blackjack, or someone attempting murder with a flower. You relate to the past and predict the future. I'm not talented as a conceptual thinker but I am in the uses of metaphor. The mythological and symbolic excite my imagination. Incidentally, Keats said, "I am not a conceptual thinker, I am a man of ideas."

DS: Is *The Assistant* mythological?

MALAMUD: Some, I understand, find it so.

DS: Did you set it up as a mythology?

MALAMUD: No. If it's mythological to some readers I have no objection. You read the book and write your ticket. I can't tell you how the words fall, though I know what I mean. Your interpretation—*pace*, S. Sontag—may enrich the book or denude it. All I ask is that it be consistent and make sense.

DS: Is it a moral allegory?

MALAMUD: You have to squeeze your brain to come up with that. The spirit is more than moral, and by the same token there's more than morality in a good man. One must make room in those he creates. So far as range is concerned, ultimately a writer's mind and heart, if any, are revealed in his fiction.

DS: What is the source of *The Assistant*?

MALAMUD: Source questions are piddling but you're my friend, so I'll tell you. Mostly my father's life as a grocer, though not necessarily my father. Plus three short stories, sort of annealed in a single narrative. "The Cost of Living" and "The First Seven Years"—both in *The Magic Barrel*. And a story I wrote in the forties, "The Place is Different Now," which I've not included in my story collections.

DS: Is *The Fixer* also related to your father's life?

MALAMUD: Indirectly. My father told me the Mendel Beilis story when I was a kid. I carried it around almost forty years and decided to use it after I gave up the idea of a Sacco and Vanzetti novel. When I began to read for the Sacco and Vanzetti it had all the quality of a structured fiction, all the necessary elements of theme and narrative. I couldn't see any way of re-forming it. I was very much interested in the idea of prison as a source of the self's freedom and thought of Dreyfus next, but he was a dullish man, and though he endured well he did not suffer well. Neither did Beilis, for that matter, but his drama was more interesting—his experiences; so I invented Yakov Bok, with perhaps the thought of him as a potential Vanzetti. Beilis, incidentally, died a bitter man, in New York—after leaving Palestine, because he thought he hadn't been adequately reimbursed for his suffering.

DS: Some critics have commented on this prison motif in your work.

MALAMUD: Perhaps I use it as a metaphor for the dilemma of all men: necessity, whose bars we look through and try not to see. Social injustice, apathy, ignorance. The personal prison of entrapment in past experience, guilt, obsession—the somewhat blind or blinded self, in other words. A man has to construct, invent, his freedom. Imagination helps. A truly great man or woman extends it for others in the process of creating his/her own.

DS: Does this idea or theme, as you call it, come out of your experience as a Jew?

MALAMUD: That's probably in it—a heightened sense of prisoner of history, but there's more to it than that. I conceive this as the major battle in life, to transcend the self—extend one's realm of freedom.

DS: Not all your characters do.

MALAMUD: Obviously. But they're all more or less engaged in the enterprise.

DS: Humor is so much a part of your work. Is this an easy quality to deal with? Is one problem that the response to humor is so much a question of individual taste?

MALAMUD: The funny bone is universal. I doubt humorists think of individual taste when they're enticing the laugh. With me, humor comes unexpectedly, usually in defense of a character, sometimes because I need cheering up. When something starts funny I can feel my imagination eating and running. I love the distancing—the guise of invention—that humor gives fiction. Comedy, I imagine, is harder to do consistently than tragedy, but I like it spiced in the wine of sadness.

DS: What about suffering? It's a subject much in your early work.

MALAMUD: I'm against it, but when it occurs, why waste the experience?

DS: Are you a Jewish writer?

MALAMUD: What is the question asking?

DS: One hears various definitions and insistences, for instance, that one is primarily a writer and any subject matter is secondary; or that one is an American-Jewish writer. There are qualifications, by Bellow, Roth, others.

MALAMUD: I'm an American, I'm a Jew, and I write for all men. A novelist has to, or he's built himself a cage. I write about Jews, when I write about Jews, because they set my imagination going. I know something about their history, the quality of their experience and belief, and of their literature, though not as much as I would like. Like many writers I'm influenced especially by the Bible, both Testaments. I respond in particular to the East European immigrants of my father's and mother's generation; many of them were Jews of the Pale as described by the classic Yiddish writers. And of course I've been deeply moved by the Jews of the concentration camps, and the refugees wandering from nowhere to nowhere. I'm concerned about Israel. Nevertheless, Jews like rabbis Kahane and

Korrf set my teeth on edge. Sometimes I make characters Jewish because I think I will understand them better as people, not because I am out to prove anything. That's a qualification. Still another is that I know that, as a writer, I've been influenced by Hawthorne, James, Mark Twain, Hemingway, more than I have been by Sholem Aleichem and I. L. Peretz, whom I read with pleasure. Of course I admire and have been moved by other writers, Dostoyevsky and Chekhov, for instance, but the point I'm making is that I was born in America and respond, in American life, to more than Jewish experience. I wrote for those who read.

DS: Thus S. Levin is Jewish and not much is made of it?

MALAMUD: He was a gent who interested me in a place that interested me. He was out to be educated.

DS: Occasionally I see a remark to the effect that he has more than a spoonful of you in him.

MALAMUD: So have Roy Hobbs, Helen Bober, Willie Spearmint, and Talking Horse. More to the point—I prefer autobiographical essence to autobiographical history. Events from life may creep into the narrative, but it isn't necessarily my life history.

DS: How much of a book is set in your mind when you begin? Do you begin at the beginning? Does its course ever change markedly from what you had in the original concept?

MALAMUD: When I start I have a pretty well developed idea what the book is about and how it ought to go, because generally I've been thinking about it and making notes for months, if not years. Generally I have the ending in mind, usually the last paragraph almost verbatim. I begin at the beginning and stay close to the track, if it is a trace and not a whalepath. If it turns out I'm in the open sea, my compass is my narrative instinct, with an assist by that astrolabe, theme. The destination, wherever it is, is, as I said, already defined. If I go astray it's not a long excursis, good for getting to know the ocean, if not the world. The original idea, altered but recognizable, on the whole remains.

DS: Do characters ever run away from you and take on identities you hadn't expected?

MALAMUD: My characters run away, but not far. Their guise is surprises.

DS: Let's go to Fidelman. You seem to like to write about painters?

MALAMUD: I know a few. I love painting.

DS: Rembrandt and who else?

MALAMUD: Too many to name, but Cézanne, Monet, and Matisse, very much, among modernists.

DS: Chagall?

MALAMUD: Not that much. He rides his nostalgic nag to death.

DS: Some have called you a Chagallean writer.

MALAMUD: Their problem. I used Chagallean imagery intentionally in one story, "The Magic Barrel," and that's it. My quality is not much like his.

DS: Fidelman first appears in "The Last Mohican," a short story. Did you already have in mind that there would be an extended work on him?

MALAMUD: After I wrote the story in Rome I jotted down ideas for several incidents in the form of a picaresque novel. I was out to loosen up—experiment a little—with narrative structure. And I wanted to see, if I wrote it at intervals—as I did from 1957 to 1968—whether the passing of time and mores would influence his life. I did not think of the narrative as merely a series of related stories, because almost at once I had the structure of a novel in mind and each part had to fit that form. Robert Scholes in *The Saturday Review* has best explained what I was up to in Fidelman.

DS: Did you use all the incidents you jotted down?

MALAMUD: No.

DS: Can you give me an example of one you left out?

MALAMUD: Yes, Fidelman administering to the dying Keats in Rome—doing Severn's job, one of the few times in his life our boy is engaged in a purely unselfish act, or acts. But I felt I had no need to predict a change in him, especially in a sort of dream sequence, so I dropped the idea. The painting element was to come in via some feverish watercolors of John Keats, dying.

DS: Fidelman is characterized by some critics as a schlemiel.

MALAMUD: Not accurately. Peter Schlemiel lost his shadow and suffered the consequences for all time. Not Fidelman. He does better. He escapes his worse fate. I dislike the schlemiel characterization as a taxonomical device. I said somewhere that it reduces to stereotypes people of complex motivations and fates. One can often behave like a schlemiel without being one.

DS: Do you read criticism of your work?

MALAMUD: When it hits me in the eye; even some reviews.

DS: Does it affect you?

MALAMUD: Some of it must. Not the crap, the self-serving pieces, but an occasional insightful criticism, favorable or unfavorable, that confirms my judgment of my work. While I'm on the subject, I dislike particularly those critics who preach their aesthetic or ideological doctrines at you. What's important to them is not what the writer has done but how it fits, or doesn't fit, the thesis they want to develop. Nobody can tell a writer what can or ought to be done, or not done, in his fiction. A living death if you fall for it.

DS: That narration, for instance, is dead or dying?

MALAMUD: It'll be dead when the penis is.

DS: What about the death of the novel?

MALAMUD: The novel could disappear, but it won't die.

DS: How does that go?

MALAMUD: I'm not saying it will disappear, just entertaining the idea. Assume it does; then someday a talented writer writes himself a long, heartfelt letter, and the form reappears. The human race needs the novel. We need all the experience we can get. Those who say the novel is dead can't write them.

DS: You've done two short stories and a novel about blacks. Where do you get your material?

MALAMUD: Experience and books. I lived on the edge of a black neighborhood in Brooklyn when I was a boy. I played with blacks in the Flatbush Boys Club. I had a friend—Buster; we used to go to his house every so often. I swiped dimes so we could go to the movies together on a couple of Saturday afternoons. After I was married I taught for a year in a black evening high school in Harlem. The short stories derive from that period. I also read black fiction and history.

DS: What set off *The Tenants*?

MALAMUD: Jews and blacks, the period of the troubles in New York City; the teachers strike, the rise of black activism, the mix-up of cause and effect. I thought I'd say a word.

DS: Why the three endings?

MALAMUD: Because one wouldn't do.

DS: Will you predict how it will be between blacks and Jews in the future?

MALAMUD: How can one? All I know is that American blacks have been badly treated. We, as a society, have to redress the balance. Those who want for others must expect to give up something. What we get in return is the affirmation of what we believe in.

DS: You give a sense in your fiction that you try not to repeat yourself.

MALAMUD: Good. In my books I go along the same paths in different worlds.

DS: What's the path—theme?

MALAMUD: Derived from one's sense of values, it's a vision of life, a feeling for people—real qualities in imaginary worlds.

DS: Do you like writing short stories more than you do novels?

MALAMUD: Just as much, though the short story has its own pleasures. I like packing a self or two into a few pages, predicating lifetimes. The drama is terse, happens faster, and is often outlandish. A short story is a way of indicating the complexity of life in a few pages, producing the surprise and effect of a profound knowledge in a short time. There's, among other things, a drama, a resonance, of the reconciliation of opposites: much to say, little time to say it, something like the effect of a poem.

DS: You write them between novels?

MALAMUD: Yes, to breathe, and give myself time to think what's in the next book. Sometimes I'll try out a character or situation similar to that in a new novel.

DS: How many drafts do you usually do of a novel?

MALAMUD: Many more than I call three. Usually the last of the first puts it in place. The second focuses, develops, subtilizes. By the third most of the dross is gone. I work with language. I love the flowers of afterthought.

DS: Your style has always seemed so individual, so recognizable. Is this a natural gift, or is it contrived and honed?

MALAMUD: My style flows from the fingers. The eye and ear approve or amend.

DS: Let's wind up. Are you optimistic about the future?

MALAMUD: My nature is optimistic but not the evidence—population misery, famine, politics of desperation, the proliferation of the atom bomb. Mylai, one minute after Hiroshima in history, was ordained. We're going through long, involved transformations of world society, ongoing upheavals of colonialism, old modes of distribution, mores, overthrowing the slave mentality. With luck we may end up in a society with a larger share of the world's goods, opportunities for education, freedom going to the presently underprivileged. Without luck there may be a vast economic redistribution without political freedom. In the Soviet Union, as it is presently constituted, that's meant the kiss of death to freedom in art and literature. I worry that democracy, which has protected us from this indignity, especially in the United States, suffers from a terrifying inadequacy of leadership, and the apathy, unimaginativeness, and hard-core selfishness of too many of us. I worry about technology rampant. I fear those who are by nature beastly.

DS: What does one write novels about nowadays?

MALAMUD: Whatever wants to be written.

DS: Is there something I haven't asked you that you might want to comment on?

MALAMUD: No.

DS: For instance, what writing has meant to you?

MALAMUD: I'd be too moved to say.

3

LONG WORK,

SHORT LIFE

◆

I intend to say something about
my life as a writer. Since I shan't go into a formal replay of the life, this
will read more like a selective short memoir.

The beginning was slow, and perhaps not quite a beginning. Some
beginnings promise a start that may take years to induce a commencement. Before the first word strikes the page, or the first decent idea
occurs, there is the complicated matter of breaking the silence. Some
throw up before they can breathe. Not all can run to the door at the
knock of announcement—granted one hears it. Not all know what it
means. Simply, not always is the gift of talent given free and clear. Some
who are marvelously passionate to write may have to spend half their
lives learning what their proper subject matter may be.

Not even geniuses know themselves in their youth. For years Emily
Dickinson was diverted from her poetry by men she felt she loved, until
one day she drew the shutters in her sunlit room and sat in loneliness at
her table. She had at last unearthed a way of beginning. Those who loved
her appeared in her home from time to time, perhaps less to love than
to cause her to write her wondrous poems of intricate feeling and intricate love.

This memoir was originally delivered at Bennington College in the Ben Belitt
Lectureship Series on October 13, 1984, and thereafter published in a limited
edition as one of *The Bennington Chapbooks in Literature*, 1985.

I began to write at an early age, yet it took me years actually to begin writing. Much diverted me. As a child I told stories for praise. I went for inspiration to the movies. I remember my mother delivering me, against her will, on a wet Sunday, to a movie house to see Charlie Chaplin, whose comedy haunted my soul. After being at the pictures I recounted their plots to school friends who would listen at dreadfully long length as I retold them. The pleasure, in the beginning, was in retelling the impossible tale.

When I overcontrived or otherwise spoiled a plot, I would substitute another of my own. I could on occasion be a good little liar who sometimes found it a burden to tell the truth. Once my father called me a "bluffer," enraging me because I had meant to tell him a simple story, not one that had elaborated itself into a lie.

In grammar school, where I lived in a state of self-enhancing discovery, I turned school assignments into stories. Once I married off Roger Williams of Rhode Island to an Indian maiden, mainly because I had worked up an early feeling for the romantic. When I was ten, I wrote a story about a ship lost in the Sargasso Sea. The vessel appeared in dreams, about to undertake a long voyage in stagnant seas. This sort of thing, to begin with, was the nature of my "gift" as a child, that I had awakened to one day, and it remained with me many years before I began to use it well. Throughout my life I struggled to define it, and to write with originality. However, once it had pointed at me and signaled the way, it kept me going even when I wasn't writing. For years it was a blessing that could bleed as a wound.

Thus began an era of long waiting.

I had hoped to start writing short stories after graduation from City College during the Depression, but they were long in coming. I had ideas and felt I was on the verge of sustained work. But at that time I had no regular means of earning a living; and as the son of a poor man, a poor grocer, I could not stand the thought of living off him, a generous and self-denying person. However, I thought the writing would take care of itself once I found steady work. I needed decent clothes; I would dream of new suits. Any work I found would make life different, I thought, and I could begin writing day or night. Yet I adamantly would not consider applying, in excess of pride, to the WPA. Years later, I judged that to have been a foolish act, or non-act.

I considered various things I might do to have time for writing, like getting up at five A.M. to work for an hour or two each morning before hitting the dreadful Sixth Avenue agencies in Manhattan to scrounge around for jobs. More often than not there were none, especially for someone with no work experience. And where there was no work there were no words.

The Second World War had begun in 1939. I was born at the beginning of the First World War, in 1914. The Second was being called "The Phony War." The French and German armies sat solemnly eyeing each other over the Maginot Line, yet almost not moving except for night forays. No one seemed about to launch a major attack. Neville Chamberlain, after Munich, was on his way out. He had rolled up his umbrella and was hastening away from the frightful future; Churchill came to power and was eloquently growling that Britain would never be conquered. Possibly diplomacy was in progress. Perhaps there would be no renewed conflict. Many Americans seemed to think the threat of war might expire. Many of us hoped so, though hoping was hard work; nor did it make too much sense, given the aberrations of Adolf Hitler. We worried about the inevitable world war but tried not to think of it.

Often young writers do not truly know what is happening in their lives and world. They know and they don't know. They are not sure what, in essence, is going on and are years in learning. Recently I was reading Ernst Pawel's book of the life of Kafka, and the author speaks of Kafka's "all-encompassing goal in which the writer searches for his own truth." Truth or no truth, I felt the years go by without accomplishment. Occasionally I wrote a short story that no one bought. I called myself a writer though I had no true subject matter. Yet from time to time I sat at a table and wrote, although it took years for my work to impress me.

By now I had registered at Columbia University for an M.A. in English, on a government loan. The work was not demanding. I told myself what I was doing was worthwhile; for no one who spends his nights and days devoted to great works of literature will be wasting his time as a writer, if he is passionate to write.

But when did I expect to begin writing?

My answer was unchanged: when I found a job that would support my habit—the self's enduring needs. I registered for a teachers' examination and afterwards worked a year at $4.50 a day as a teacher-in-training in a high school in Brooklyn. I was also applying for, and took, several civil service examinations, including those leading to jobs of postal clerk and letter carrier. This is mad, I thought, or I am. Yet I told myself the kind of work I might get didn't matter so long as I was working for time to write. Throughout these unsatisfying years, writing was still my gift and persuasion.

It was now four years after my graduation from college, but the four felt like fifty when I was counting. However, in the spring of 1940 I was offered work in Washington, D.C., as a clerk in the Census Bureau. I accepted at once though I soon realized the "work" was a laugh. All morning I conscientiously checked estimates of drainage ditch statistics, as they appeared in various counties of the United States. Although the job hardly thrilled me, I worked diligently and was promoted, at the end of three months, to receive a salary of $1,800 per annum. That, in those times, was good money. What was better was that I had begun to write seriously on company time. No one seemed to care what I was doing so long as the record showed I had finished a full day's work; therefore after lunch time I kept my head bent low while I was writing short stories at my desk.

At about this time I wrote a piece for the *Washington Post*, mourning the fall of France after the German Army had broken through the Maginot Line and was obscenely jubilant in conquered Paris. I felt unhappy, as though mourning the death of a civilization I loved; yet somehow I managed to celebrate on-going life and related acts.

Although my writing seemed less than inspiring to me, I stayed with it and tried to breathe into it fresh life and beauty, hoping that the gift was still in my possession, if by some magic act I could see life whole. And though I was often lonely, I stayed in the rooming house night after night trying to invent stories I needn't be ashamed of.

One night, after laboring in vain for hours attempting to bring a short story to life, I sat up in bed at an open window looking at the stars after a rainfall. Then I experienced a wave of feeling, of heartfelt emotion bespeaking commitment to life and art, so deeply it brought tears to my eyes. For the hundredth time I promised myself that I would someday be a very good writer. This renewal, and others like it, kept me alive in art years from fulfillment. I must have been about twenty-five then, and was still waiting, in my fashion, for the true writing life to begin. I'm reminded of Kafka's remark in his mid-twenties: "God doesn't want me to write, but I must write."

There were other matters to consider. What about marriage—should I, shouldn't I? I sometimes felt that the young writers I knew were too much concerned with staying out of marriage, whereas they might have used it, among other things, to order their lives and get on with their work. I wondered whether I could make it a necessary adjunct of my writing. But marriage was not easy: wouldn't it hurt my career if I urged on myself a way of life I could hardly be sure of? One has his gift—the donnée—therefore he'd better protect it from those who seem to be without a compelling purpose in life. Many young women I met had no clear idea what they wanted to do with their lives. If such a woman became a writer's wife, would she, for instance, know what was going on in his thoughts as he worked in his sleep? Would she do her part in keeping the family going? I was often asking myself these and related questions—though not necessarily of someone who might answer them. And I was spending too much time being in love, as an uneasy way of feeling good when I wasn't writing. I needed someone to love and live with, but I wasn't going out of my way to find her.

Meanwhile, I had nailed down an evening school job in September of 1940; I then completed an M.A. thesis and began to think of writing a novel. By now I had finished about a dozen stories, a few of which began to appear in university quarterlies. One of these, "The Place is Different Now," was the forerunner of *The Assistant*. And a novel I had started while I was teaching in Erasmus Hall Evening High School, in Brooklyn, was called *The Light Sleeper*. It was completed but not sold. Later, I burned it one night in Oregon because I felt I could do better. My son, who was about four at that time, watched me burning the book. As we looked at the sparks fly upward I was telling him about death; but he denied the concept.

Several years before that, not long after Pearl Harbor, while I was teaching at night and writing this novel, I met a warm, pretty young woman at a party. I was told she was of Italian descent and lived in a hotel with her mother and step-father, who was a musician. I observed my future wife for a while before we talked.

Soon we began to meet. Some nights she would come to Flatbush to watch me teach. We ate at Sears, or Oetgen's, and sometimes walked across the Parade Grounds to my room. We wrote each other during the week. Her letters were intense and witty, revealing an informed interest in politics and literature; in love and marriage. After the death of my own mother, I had had a step-mother and a thin family life; my wife, the child of a woman divorced young, had experienced a richer cultural life than I. And since we both wanted children we wondered how we would fare in a mixed marriage. She had been Catholic. I defined myself as Jewish.

Life in New York City was not easy or pleasant during the Second World War. Our friends Rose and James Lechay, the painter, rented a small walk-up flat on King Street, in the Village, which we took over when they went off to live in Iowa, Jim to take Grant Wood's place as Professor of Painting at the university. After we were married we both continued working until my wife was pregnant. I taught day and evening classes, with practically no time to write. A few years later I left the evening high school and spent a year teaching in Harlem, incidentally picking up ideas for short stories (like "Black Is My Favorite Color") before we decided to go west. I had now received an offer to teach at Oregon State College though I had no Ph.D. degree. In 1949, when my son was two, we moved to Corvallis, Oregon, where I taught three days a week and wrote four. In my own eyes I had become seriously a writer earning his living, though certainly not from his writing.

I think I discovered the Far West and some subject matter of my earlier fiction at almost the same time, an interesting conjunction, in imagination, of Oregon and the streets of New York. One's fantasy goes for a walk and returns with a bride.

During my first year at Oregon State I wrote *The Natural*, begun before leaving New York City. Baseball had interested me, especially its comic aspects, but I wasn't able to write about the game until I transformed game into myth, via Jessie Weston's Percival legend with an assist by T. S. Eliot's "The Waste Land" plus the lives of several ballplayers I had read, in particular Babe Ruth's and Bobby Feller's. The myth enriched the baseball lore as feats of magic transformed the game.

Soon we were making plans to go abroad. We had wanted to go earlier, but could not afford it until we experienced the fortunate coincidence of a sabbatical leave from Oregon State with a *Partisan Review*-Rockefeller Foundation grant.

We left in late August, 1956, for Italy. On board the SS CONSTITUTION I spent hours studying the horizon, enjoying the sight of ocean as the beginning of more profound adventure, amid thoughts of new writing. One night we passed our sister ship, the SS AMERICA, steaming along in the mid-Atlantic, all decks alight. I felt I was on the verge of a long celebration.

Previously my wife had been abroad twice, once at age eight for a year in Italy, and at another time for her college junior year in France.

I was ready for a broader kind of living with as much range in writing as I could manage. Before leaving Oregon to go abroad, I had completed *The Assistant*, and had begun to develop several of the stories that became *The Magic Barrel*, some of which I wrote in Rome.

Italy unrolled like a foreign film; what was going on before my eyes seemed close to unreality. An ancient city seemed to be alive in present time. It was larger than life, yet defined itself as our new life. I felt the need to live in a world that was more than my world to live in. I walked all over the city. I walked in the ghetto. I met Italian Jews who had been tortured by Nazis; one man held up his hand to show his finger-shorn fist. I felt I was too much an innocent American. I wandered along Roman streets and studied Roman faces, hoping to see what they saw when they looked; I wanted to know more of what they seemed to know. On All Soul's, I walked in the Campo Verano cemetery. I visited the Ardeatine Caves where the Nazis had slaughtered Italians and Jews. Rome had its own sad way of sharing Jewish experience.

Mornings I walked my eight-year-old son to Piazza Bologna where he took his bus to the American school. At noon, after finishing my morning's work, I picked up my four-year-old daughter at her kindergarten. She would hand me her drawings as we walked home. Home was 88 Via Michelo Di Lando, not far from where Mussolini had lived with Clara Petacci, his mistress. We had made friends of our landlords. Mr. Gianolla was an old Socialist who had been forced to swallow castor oil by Mussolini's Fascist thugs. His wife, thin and energetic, talkative, courteous, was one of the rare women university graduates of her time.

I returned to Oregon to an improved situation after our year abroad. From a teacher of freshman grammar and technical report writing, I was transformed into a teacher of English literature, as though a new talent had been discovered in a surprised self. What had happened was that the two gentlemen who administered the English department had heard I was acquiring a small reputation as a serious writer of fiction, and therefore I was no longer required to teach composition only, but might be allowed, even without a doctoral degree, to teach unsuspecting sophomores a little poetry, with even a touch of Shakespeare in the night. For this relief I gave happy thanks.

Let me, at this point, say a short word about the yeas and nays of a writer teaching what is called Creative Writing. I have done it because I teach decently well, but I wouldn't recommend that anyone devote his life to teaching writing if he takes little pleasure in informing others. Elsewhere I've said about teaching creative writing, that one ought to keep in mind he is not so much teaching the art of imaginative writing as he is encouraging people with talent how to work as writers. Writing courses are of limited value although in certain cases they may encourage young writers to read good fiction with the care it deserves. However, I think about a year of these courses should be enough for any serious student. Thereafter writing must become a way of life.

When my Western-born daughter appeared, my father sent us $350 for a washing machine. Once when I was twenty, he trudged up the hall stairs from his grocery store one morning. I had a summer cold and was stretched out in bed. I had been looking for a job without success. My father reached for my foot and grasped it with his hand.

"I wish it was me with that cold instead of you."

What does a writer need most? When I ask the question, I think of my father.

I had already begun to receive literary awards. It seemed to me that I did nothing to get them other than stay at the writing table, and the prizes would mysteriously appear. One day I had a phone call from New York. My publisher, Roger Straus, asked me whether I was sitting down. I said I was. He told me I had just won the National Book Award for *The Magic Barrel*.

I must know how to write, I told myself, almost surprised.

I was in a happy mood when I began to work on *A New Life*, my fourth book. Once, at Yaddo, while I was writing it, a visitor knocked at my door. I had just written something that moved me. He saw my wet eyes. I told him I was enjoying writing my book. Later the legend grew that I had wept my way through it.

During my early years at Oregon State I had gone nowhere, with the exception of our trip abroad, and a six-week visit to Montana, when Leslie Fiedler was there in the 1950s. He had sent me a copy of an article he had published in *Folio*, in Indiana. His was the first appreciation of *The Natural* that I had read by someone who knew how to read. Fiedler was always sui generis, but on the whole generous in his judgment of my work. I shan't forget that he appreciated the quality of my imaginative writing before anyone else wrote about it. That was long before Robert Redford, in his sad hat of failure, appeared on the scene, socking away at a ball that went up in the lights.

Not long after our return to Corvallis from Italy, I had a telephone call from Howard Nemerov, at Bennington College, where I was invited to teach for a year. I was glad to go. After our year abroad, stimulated by the life and art I had seen, I wasn't very patient with my experience in a small town, though my wife, after a difficult start, now enjoyed Western life. I seized the opportunity to return to the East. She would have liked living in San Francisco, but there were no job offers. So we traveled to Vermont by way of Harvard Summer School, where I substituted for Albert Guérard. When the class filled quickly, someone at Harvard asked John Hawkes, the novelist at Brown University, to teach a second section of the course. Before long we were walking together in Cambridge streets, talking about fiction. Hawkes is a gallant man and imaginative writer. His work should be better known than it is.

In September, 1961, my wife and I arrived with our kids in Bennington, Vermont. The college, an unusual place to work and learn, soon became a continuing source of education for me. My teachers were my new colleagues: Howard Nemerov, poet and faithful friend; Stanley Edgar Hyman, a unique scholar and fine critic; and Ben Belitt, a daring, original poet and excellent teacher—from all of whom I learned. My other teachers were my students, whom I taught to teach me.

Stanley Hyman reminded me of Leslie Fiedler in more ways than one. They both knew a great deal about literature, and neither found it difficult to say what. Hyman was an excellent theoretician of myth and literature. His humor kept him young and so did his appetite. Once my wife and I invited him and his wife, the writer Shirley Jackson, to a restaurant, to help us celebrate our wedding anniversary. Stanley ordered the champagne. He and Shirley lived hard, and—I think they thought—well; and almost did not regret dying young. Flannery O'Connor once described them as two large people in a small car, when they came to call on her in Milledgeville, Georgia. She showed them her peacocks.

When I think of Hyman as a critic of literature, what stands out was his honesty of self and standards. One of his favorite words was "standards," and you weren't in his league if you didn't know what he meant. He defined and explicated. He was proud of what he knew, though I remember his saying, speaking of himself, "knowledge is not wisdom." He enjoyed the fun of wit, merriment, poker, horseplay, continuous laughter. He died young.

Before I come to the end of this casual memoir, perhaps I ought to say that I served as president of American PEN (Poets, Editors, and Novelists) from 1979 to 1981. PEN had come to life in 1921 as an international organization founded in London by John Galsworthy, the

British novelist and dramatist. Basically, PEN brings together writers from all over the world to meet as a fraternity, to foster literature, and to defend the written word wherever threatened.

When I was president, I began to deal more frequently with publishers after the difficult period that followed a time of consolidation in the book industry. The consolidation I refer to was not always helpful to those who wrote, and much remains to be done to improve the situation of writers, dealing in whatever way with their own publishers.

Though my publisher is a good one, I fear that too many of them are much more concerned with making money than with publishing good books that will seriously influence generations of writers in the future. Stanley Hyman had preached standards, but one tendency in publishing today is that standards are forgotten. I can't tell you how badly some books are edited these days; one excuse given is "We can't afford too much time on one book. We've got to make our profit." I'm all for profit from the work of writers, but the simple fact is that we have begun to pay more in a loss of quality in publishing than our culture can afford. Happily, many people of good will, dissatisfied with present day publishing, are trying to find new ways to improve the industry. And some of the new presses that have begun to publish are quite good, a few even daring.

If I may, I would at this point urge young writers not to be too much concerned with the vagaries of the marketplace. Not everyone can make a first-rate living as a writer, but a writer who is serious and responsible about his work, and life, will probably find a way to earn a decent living, if he or she writes well. And there's great pleasure in writing, if one writes well. A good writer will be strengthened by his good writing at a time, let us say, of the resurgence of ignorance in our culture. I think I have been saying that the writer must never compromise with what is best in him in a world defined as free.

I have written almost all my life. My writing has drawn, out of a reluctant soul, a measure of astonishment at the nature of life. And the more I wrote well, the better I felt I had to write.

In writing I had to say what had happened to me, yet present it as though it had been magically revealed. I began to write seriously when I had taught myself the discipline necessary to achieve what I wanted. When I touched that time, my words announced themselves to me. I have given my life to writing without regret, except when I consider what in my work I might have done better. I wanted my writing to be as good as it must be, and on the whole I think it is. I would write a book, or a short story, at least three times—once to understand it, the second time to improve the prose, and a third to compel it to say what it still must say.

Somewhere I put it this way: first drafts are for learning what one's fiction wants him to say. Revision works with that knowledge to enlarge and enhance an idea, to re-form it. Revision is one of the exquisite pleasures of writing: "The men and things of today are wont to lie fairer and truer in tomorrow's meadow," Henry Thoreau said.

I don't regret the years I put into my work. Perhaps I regret the fact that I was not two men, one who could live a full life apart from writing; and one who lived in art, exploring all he had to experience and know how to make his work right; yet not regretting that he had put his life into the art of perfecting the work.

Part 2

THE MAN ON HIS WORK

◆

◆

Bernard Malamud, during his
lifetime as an artist and writer, said little in private about his own work.
In public he said even less. But he kept up a constant dialogue with himself about work in progress, in notes, notes, and more notes, most of
them handwritten, a few of them typed and used late in life as illustra-
tive teaching lectures. In the section that follows we become privy to
some of that privileged dialogue with himself on the subject of the composition of his first novel, *The Natural*, and his only work of historical
fiction, *The Fixer*. In the two teaching lectures printed here—possibly
from his time as a lecturer at Harvard, possibly prepared for one of his
campus appearances elsewhere—he includes a reading of some of his stories and a subsequent workout on the nature of the composition of those
stories as a way of suggesting to writing students a model of how to
make found material, anecdote, and conjecture into the stuff of art. The
only item in this section that has appeared in print before is the brief
addendum to the Norwegian edition of his second novel, "A Note to my
Norwegian Readers on *The Assistant*."

But as the title of the talk on a major element in some of his fiction
("Why Fantasy?") suggests, the teaching lectures still take the form of a
dialogue between himself and himself on the nature of his own style.
And in the talk on the story "The Magic Barrel," he walks his audience—
and thus himself—through the various stages of composition. In the
"Malamud Finding" in the Manuscript Room at the Library of Congress
there are a number of stories in draft that scholars may one day approach

and explicate in detail—as a way of understanding the meticulous and dedicated aesthetic practice of our dear late master. For instance, this volume's title tale ("Talking Horse") has several drafts in holograph and several more in typescript, with Malamud's inked-in corrections even on the first published version in the *Atlantic Monthly Magazine*; from original title to last sentence, everything's subject to change.

In this next section students of fiction writing and serious readers also will find themselves in the midst of Malamud's writing mind as he allows his imagination to speak up in an unusually frank way about the serene and successful methods it followed in the wild and swirl of what we call our labors at making stories work. —*Alan Cheuse*

4

The Natural: **RAISON D'ETRE**

AND MEANING

◆

1. Situation and challenge: previous novel a realistic study; short stories realistic, to begin with, veering towards experimentation in symbolism and style; challenge a work of imagination—more freedom than in previous realistic studies. The freedom to handle material imaginatively; to achieve the impression of life or reality, yet to realize something above or beyond life (though within life) that we call art.

2. Why baseball? Considering my background and interests. Part of the challenge—to test the power of the imagination. Bellow: a good writer can write about anything. This is true of only a certain type of good writer. (Can Hemingway, for instance, write humor?) The poignant Jackson story. Books are about people. Baseball is a meaningful part of the American scene.

3. How to handle the material:

a. how treated in the past—superficially by Lardner, Broun, and others. The characters were close to grotesques or caricatures; they were oversimplified, as one might expect. The humor was based on their inadequacies as people; it was basically cruel. Baseball when described realistically as a game is boring. How to enrich characterization, humor, and the game itself?

b. decision—treat the material symbolically to give it a more meaningful quality for me.

c. What is meant by symbolism? Symbolism is a device used to deepen the meanings of facts and experience. In one thing we see more than one thing: we see a thing plus an idea. Symbolism may be played lightly in a story or played heavily, or somewhere in between. One object or a few objects may be symbolic, or every object, person, and movement in a story; or symbolism itself may be hinted. It depends on the purpose and feeling of the artist. In other words, there are degrees of symbolism. Symbolism simplifies complexity; it, at the same time, adds to the richness of meaning when handled right. Note that there is symbolism in realistic or naturalistic writing—just as there is in life—we make our own symbols out of experience—and there must be a realism as the basis of symbolism, otherwise the symbolism is ineffective.

d. Mark Schorer on symbolism:

"Physical facts are the material which the story writer must, somehow, make mean, which is only another way of saying that fiction must express moral and spiritual conflicts in terms of objective nature.

"Between naturalism and symbolism, then, there is no radical difference—however extreme particular examples may sometimes make the difference seem, it is a difference of degree. Some writers throw their weight on the facts, some on the meanings. It is probably true that the most interesting recent fiction has become more concerned with meanings of experience than earlier and more primitive fiction where the delight in the pure narrative of events for their own sake dominates. This is simply to say that more writers today use, and use more eagerly and self-consciously, the resources of symbolism than writers in the past. It hardly means the works of earlier writers of fiction . . . are, in the final result, less symbolic; it does mean that the words of these less self-conscious writers are more symbolical of their own selves, less symbolical of imaginatively considered and defined themes. Contrariwise, some of the earlier writers, John Bunyan, or, much later in America, Nathaniel Hawthorne, were often very strongly inclined to use symbolism in its baldest form, to begin, that is, with an urgent moral or theological "idea" and dress that in the minimum physical circumstances sufficient to produce a fable or an allegory. But these forms are not stories as we think of stories today, even though one can argue that every story has, however deeply buried in its immediate and particularized realism, a fable, an allegory, a mythical generalization. Fiction today characteristically tries to give us the believable surface of experience and yet to select and to emphasize its details in such a fashion as to make that experience mean most. Symbolism, then, is not an act of translation, where one thing is represented by something else: it is not a form of literary or philosophical disguise, but of presentation and revelation."

e. R. P. Blackmur says much the same thing in a different way:
"What writing drags into being and holds there while the writing lasts may be called the experience of the actual; what writing creates—what goes on after the writing has stopped—may sometimes be called symbol. It is symbol when it stands, not for what has been said or stated, but for what has not been said and could not be said, for what has been delivered by the writing into what seems an autonomous world of its own. Symbol is the most exact possible meaning, almost tautologically exact, for what stirred the words to move and what the moving words made. Symbol stands for nothing previously known, but for what is "here" made known and what is about to be made known. If symbol stands for anything else than itself, continuing, it stands for that within me the reader which enables me to recognize it and to illuminate it with my own experience at the same moment that what it means illuminates further corridors in my sense of myself."

4. I ought perhaps to say a word here about Freud and symbolism, since a good deal has been said of the Freudian quality of my book, principally by people ignorant of Freud's writing. Freud . . . was really the first one to discover the laws by which symbolism operates—in a word how symbols are manufactured by the human mind, and for what reason, and under what circumstances. Freud has discovered the meaning of symbolism in our dreams and in the unconscious generally. He has further discovered a whole category of symbols which he feels are sexual in origin. Some of these symbols are quite arbitrary, and according to Freud, they never change in their symbolic meaning. But for the most part symbols as they occur in our experience are subject to the inventiveness of our psyches and may mean a variety of things depending on the circumstances under which they appear. The writer who sticks entirely to Freud's arbitrary symbols is sacrificing freedom of choice and creativity—the freedom and creativity to manufacture his own symbols; or to put it another way, to find universals in symbols of his own choosing. This sort of thing would be tantamount to writing a story in terms of Freudian theory, which would make it a case study, hence a not fully imagined piece of writing. That should be avoided by the truly creative writer. The only thing else I can say of Freud and symbolism is that Freud has made it easier . . . to translate symbols and to relate them to other layers of our experience. In other words you can take what we would call universal symbols, perhaps Christian symbols, and because of

Freud you can now relate these symbols to more primitive levels of human experience.

5. Now what use have I made of Freud in this book? Remember, the only sin for a writer in connection with Freud is the sin of arbitrary symbolism. Have I any arbitrary symbols of a Freudian nature in this book? Yes, there are one or two—the bat, for example, is an obviously phallic symbol, and water is as in Freud [a] symbol of fertility. However, they were not chosen from Freud but are in a sense elements of rituals described not by Freudians but by literary historical critics like Jessica Weston in her *Ritual and Romance*. To Miss Weston the Gawain, or Perceval legend is essentially a fertility ritual, and she states that the grail and the spear may be translated into sexual symbols. So far as I know her point of view is anthropological and not psychoanalytical, in the Freudian sense. My choice of the bat and water as symbols were motivated by the knight story, as part of that story and not arbitrarily from Freud. What the knight story meant to me I will describe later.

6. However, I must confess that is not all the use I have made of Freud; that is, the bat and water symbol—for instance the possibility of Roy's rebirth in the waters of Lake Michigan, in the presence of Iris. Another use I have made of Freud is to amplify my understanding of unconscious motivations through what he has taught me. Notice that I use the word amplify. Most writers, if they are truly writers, have the kind of insight that causes them to see the true meaning of certain actions, or if you will, symptoms. Dostoyevsky, for example, had an almost uncanny knowledge of human motivations, based, I would say, on a good deal of self-observation. To show you more clearly what I mean, take the scene in which Roy eats himself sick. Have you noticed how we sometimes eat when we are disturbed? That is the most important meaning that lies behind this prodigious overeating. Essentially Roy is disturbed over his treatment of Iris. He knows she is good and therefore good for him, but he avoids her because she is a grandmother. This reflects on his values. He judges her by something more superficial than her obvious love for him, less superficial than the totality of herself—the accident of her being a grandmother; furthermore he feels a certain guilt for being present at the party after being forbidden to celebrate by Pop Fisher. Pop is by definition a father figure, and Roy is always responsive to any father figure for reasons established in childhood—especially because his mother was not much of a mother to him. He gets

drunk, we are told, with food. That is an insight that Freud helped me to, but I might have come on it without Freud, and I am sure that there are some sensitive readers who do so too. One might say they sense the meaning of his overeating. Such sensing implies a decent sensitivity to life. It should be easy for the reader to figure out some of the hidden meanings of the book because the meanings are planned for by the writer; that is, he gives the reader clues to their presence. If you read carefully and put the clues together the meanings will open themselves to you as they have to other of my readers. However, I do confess the reading requires an effort, and some resent having to make the effort because they want to be entertained without any effort on their part. I shall have a word more to say about this at the end of my talk.

7. One last word about Freud. Some reviewers have used the word surrealistic about my writing, using it as interchangeable with Freudian, which it is not. Freud is not surrealistic and neither is my book. People who use the word in connection with my writing don't know what they are talking about. Webster defines surrealism as follows: "A modern French movement in art and literature, influenced by Freudianism, purporting to express the subconscious mental activities by presenting images without order or sequence, as in a dream." The important words are the last—as in a dream. In other words surrealism seeks a quality of dream in reality; it makes of reality a dream. I see the dream as only one aspect of reality. If a man dreams, then dreaming is real and thus gives, in the dreaming, a fuller picture of the person. There was no attempt in my book at dream presentation for dream's sake. There is no use of the so-called stream of consciousness as Joyce used it—though in a work of art, I would limit the artist to no one particular technique so long as he seeks to be intelligible—intelligible to intelligent readers.

8. To come back then to the subject of my handling of the material: I decided to work on three levels; deeply and firmly on the narrative level; and less deeply on two other levels—what one might call the historical and legendary, and also to sketch or outline a symbolic or mythic level. I will explain just where these levels of meaning may be found in my book.

9. Let me speak about the first, or narrative level, first. This, of course, is the most important one. Here is reality, the whole basis for any symbolism that I incorporate into the book. Here is the story texture, and I am storyteller enough to know that the tie between reader

and writer is story. I do not scorn the story as some writers say they do; in fact, I love writing the story. The story is so important to me that I am perfectly happy as a writer if my reader enjoys it, whether he suspected or not, as he read, that there was more to the book than story. If a reader tells me that he was entertained by my narrative I am happy.

10. However, and I must say somewhat to my surprise there were some readers who told me, or wrote in reviews that they did not understand the story. I know the story is understandable because I have talked with people who have understood it. Those people were editors, writers, critics, my colleagues, and some of my students. Yet I discovered that some of my readers, of course those who would not like the book because of gaps in their comprehension of the story, did not fully understand the story as story; that is to say they did not fully comprehend the theme of the book, as it is revealed in the story itself, though I do admit that the revelation is deepened in the symbolic stratum. Some of my friends who have read the book have never mentioned their reading of the book to me because they have not understood it. One of my colleagues told me he did not like the book because he felt it did not deal with a moral man. Of course he is entitled to his taste for the moral—it is my taste too—but the very fact that he said it had little of the moral in it is proof to me that he did not comprehend the theme of the narrative.

5

WHY FANTASY?

◆

Some people can't abide the improbable, and shy away especially from any contemporary short story or novel that is written as fantasy. I suppose they wonder why the writer bothers. On the whole they want their fiction to be "real" (although fiction is not real but only pretends to be); anyway they want it "realistic," and there are some critics nowadays who feel a man can write nothing of importance unless he is dealing with some aspect of society using the method we call social realism. And some people don't want "reality" tampered with, particularly if it is everyday reality and seems fantastic to them, not because of monstrous acts of inhumanity or the flights of missiles through space, made to carry atomic warheads, but because something improbable happens: an angel appears in a story, or maybe a ghost; that of course is personally threatening although the death of multitudes and the everyday threat of the end of the world may not be. In some kinds of fiction, certainly fantasy, the imaginative element is too patently visible for some; or to put it another way, the story becomes for them too obviously a work of imagination. One might say they don't want to be distracted from what the book is saying, from the book's content, if that can possibly be separate from form. Perhaps they don't want to feel uncertain about what is real, or seems to be—for fear nightmare will seep in. I once knew a man who could never read a novel because novels weren't real; he of course, went a step farther than those who can read realistic fiction, but I'll tell you about him because it will help you to understand what I'm driving at, for the difference between him and those who can't read or appreciate fantasy is one of degree. Once this man I knew was halfway through an interesting book he had picked up in the library about a voyage of some sort—I think to the Arctic—but he had to abandon it when he discovered he was reading a novel. He was apparently uncomfortable with illusion in fiction especially when *he knew* it was illusion, a quality that is essential to all good fiction, let me say in passing, and one which none but the best writers are able to brew up so that it is visible yet invisible. My friend reminds me of those tribesmen I read about who were disturbed by an incomplete picture— incomplete in their minds—which an anthropologist showed them; let me say of three deer bunched together in such a way that only two legs of one of the animals were visible; this bothered these tribesmen because one deer was not all there. How could it stand on two legs? And if the deer really was standing on two legs, then it wasn't a deer but possibly a god disguised as one, hence a supernatural threat.

Or perhaps some object to the fantasy as childish, which may mean they recall when they hear the word, fairy tales, stories of gods wandering the earth, miraculous Biblical stories and morality tales, stories of knightly adventure, fables of various sorts, ghost stories—the world of the presently unreal. They've put aside childish things and want no more of them; and, if such *is* the case they've put aside poetry too. However I don't think that's the way it usually works. I feel that people who have read these imaginative stories in childhood and early youth will tend to be receptive to fantasy, myth, symbolism, and other devices of literature, wherever they are effectively used. They have, so to speak, built up a taste for the highly inventive and don't discriminate against a work of art because of its genre or methodology. The simple fact is, I imagine, that some people haven't had the variety of reading experiences necessary to appreciate the quality of fantasy or the fantastic, just as there are people, I suppose, who have not been taught, nor taught themselves, what is funny, and are hard put to laugh. They grow up as non-laughers. In the same way some people haven't learned to take pleasure in certain kinds of fiction, especially that in which the fiction seems most visible.

Every so often I write a short fantasy and am later surprised to hear that an editor who had read the story had asked my agent why I was still on that kick; or after it is published I am surprised by a remark of a reviewer who happens to mention the story, that he sees no good in my going on with fantasy at this stage of my career. The ideological reasons for this, which are more complex than merely the matter of taste, though they are, of course, related to taste, I'll go into in a little while. Let me say here that when Saul Bellow's *Henderson the Rain King* came out, an enormously inventive book, not formally fantasy but symbolic, mythic, and characterized by the reviewer for the Sunday *New York Times* as "in the direction of fantasy," he felt it necessary to add, "a form of discourse to which the present reviewer is not strongly drawn." He had some very good things to say about the novel yet was impelled to write, "Mr. Bellow, forcing his hand to invent, has here entered a corridor into wonderland none of whose doors open into new possibilities for serious fiction." It would seem to me that the ideal is a profusion of possibilities for serious fiction, not necessarily "new" ones. As a character Henderson borders on the gargantuan fantastic; more than one of his experiences is exaggerated to the edge of belief; the setting is an Africa that never was or will be, yet the novel is a serious one with a serious and important meaning and is, in the best sense of the term, a successful piece of fiction. It may not help us to understand Africa but it will help us to understand man and if so perhaps society.

Why did Bellow write the novel as he did? Naturally there are reasons I don't know; however, I wonder if it will please anyone if I say he had to; that's the way the book came to him. Once he thought of it as that kind of book, idea after idea, incident after incident grew in his mind, proving it was that kind of book. He could not, in truth, have written it any other way. Would those readers who aren't drawn to fantasy, who won't go to certain books of Mark Twain, Kafka, Thomas Mann, for instance, would they want us not to write a particular novel or short story—*Henderson*, for instance, or my story "Idiots First," which an English reviewer who had happened to read it characterized as a regressive step for me, not because it was a bad story but because it was fantasy? I doubt they would want to stop us before we start; they might want us to write it so that some of them might wonder in print why we bothered to write a fantasy. I would then have to say again that if the story comes to the writer as fantasy it will pay him to write it as such. I tried unsuccessfully for years to write the story that I call "Take Pity." When I finally saw it as a fantasy, I wrote it easily and made not the slightest sacrifice of truth for having done so; got it to say everything I had wanted it to say as a realistic piece. All the conception of it as a fantasy did for me was to kindle my imagination so that I could write it effectively and richly.

Let me say a little more about the effect of writing fantasy on the writer; or of his being engaged in producing any work of rich inventiveness, the sort that some people would characterize as fantastic. It does for the writer what Shelley says fantasy does: "quickens and enlarges the mind." It excites and releases imagination. We think of imagination as that which is released to begin with, but that isn't always so. The imagination can lie like a dead dog until certain ideas, connecting and unifying, or suggesting others in interesting and exciting combinations, a sudden opening of the doors of possibility, cause the dog to awake and prance. Enlarge? Fantasy, since it is out of bounds of the ordinary, invites the writer to take chances, to venture beyond habitual limits or limitations, to do things he hasn't previously done—to play with fire and magic. Fantasy, whose essence is possibility, affords the writer the pleasure of creating people and events reacting on each other in ways that seem original, perhaps unique. The writer may readily feel that he is manipulating reality itself, yet safely because controlled by art; I needn't say how the effect of this, if he dares, will enrich his realistic writing. Fantasy challenges him to make use of the earthly wonderful as well as the supernatural; to tie them together in unpredictable combinations with the commonplace, the ordinary, and out of this still produce a real enough truth about life. That he may go too far and bring it all tumbling down is a danger, but he will encounter the same danger in realistic fiction, or in any art. Whether the writer goes too far or just far enough depends on his sense of proportion and good judgment. If he has these he needn't be afraid to handle fantasy.

And fantasy does for the reader pretty much what it does for the writer. He participates in the manipulatory pleasure of the writer. He experiences the poetry of the unearthly strange and mysterious; he senses the effect of the supernatural whether he believes in it or not; he enjoys the fact that the impossible happens. He takes pleasure in discovering a real meaning in a mixture of real and unreal events acted out by unreal people or agents, and those who seem real. He may think about illusion and perhaps admit to himself how vast an illusion our selves live in. He will taste the true taste of fiction, the taste that is weak or nonexistent in the merely journalistic or documentary and in other kinds of almost unimagined, or thinly imagined writing.

I've already mentioned some of the ingredients and proportions of fantasy but without pretending to be comprehensive or systematic I would like to add a few more observations. Of course fantasies differ. Some are comic, some tragic; many modern fantasies are horror pieces. They speak the truth of the times. In some the elements of fantasy— what we call the improbable—are used merely decoratively; in some, fantasy becomes the bones of the story structure. Of my three short-story fantasies, "Take Pity" is quantitatively the least fantastic; "Idiots First," more so; "Angel Levine," the most quantitatively fantastic. There can be fantastic backgrounds, events, people, but there needn't be all of these at once. Each fantasy, obviously, must contain a body or portion of the real; the real as we know it in fiction. Usually the people are real beings, no matter what miracles they endure, and it is their reality that persuades the reader that what is happening to them is real too, even when it is not. (In essence believable characterization is the secret of believable fiction.) It doesn't seem to work the other way; unreal events making real people unreal. Some fantasies make more of the real elements of life; some emphasize the miraculous and supernatural. One effect of fantasy is to give a feeling of timelessness, another of universality, effects in fiction that are presently under attack by certain critics. There are of course, though not necessarily, symbolic and mythic elements in fantasy. The symbols can be undisguised; sometimes they are disguised. And there is often a poetic component, often lyrical, sometimes, as in Kafka's *Metamorphosis*, the poetry of horror. One is conscious, as I said before, of the visible fiction (visible also to differing degrees in various realistic fictions): the reader knows all along this is imagined. That is the convention and no attempt other than bringing the tale to life is made to hide the fact. The important thing is that in a good fantasy the reader forgets the openness of the magic. And to conclude this short descriptive summary, if the fantasy has a meaning, as every work of literary art must . . . then the meaning need not be accounted unreal.

I'm going to read a short story to you—"Take Pity," one of my own—and then ask you to tell me what you think it means. This ties up with Kenneth Burke's remark that the author doesn't necessarily know all that goes on in his fiction. For example, the quality of an author's vocabulary at a certain time when he is writing some work, or the unconscious forces that influence that particular story or work may be unknown to him, so that besides the story he is doing consciously there would be elements that he is not aware of.

D. H. Lawrence said, "Never trust the artist. Trust the tale. The proper function of the critic is to save the tale from the artist who created it."

What I gather from this remark is that one ought not to trust the author's explanation of the tale; also perhaps his interference with it simply by existing, that is by having a history, a personal history by means of which the tale may be interpreted. The first explanation is the more likely one.

With these thoughts in mind I will read my story to you.

◆

Take Pity

Davidov, the census-taker, opened the door without knocking, limped into the room, and sat wearily down. Out came his notebook and he was on the job. Rosen, the ex-coffee salesman, wasted, eyes despairing, sat motionless, cross-legged, on his cot. The square, clean but cold room, lit by a dim globe, was sparsely furnished: the cot, a folding chair, small table, old unpainted chests—no closets but who needed them?—and a small sink with a rough piece of green, institutional soap on its holder—you could smell it across the room. The worn black shade over the single narrow window was drawn to the ledge, surprising Davidov.

"What's the matter you don't pull the shade up?" he remarked.

Rosen ultimately sighed. "Let it stay."

"Why? Outside is light."

"Who needs light?"

"What then you need?"

"Light I don't need," replied Rosen.

Davidov, sour-faced, flipped through the closely scrawled pages of his notebook until he found a clean one. He attempted to scratch in a word with his fountain pen but it had run dry, so he fished a pencil stub out of his vest pocket and sharpened it with a cracked razor blade. Rosen paid no attention to the feathery shavings falling to the floor. He looked restless, seemed to be listening to or for something, although Davidov was convinced there was absolutely nothing to listen to. It was only when the census-taker somewhat irritably and with increasing loudness repeated a question that Rosen stirred and identified himself. He was about to furnish an address but caught himself and shrugged.

Davidov did not comment on the salesman's gesture. "So begin," he nodded.

"Who knows where to begin?" Rosen stared at the drawn shade. "Do they know where to begin?"

"Philosophy we are not interested," said Davidov. "Start in how you met her."

"Who?" pretended Rosen.

"Her," he snapped.

"So if I got to begin, how you know about her already?" Rosen asked triumphantly.

Davidov spoke wearily, "You mentioned before."

Rosen remembered. They had questioned him upon his arrival and he now recalled blurting out her name. It was perhaps something in the air. It did not permit you to retain what you remembered. That was part of the cure, if you wanted a cure.

"Where I met her—?" Rosen murmured. "I met her where she always was—in the back room there in that hole in the wall that it was a waste of time for me I went there. Maybe I sold them a half a bag of coffee a month. This is not business."

"In business we are not interested."

"What then you are interested?" Rosen mimicked Davidov's tone.

Davidov clammed up coldly.

Rosen knew they had him where it hurt, so he went on: "The husband was maybe forty, Axel Kalish, a Polish refugee. He worked like a blind horse when he got to America, and saved maybe two, three thousand dollars that he bought with the money this pisher grocery in a dead neighborhood where he didn't have a chance. He called my company up for credit and they sent me I should see. I recommended okay because I felt sorry. He had a wife, Eva, you know already about her, and two darling girls, one five and one three, little dolls, Fega and Surale, that I didn't want them to suffer. So right away I told him, without tricks, 'Kiddo, this is a mistake. This place is a grave. Here they will bury you if you don't get out quick!' "

Rosen sighed deeply.

"So?" Davidov had thus far written nothing, irking the ex-salesman.

"So?—Nothing. He didn't get out. After a couple months he tried to sell but nobody bought, so he stayed and starved. They never made expenses. Every day they got poorer you couldn't look in their faces. 'Don't be a damn fool,' I told him, 'go in bankruptcy.' But he couldn't stand to lose all his capital, and he was also afraid it would be hard to find a job. 'My God,' I said, 'do anything. Be a painter, a janitor, a junk man, but get out of here before everybody is a skeleton.'

"This he finally agreed with me, but before he could go in auction he dropped dead."

Davidov made a note. "How did he die?"

"On this I am not an expert," Rosen replied. "You know better than me."

"How did he die?" Davidov spoke impatiently. "Say in one word."

"From what he died?—he died, that's all."

"Answer, please, this question."

"Broke in him something. That's how."

"Broke what?"

"Broke what breaks. He was talking to me how bitter was his life, and he touched me on my sleeve to say something else, but the next minute his face got small and he fell down dead, the wife screaming, the little girls crying that it made in my heart pain. I am myself a sick man and when I saw him laying on the floor, I said to myself, 'Rosen, say goodbye, this guy is finished.' So I said it."

Rosen got up from the cot and strayed despondently around the room, avoiding the window. Davidov was occupying the only chair, so the ex-salesman was finally forced to sit on the edge of the bed again. This irritated him. He badly wanted a cigarette but disliked asking for one.

Davidov permitted him a short interval of silence, then leafed impatiently through his notebook. Rosen, to needle the census-taker, said nothing.

"So what happened?" Davidov finally demanded.

Rosen spoke with ashes in his mouth. "After the funeral—" He paused, tried to wet his lips, then went on, "He belonged to a society that they buried him, and he also left a thousand dollars insurance, but after the funeral I said to her, 'Eva, listen to me. Take the money and your children and run away from here. Let the creditors take the store. What will they get?—Nothing.'

"But she answered me, 'Where will I go, where, with my two orphans that their father left them to starve?'

" 'Go anywhere,' I said. 'Go to your relatives.'

"She laughed like laughs somebody who hasn't got no joy. 'My relatives Hitler took away from me.'

" 'What about Axel—surely an uncle somewheres?'

" 'Nobody,' she said. 'I will stay here like my Axel wanted. With the insurance I will buy new stock and fix up the store. Every week I will decorate the window, and in this way gradually will come in new customers—'

" 'Eva, my darling girl—'

" 'A millionaire I don't expect to be. All I want is I should make a little living and take care on my girls. We will live in the back here like before, and in this way I can work and watch them, too.'

" 'Eva,' I said, 'you are a nice-looking young woman, only thirty-eight years. Don't throw away your life here. Don't flush in the toilet—you should excuse me—the thousand poor dollars from your dead husband. Believe me, I know from such stores. After thirty-five years' experience I know a graveyard when I smell it. Go better someplace and find a job. You're young yet. Sometime you will meet somebody and get married.'

" 'No, Rosen, not me,' she said. 'With marriage I am finished. Nobody wants a poor widow with two children.'

" 'This I don't believe it.'

" 'I know,' she said.

"Never in my life I saw so bitter a woman's face.

" 'No,' I said. 'No.'

" 'Yes, Rosen, yes. In my whole life I never had anything. In my whole life I always suffered. I don't expect better. This is my life.'

"I said no and she said yes. What could I do? I am a man with only one kidney, and worse than that, that I won't mention it. When I talked she didn't listen, so I stopped to talk. Who can argue with a widow?"

The ex-salesman glanced up at Davidov but the census-taker did not reply. "What happened then?" he asked.

"What happened?" mocked Rosen. "Happened what happens."

Davidov's face grew red.

"What happened, happened," Rosen said hastily. "She ordered from the wholesalers all kinds goods that she paid for them cash. All week she opened boxes and packed on the shelves cans, jars, packages. Also she cleaned, and she washed, and she mopped with oil the floor. With tissue paper she made new decorations in the window, everything should look nice—but who came in? Nobody except a few poor customers from the tenement around the corner. And when they came? When was closed the supermarkets and they needed some little item that they forgot to buy, like a quart milk, fifteen cents' cheese, a small can sardines for lunch. In a few months was again dusty the cans on the shelves, and her money was gone. Credit she couldn't get except from me, and from me she got because I paid out of my pocket the company. This she didn't know. She worked, she dressed clean, she waited that the store should get better. Little by little the shelves got empty, but where was the profit? They ate it up. When I looked on the little girls I knew what she didn't tell me. Their faces were white, they were thin, they were hungry. She kept the little food that was left, on the shelves. One night I brought in a nice piece of sirloin, but I could see from her eyes that she didn't like that I did it. So what else could I do? I have a heart and I am human."

Here the ex-salesman wept.

Davidov pretended not to see though once he peeked.

Rosen blew his nose, then went on more calmly, "When the children were sleeping we sat in the dark there, in the back, and not once in four hours opened the door should come in a customer. 'Eva, for Godsakes, *run away*,' I said.

" 'I have no place to go,' she said.

" 'I will give you where you can go, and please don't say to me no. I am a bachelor, this you know. I got whatever I need and more besides. Let me help you and the children. Money don't interest me. Interests me good health, but I can't buy it. I'll tell you what I will do. Let this place go to the creditors and move into a two-family house that I own, which the top floor is now empty. Rent will cost you nothing. In the meantime you can go and find a job. I will also pay the downstairs lady to take care of the girls—God bless them—until you will come home. With your wages you will buy the food, if you need clothes, and also save a little. This you can use when you get married someday. What do you say?'

"She didn't answer me. She only looked on me in such a way, with such burning eyes, like I was small and ugly. For the first time I thought to myself, 'Rosen, this woman don't like you.'

" 'Thank you very kindly, my friend Mr. Rosen,' she answered me, 'but charity we are not needing. I got yet a paying business, and it will get better when times are better. Now is bad times. When comes again good times will get better the business.'

" 'Who charity?' I cried to her. 'What charity? Speaks to you your husband's a friend.'

" 'Mr. Rosen, my husband didn't have no friends.'

" 'Can't you see that I want to help the children?'

" 'The children have their mother.'

" 'Eva, what's the matter with you?' I said. 'Why do you make sound bad something that I mean it should be good?'

"This she didn't answer. I felt sick in my stomach, and was coming also a headache so I left.

"All night I didn't sleep, and then all of a sudden I figured out a reason why she was worried. She was worried I would ask for some kind of payment except cash. She got the wrong man. Anyway, this made me think of something that I didn't think about before. I thought now to ask her to marry me. What did she have to lose? I could take care of myself without any trouble to them. Fega and Surale would have a father he could give them for the movies, or sometime to buy a little doll to play with, and when I died, would go to them my investments and insurance policies.

"The next day I spoke to her.

" 'For myself, Eva, I don't want a thing. Absolutely not a thing. For you and your girls—everything. I am not a strong man, Eva. In fact, I am sick. I tell you this you should understand I don't expect to live long. But even for a few years would be nice to have a little family.'

"She was with her back to me and didn't speak.

"When she turned around again her face was white but the mouth was like iron.

" 'No, Mr. Rosen.'

" 'Why not, tell me?'

" 'I had enough with sick men.' She began to cry. 'Please, Mr. Rosen. Go home.'

"I didn't have strength I should argue with her, so I went home. I went home but hurt me in my mind. All day long and all night I felt bad. My back pained me where was missing my kidney. Also too much smoking. I tried to understand this woman but I couldn't. Why should somebody that her two children were starving always say no to a man that he wanted to help her? What did I do to her bad? Am I maybe a murderer she should hate me so much? All that I felt in my heart was pity for her and the children, but I couldn't convince her. Then I went back and begged her she should let me help them, and once more she told me no.

" 'Eva,' I said, 'I don't blame you that you don't want a sick man. So come with me to a marriage broker and we will find you a strong, healthy husband that he will support you and your girls. I will give the dowry.'

"She screamed, 'On this I don't need your help, Rosen!'

"I didn't say no more. What more could I say? All day long, from early in the morning till late in the night she worked like an animal. All day she mopped, she washed with soap and a brush the shelves, the few cans she polished, but the store was still rotten. The little girls I was afraid to look at. I could see in their faces their bones. They were tired, they were weak. Little Surale held with her hand all the time the dress of Fega. Once when I saw them in the street I gave them some cakes, but when I tried the next day to give them something else, the mother shouldn't know, Fega answered me, 'We can't take, Momma says today is a fast day.'

"I went inside. I made my voice soft. 'Eva, on my bended knees, I am a man with nothing in this world. Allow me that I should have a little pleasure before I die. Allow me that I should help you to stock up once more the store.'

"So what did she do? She cried, it was terrible to see. And after she cried, what did she say? She told me to go away and I shouldn't come back. I felt like to pick up a chair and break her head.

"In my house I was too weak to eat. For two days I took in my mouth nothing except maybe a spoon of chicken noodle soup, or maybe a glass tea without sugar. This wasn't good for me. My health felt bad.

"Then I made up a scheme that I was a friend of Axel's who lived in Jersey. I said I owed Axel seven hundred dollars that he lent me this money fifteen years ago, before he got married. I said I did not have the whole money now, but I would send her every week twenty dollars till it was paid up the debt. I put inside the letter two tens and gave it to a friend of mine, also a salesman, he should mail it in Newark so she wouldn't be suspicious who wrote the letters."

To Rosen's surprise Davidov had stopped writing. The book was full, so he tossed it onto the table, yawned, yet listened amiably. His curiosity had died.

Rosen got up and fingered the notebook. He tried to read the small distorted handwriting but could not make out a single word.

"It's not English and it's not Yiddish," he said. "Could it be in Hebrew?"

"No," answered Davidov. "It's an old-fashioned language they don't use it nowadays."

"Oh?" Rosen returned to the cot. He saw no purpose in going on now that it was not required, but he felt he had to.

"Came back all the letters," he said dully. "The first she opened it, then pasted back again the envelope, but the rest she didn't even open."

" 'Here,' I said to myself, 'is a very strange thing—a person that you can never give her anything.—*But I will give.*'

"I went then to my lawyer and we made out a will that everything I had—all my investments, my two houses that I owned, also furniture, my car, the checking account—every cent would go to her, and when she died, the rest would be left for the two girls. The same with my insurance. They would be my beneficiaries. Then I signed and went home. In the kitchen I turned on the gas and put my head in the stove.

"Let her say now no."

Davidov, scratching his stubbled cheek, nodded. This was the part he already knew. He got up and, before Rosen could cry no, idly raised the window shade.

It was twilight in space but a woman stood before the window. Rosen with a bound was off his cot to see.

It was Eva, staring at him with haunted, beseeching eyes. She raised her arms to him.

Infuriated, the ex-salesman shook his fist.

"Whore, bastard, bitch," he shouted at her. "Go 'way from here. Go home to your children."

Davidov made no move to hinder him as Rosen rammed down the window shade.

Permit me now to say a few words about the story I read you a few minutes ago. "Take Pity" is one of the three short-story fantasies I've written, of the twenty stories I've published up to now. They can be described as folk fantasies; that is to say, except for the miraculous element, what happens happens to ordinary people in more or less ordinary circumstances, usually during periods of difficulty or stress. To solve the trouble certain unreal or supernatural beings appear, inducing miraculous events. The classic Yiddish writers wrote stories of this kind. Basically they show how God tries the Jews and are clearly derived from certain books of the Bible. I tried writing a few because I like the human taste of them. What stayed with me, in other words, was not so much the miraculous element, but the sense of the trials and suffering of poor people. It may be interesting to analyze the story to see what constitutes its fantasy, reality, and final truth.

First of all, the setting is part of the fantasy; it's an institutional place in limbo. It is limbo. The reader does not know this at first but he may sense it before he catches on. Once he does, the fact excites him because it seems like an ordinary institutional place, something like a hospital or old folks' home, or possibly a room in a police station; and the reader wonders what sort of concoction the author is attempting. At this point, too, some readers are annoyed and perhaps get off the train. Having arrived in this institution—we have no idea if he will ever leave—Rosen is being judged, perhaps even paying for the act he committed—his suicide. Perhaps he is also being punished for his pride, for insisting on giving when it wasn't wanted; but if he is being punished for that reason that's no doing of mine. Of course it's fantastic for Rosen to be where he is, an institutional place in limbo, and for that matter, for the reader to see him there, but any fiction, once you open the book and find yourself elsewhere, is that fantastic.

Davidov is a figure of fantasy; that is, his function is that of a recording angel. He looks human but may never have lived on earth; not so Rosen. Davidov nowhere in the story reveals his true occupation or purpose, except through certain hints or details given in the story. For example, Rosen tries to read his writing and can't understand the language, probably Aramaic; and Davidov has heard it all before anyway. The purpose of Davidov in the structure of the story, is, obviously, to act the listener. He gives Rosen a chance to tell the story after his death— in effect a fantastic twist we accept more or less without effort, because the same effect could be achieved through our reading, after he had killed himself, Rosen's diary, if he had kept one, or perhaps his letters. Having Davidov present gives the telling of Rosen's story a certain tension because Davidov is obviously someone in authority. We don't know about Rosen's suicide in the beginning but the problem seems to be, will Davidov approve Rosen's act?—we sense something like that. Davidov also provides the opportunity for some ironic dialogue. He is used too to further the plot—bringing together Rosen and Eva at the end—because he is the one who mentions the window shade in the beginning and he raises it in the end to let Rosen see Eva.

Her appearance becomes part of the fantasy because we're not sure whether she's alive or dead. I'm often asked about her. Has she too committed suicide—or is she a figure drummed up by Davidov, the major-domo, whatever his ironic purpose; or is she a figment of a dead man's imagination—if you want to add that dimension to the already improbable. The questions that fantasy induces are themselves extraordinary, and the beauty is that they can be answered according to the logic of the story, another odd requirement of fantasy. It may therefore disappoint you to have me say about Eva that I don't know how she got there. All I know is that her presence is necessary at this point and that's why she's there, and that she is there is believable.

That about exhausts the fantasy as fantasy; now what about the realistic elements? I think they're obvious: Axel, the store, Eva's fight to exist, the hungry children, Rosen. If we exclude Davidov, who ultimately is a symbolic figure with a supernatural quality, but who could be anybody listening to a tale, the story is about real people, principally Eva and Rosen, the coffee salesman. The now dead man tells us something about his life and we believe him even though he is dead. We believe he slams down the shade at the end; let us say we believe in his spirit. I've said this before in another context but I'd like to repeat that the curious thing about fiction is that once we believe in the reality of a person—that there could be such a person, we believe in what he does no matter how inventive the author is; I mean of course within the framework of the character's possibilities, even his fantastic possibilities. The character stands before us, created, and if he is human and we can feel for him, we believe. We believe his fantastic tilts with windmills. We accept the fact that he arranges his own trial and execution, or that he has become metamorphosed into a gigantic bedbug; or that he is Henderson and is lifting a fantastically heavy statue in order to become Rain King. What we can't believe are poorly conceived characters. "Take Pity," then, is (among other things) about a woman who for one reason or another—perhaps her embittered quality, stubbornness, pride, or simple incapacity, through lack of generosity, to accept any man's generosity or compassion—cannot accept what he offers in goodwill for herself and her children to alleviate their distress and suffering. In essence to teach her what she is, as well as to thwart her will and save her children, to give pity where none is desired, Rosen takes his life.

Might this happen, if it hasn't a thousand times already? I think so. The fantasy, therefore, is not necessary to the situation; the fantasy enriches the fiction without altering the truth about certain human beings. The truth is of this world, not beyond, and it is a moral truth.

Fantastic, symbolic, mythic, timeless, universal, poetic, or anything else the fantasy may be, the truth it tells is true.

6

The Magic Barrel

◆

I want to talk about the origin of the story and some of the sources of its material.

One's subject matter is not always easy to come by. It sometimes takes years to discover, and it may be that its development and the use made of it are ultimately connected with the discovery of self and the consequent or parallel development of a personal philosophy of life. Thus is the matrix formed for collecting experiences or ideas. You are more attentive, of course, to what is important to you. Sometimes the discovery of what one will write about—his kind of subject matter— may come as a startling insight, but usually the insight occurs after the accumulation of a certain amount of understanding of oneself and the world.

I have never made a study of the main sources of literary material but I imagine they can be divided into two obvious categories: that of autobiography and sources other than oneself.

Autobiography uses a good deal of the material of the past, particularly adolescence and childhood; the material of the past often centers around an environment and can be very fruitful if it includes that of a second culture. It also uses, of course, the material of present time, centered a good deal in observations, we hope mature, of amorous experience, not often enough on matters of belief and principle, quite often in trauma. Sometimes this material, of present time, can become journalistically thin if it is not handled with some reference to symbol or archetype or history, personal or cultural; that is to say if it is handled without imaginative plumbing for depth, or with little awareness of the complexity of human experience.

If one depends on his memory to provide him with a subject matter, or documentation of some sort, it is wise to remember that memory alone cannot in itself provide the writer with a work of art. If memory is practically all, the writer becomes a sort of recording device, in much the way Thomas Wolfe was, and Proust was not.

Memory, when too strongly relied on, destroys a necessary invention; and it slows objectification and symbolism. As a matter of fact, it is the purpose of the symbol to fight memory: to reduce experience to its essentials at the same time as it derives all the meanings (and contains them) that it can. It is, let me call it, the quickest route out of the self into the past, the lives of others, and into universal experience generally.

The second category—sources other than oneself—will center around people whom one has observed in the world outside the family, at work or in society; people one has not become much involved with, to whom one responds as a sort of listener, if confidante is too formal a term.

Next, I suppose, would be hearsay—hearing stories about people you don't know. Henry James very much liked this sort of thing—the donnée whose kernel only he wanted to hear so that he could work out the rest.

Then would come ideas from one's reading, everything from newspaper stories to literature; and it too can form a treasure of the past which the writer will, on occasion, tap.

The use of this second category does not mean of course the exclusion of the autobiographical. The autobiographical will interweave with this material; it will work in as needed, not as a mere record.

This account is far from complete, but is enough to go on for purposes of discussing my story. I will now read "The Magic Barrel."

◆

The Magic Barrel

Not long ago there lived in uptown New York, in a small, almost meager room, though crowded with books, Leo Finkle, a rabbinical student at the Yeshiva University. Finkle, after six years of study, was to be ordained in June and had been advised by an acquaintance that he might find it easier to win himself a congregation if he were married. Since he had no present prospects of marriage, after two tormented days of turning it over in his mind, he called in Pinye Salzman, a marriage broker whose two-line advertisement he had read in *The Forward*.

The matchmaker appeared one night out of the dark fourth-floor hallway of the graystone rooming house where Finkle lived, grasping a black, strapped portfolio that had been worn thin with use. Salzman, who had been long in the business, was of slight but dignified build, wearing an old hat, and an overcoat too short and tight for him. He smelled frankly of fish, which he loved to eat, and although he was missing a few teeth, his presence was not displeasing, because of an amiable manner curiously contrasted with mournful eyes. His voice, his lips, his wisp of beard, his bony fingers were animated, but give him a moment of repose and his mild blue eyes revealed a depth of sadness, a characteristic that put Leo a little at ease although the situation, for him, was inherently tense.

He at once informed Salzman why he had asked him to come, explaining that but for his parents, who had married comparatively late in life, he was alone in the world. He had for six years devoted himself almost entirely to his studies, as a result of which, understandably, he had found himself without time for social life and the company of young women. Therefore he thought it the better part of trial and error—of embarrassing fumbling—to call in an experienced person to advise him on these matters. He remarked in passing that the function of the marriage broker was ancient and honorable, highly approved in the Jewish community, because it made practical the necessary without hindering joy. Moreover, his own parents had been brought together by a matchmaker. They had made, if not a financially profitable marriage—since neither had possessed any worldly goods to speak of—at least a successful one in the sense of their everlasting devotion to each other. Salzman listened in embarrassed surprise, sensing a sort of apology. Later, however, he experienced a glow of pride in his work, an emotion that had left him years ago, and he heartily approved of Finkle.

The two went to their business. Leo had led Salzman to the only clear place in the room, a table near a window that overlooked the lamp-lit city. He seated himself at the matchmaker's side but facing him, attempting by an act of will to suppress the unpleasant tickle in his throat. Salzman eagerly unstrapped his portfolio and removed a loose rubber band from a thin packet of much-handled cards. As he flipped through them, a gesture and sound that physically hurt Leo, the student pretended not to see and gazed steadfastly out the window. Although it was still February, winter was on its last legs, signs of which he had for the first time in years begun to notice. He now observed the round white moon, moving high in the sky through a cloud menagerie, and watched with half-open mouth as it penetrated a huge hen, and dropped out of her like an egg laying itself. Salzman, though pretending through eyeglasses he had just slipped on to be engaged in scanning the writing on the cards, stole occasional glances at the young man's distinguished face, noting with pleasure the long, severe scholar's nose, brown eyes heavy with learning, sensitive yet ascetic lips, and a certain almost hollow quality of the dark cheeks. He gazed around at shelves upon shelves of books and let out a soft, contented sigh.

When Leo's eyes fell upon the cards, he counted six spread out in Salzman's hand.

"So few?" he asked in disappointment.

"You wouldn't believe me how much cards I got in my office," Salzman replied. "The drawers are already filled to the top, so I keep them now in a barrel, but is every girl good for a new rabbi?"

Leo blushed at this, regretting all he had revealed of himself in a curriculum vitae he had sent to Salzman. He had thought it best to acquaint him with his strict standards and specifications, but in having done so, felt he had told the marriage broker more than was absolutely necessary.

He hesitantly inquired, "Do you keep photographs of your clients on file?"

"First comes family, amount of dowry, also what kind promises," Salzman replied, unbuttoning his tight coat and settling himself in the chair. "After comes pictures, rabbi."

"Call me Mr. Finkle. I'm not yet a rabbi."

Salzman said he would, but instead called him doctor, which he changed to rabbi when Leo was not listening too attentively.

Salzman adjusted his horn-rimmed spectacles, gently cleared his throat, and read in an eager voice the contents of the top card:

"Sophie P. Twenty-four years. Widow one year. No children. Educated high school and two years college. Father promises eight thousand dollars. Has wonderful wholesale business. Also real estate. On the mother's side comes teachers, also one actor. Well known on Second Avenue."

Leo gazed up in surprise. "Did you say a widow?"

"A widow don't mean spoiled, rabbi. She lived with her husband maybe four months. He was a sick boy she made a mistake to marry him."

"Marrying a widow has never entered my mind."

"This is because you have no experience. A widow, especially if she is young and healthy like this girl, is a wonderful person to marry. She will be thankful to you the rest of her life. Believe me, if I was looking now for a bride, I would marry a widow."

Leo reflected, then shook his head.

Salzman hunched his shoulders in an almost imperceptible gesture of disappointment. He placed the card down on the wooden table and began to read another:

"Lily H. High school teacher. Regular. Not a substitute. Has savings and new Dodge car. Lived in Paris one year. Father is successful dentist thirty-five years. Interested in professional man. Well-Americanized family. Wonderful opportunity.

"I know her personally," said Salzman. "I wish you could see this girl. She is a doll. Also very intelligent. All day you could talk to her about books and theyater and what not. She also knows current events."

"I don't believe you mentioned her age?"

"Her age?" Salzman said, raising his brows. "Her age is thirty-two years."

Leo said after a while, "I'm afraid that seems a little too old."

Salzman let out a laugh. "So how old are you, rabbi?"

"Twenty-seven."

"So what is the difference, tell me, between twenty-seven and thirty-two? My own wife is seven years older than me. So what did I suffer?—Nothing. If Rothschild's a daughter wants to marry you, would you say on account her age, no?"

"Yes," Leo said dryly.

Salzman shook off the no in the yes. "Five years don't mean a thing. I give you my word that when you will live with her for one week you will forget her age. What does it mean five years—that she lived more and knows more than somebody who is younger? On this girl, God bless her, years are not wasted. Each one that it comes makes better the bargain."

"What subject does she teach in high school?"

"Languages. If you heard the way she speaks French, you will think it is music. I am in the business twenty-five years, and I recommend her with my whole heart. Believe me, I know what I'm talking, rabbi."

"What's on the next card?" Leo said abruptly.

Salzman reluctantly turned up the third card:

"Ruth K. Nineteen years. Honor student. Father offers thirteen thousand cash to the right bridegroom. He is a medical doctor. Stomach specialist with marvelous practice. Brother-in-law owns own garment business. Particular people."

Salzman looked as if he had read his trump card.

"Did you say nineteen?" Leo asked with interest.

"On the dot."

"Is she attractive?" He blushed. "Pretty?"

Salzman kissed his fingertips. "A little doll. On this I give you my word. Let me call the father tonight and you will see what means pretty."

But Leo was troubled. "You're sure she's that young?"

"This I am positive. The father will show you the birth certificate."

"Are you positive there isn't something wrong with her?" Leo insisted.

"Who says there is wrong?"

"I don't understand why an American girl her age should go to a marriage broker."

A smile spread over Salzman's face.

"So for the same reason you went, she comes."

Leo flushed. "I am pressed for time."

Salzman, realizing he had been tactless, quickly explained. "The father came, not her. He wants she should have the best, so he looks around himself. When we will locate the right boy he will introduce him and encourage. This makes a better marriage than if a young girl without experience takes for herself. I don't have to tell you this."

"But don't you think this young girl believes in love?" Leo spoke uneasily.

Salzman was about to guffaw but caught himself and said soberly, "Love comes with the right person, not before."

Leo parted dry lips but did not speak. Noticing that Salzman had snatched a glance at the next card, he cleverly asked, "How is her health?"

"Perfect," Salzman said, breathing with difficulty. "Of course, she is a little lame on her right foot from an auto accident that it happened to her when she was twelve years, but nobody notices on account she is so brilliant and also beautiful."

Leo got up heavily and went to the window. He felt curiously bitter and upbraided himself for having called in the marriage broker. Finally, he shook his head.

"Why not?" Salzman persisted, the pitch of his voice rising.

"Because I detest stomach specialists."

"So what do you care what is his business? After you marry her do you need him? Who says he must come every Friday night in your house?"

Ashamed of the way the talk was going, Leo dismissed Salzman, who went home with heavy, melancholy eyes.

Though he had felt only relief at the marriage broker's departure, Leo was in low spirits the next day. He explained it as arising from Salzman's failure to produce a suitable bride for him. He did not care for his type of clientele. But when Leo found himself hesitating whether to seek out another matchmaker, one more polished than Pinye, he wondered if it could be—his protestations to the contrary, and although he honored his father and mother—that he did not, in essence, care for the matchmaking institution? This thought he quickly put out of mind yet found himself still upset. All day he ran around in the woods—missed an important appointment, forgot to give out his laundry, walked out of a Broadway cafeteria without paying and had to run back with his ticket in his hand; had even not recognized his landlady in the street when she passed with a friend and courteously called over, "A good evening to you, Doctor Finkle." By nightfall, however, he had regained sufficient calm to sink his nose into a book and there found peace from his thoughts.

Almost at once there came a knock on the door. Before Leo could say enter, Salzman, commercial cupid, was standing in the room. His face was gray and meager, his expression hungry, and he looked as if he would expire on his feet. Yet the marriage broker managed, by some trick of the muscles, to display a broad smile.

"So good evening. I am invited?"

Leo nodded, disturbed to see him again, yet unwilling to ask the man to leave.

Beaming still, Salzman laid his portfolio on the table. "Rabbi, I got for you tonight good news."

"I've asked you not to call me rabbi. I'm still a student."

"Your worries are finished. I have for you a first-class bride."

"Leave me in peace concerning this subject." Leo pretended lack of interest.

"The world will dance at your wedding."

"Please, Mr. Salzman, no more."

"But first must come back my strength," Salzman said weakly. He fumbled with the portfolio straps and took out of the leather case an oily paper bag, from which he extracted a hard, seeded roll and a small smoked whitefish. With a quick motion of his hand he stripped the fish out of its skin and began ravenously to chew. "All day in a rush," he muttered.

Leo watched him eat.

"A sliced tomato you have maybe?" Salzman hesitantly inquired.

"No."

The marriage broker shut his eyes and ate. When he had finished he carefully cleaned up the crumbs and rolled up the remains of the fish, in the paper bag. His spectacled eyes roamed the room until he discovered, amid some piles of books, a one-burner gas stove. Lifting his hat he humbly asked, "A glass tea you got, rabbi?"

Conscience-stricken, Leo rose and brewed the tea. He served it with a chunk of lemon and two cubes of lump sugar, delighting Salzman.

After he had drunk his tea, Salzman's strength and good spirits were restored.

"So tell me, rabbi," he said amiably, "you considered some more the three clients I mentioned yesterday?"

"There was no need to consider."

"Why not?"

"None of them suits me."

"What then suits you?"

Leo let it pass because he could give only a confused answer.

Without waiting for a reply, Salzman asked, "You remember this girl I talked to you—the high school teacher?"

"Age thirty-two?"

But, surprisingly, Salzman's face lit in a smile. "Age twenty-nine."

Leo shot him a look. "Reduced from thirty-two?"

"A mistake," Salzman avowed. "I talked today with the dentist. He took me to his safety deposit box and showed me the birth certificate. She was twenty-nine years last August. They made her a party in the mountains where she went for her vacation. When her father spoke to me the first time I forgot to write the age and I told you thirty-two, but now I remember this was a different client, a widow."

"The same one you told me about, I thought she was twenty-four?"

"A different. Am I responsible that the world is filled with widows?"

"No, but I'm not interested in them, nor, for that matter, in schoolteachers."

Salzman pulled his clasped hands to his breast. Looking at the ceiling he devoutly exclaimed, "Yiddishe kinder, what can I say to somebody that he is not interested in high school teachers? So when then are you interested?"

Leo flushed but controlled himself.

"In what else will you be interested," Salzman went on, "if you not interested in this fine girl that she speaks four languages and has personally in the bank ten thousand dollars? Also her father guarantees further twelve thousand. Also she has a new car, wonderful clothes, talks on all subjects, and she will give you a first-class home and children. How near do we come in our life to paradise?"

"If she's so wonderful, why wasn't she married ten years ago?"

"Why?" said Salzman with a heavy laugh. "—Why? Because she is *partikiler*. This is why. She wants the *best*."

Leo was silent, amused at how he had entangled himself. But Salzman had aroused his interest in Lily H., and he began seriously to consider calling on her. When the marriage broker observed how intently Leo's mind was at work on the facts he had supplied, he felt certain they would soon come to an agreement.

$\approx$

Late Saturday afternoon, conscious of Salzman, Leo Finkle waked with Lily Hirschorn along Riverside Drive. He walked briskly and erectly, wearing with distinction the black fedora he had that morning taken with trepidation out of the dusty hat box on his closet shelf, and the heavy black Saturday coat he had thoroughly whisked clean. Leo also owned a walking stick, a present from a distant relative, but quickly put temptation aside and did not use it. Lily, petite and not unpretty, had on something signifying the approach of spring. She was au courant, animatedly, with all sorts of subjects, and he weighed her words and found her surprisingly sound—score another for Salzman, whom he uneasily sensed to be somewhere around, hiding perhaps in a tree along the street, flashing the lady signals with a pocket mirror; or perhaps a cloven-hoofed Pan, piping nuptial ditties as he danced his invisible way before them, strewing wild buds on the walk and purple grapes in their path, symbolizing fruit of a union, though there was of course still none.

Lily startled Leo by remarking, "I was thinking of Mr. Salzman, a curious figure, wouldn't you say?"

Not certain what to answer, he nodded.

She bravely went on, blushing, "I for one am grateful for his introducing us. Aren't you?"

He courteously replied, "I am."

"I mean," she said with a little laugh—and it was all in good taste, or at least gave the effect of being not in bad—"do you mind that we came together so?"

He was not displeased with her honesty, recognizing that she meant to set the relationship aright, and understanding that it took a certain amount of experience in life, and courage, to want to do it quite that way. One had to have some sort of past to make that kind of beginning.

He said that he did not mind. Salzman's function was traditional and honorable—valuable for what it might achieve, which, he pointed out, was frequently nothing.

Lily agreed with a sigh. They walked on for a while and she said after a long silence, again with a nervous laugh, "Would you mind if I asked you something a little bit personal? Frankly, I find the subject fascinating." Although Leo shrugged, she went on half embarrassedly, "How was it that you came to your calling? I mean, was it a sudden passionate inspiration?"

Leo, after a time, slowly replied, "I was always interested in the Law."

"You saw revealed in it the presence of the Highest?"

He nodded and changed the subject. "I understand that you spent a little time in Paris, Miss Hirschorn?"

"Oh, did Mr. Salzman tell you, Rabbi Finkle?" Leo winced but she went on, "It was ages ago and almost forgotten. I remember I had to return for my sister's wedding."

And Lily would not be put off. "When," she asked in a slightly trembly voice, "did you become enamored of God?"

He stared at her. Then it came to him that she was talking not about Leo Finkle but a total stranger, some mystical figure, perhaps even passionate prophet that Salzman had dreamed up for her—no relation to the living or dead. Leo trembled with rage and weakness. The trickster had obviously sold her a bill of goods, just as he had him, who'd expected to become acquainted with a young lady of twenty-nine, only to behold, the moment he had laid eyes upon her strained and anxious face, a woman past thirty-five and aging rapidly. Only his self-control had kept him this long in her presence.

"I am not," he said gravely, "a talented religious person," and in seeking words to go on, found himself possessed by shame and fear. "I think," he said in a strained manner, "that I came to God not because I loved him but because I did not."

This confession he spoke harshly because its unexpectedness shook him.

Lily wilted. Leo saw a profusion of loaves of bread go flying like ducks high over his head, not unlike the winged loaves by which he had counted himself to sleep last night. Mercifully, then, it snowed, which he would not put past Salzman's machinations.

~

He was infuriated with the marriage broker and swore he would throw him out of the room the moment he reappeared. But Salzman did not come that night, and when Leo's anger had subsided, an unaccountable despair grew in its place. At first he thought this was caused by his disappointment in Lily, but before long it became evident that he had involved himself with Salzman without a true knowledge of his own intent. He gradually realized—with an emptiness that seized him with six hands—that he had called in the broker to find him a bride because he was incapable of doing it himself. This terrifying insight he had derived as a result of his meeting and conversation with Lily Hirschorn. Her probing questions had somehow irritated him into revealing—to himself more than her—the true nature of his relationship to God, and from that it had come upon him, with shocking force, that apart from his parents, he had never loved anyone. Or perhaps it went the other way, that he did not love God so well as he might, because he had not loved man. It seemed to Leo that his whole life stood starkly revealed and he saw himself for the first time as he truly was—unloved and loveless. This bitter but somehow not fully unexpected revelation brought him to a point of panic, controlled only by extraordinary effort. He covered his face with his hands and cried.

The week that followed was the worst of his life. He did not eat and lost weight. His beard darkened and grew ragged. He stopped attending seminars and almost never opened a book. He seriously considered leaving the Yeshiva, although he was deeply troubled at the thought of the loss of all his years of study—saw them like pages torn from a book, strewn over the city—and at the devastating effect of this decision upon his parents. But he had lived without knowledge of himself, and never in the Five Books and all the Commentaries—mea culpa—had the truth been revealed to him. He did not know where to turn, and in all this desolating loneliness there was no *to whom*, although he often thought of Lily but not once could bring himself to go downstairs and make the call. He became touchy and irritable, especially with his landlady, who asked him all manner of personal questions; on the other hand, sensing his own disagreeableness, he waylaid her on the stairs and apologized abjectly, until, mortified, she ran from him. Out of this, however, he drew the consolation that he was a Jew and that a Jew suffered. But gradually, as the long and terrible week drew to a close, he regained his composure and some idea of purpose in life: to go on as planned. Although he was imperfect, the ideal was not. As for his quest of a bride, the thought of continuing afflicted him with anxiety and heartburn, yet perhaps with this new knowledge of himself he would be more successful than in the past. Perhaps love would now come to him and a bride to that love. And for this sanctified seeking who needed a Salzman?

The marriage broker, a skeleton with haunted eyes, returned that very night. He looked, withal, the picture of frustrated expectancy—as if he had steadfastly waited the week at Miss Lily Hirschorn's side for a telephone call that never came.

Casually coughing, Salzman came immediately to the point: "So how did you like her?"

Leo's anger rose and he could not refrain from chiding the matchmaker: "Why did you lie to me, Salzman?"

Salzman's pale face went dead white, the world had snowed on him.

"Did you not state that she was twenty-nine?" Leo insisted.

"I give you my word—"

"She was thirty-five, if a day. At *least* thirty five."

"Of this don't be too sure. Her father told me—"

"Never mind. The worst of it is that you lied to her."

"How did I lie to her, tell me?"

"You told her things about me that weren't true. You made me out to be more, consequently less than I am. She had in mind a totally different person, a sort of semi-mystical Wonder Rabbi."

"All I said, you was a religious man."

"I can imagine."

Salzman sighed. "This is my weakness that I have," he confessed. "My wife says to me I shouldn't be a salesman, but when I have two fine people that they would be wonderful to be married, I am so happy that I talk too much." He smiled wanly. "This is why Salzman is a poor man."

Leo's anger left him. "Well, Salzman, I'm afraid that's all."

The marriage broker fastened hungry eyes on him.

"You don't want any more a bride?"

"I do," said Leo, "but I have decided to seek her in another way. I am no longer interested in an arranged marriage. To be frank, I now admit the necessity of premarital love. That is, I want to be in love with the one I marry."

"Love?" said Salzman, astounded. After a moment he remarked, "For us, our love is our life, not for the ladies. In the ghetto they—"

"I know, I know," said Leo. "I've thought of it often. Love, I have said to myself, should be a product of living and worship rather than its own end. Yet for myself I find it necessary to establish the level of my need and fulfill it."

Salzman shrugged but answered, "Listen, rabbi, if you want love, this I can find for you also. I have such beautiful clients that you will love them the minute your eyes will see them."

Leo smiled unhappily. "I'm afraid you don't understand."

But Salzman hastily unstrapped his portfolio and withdrew a manila packet from it.

"Pictures," he said, quickly laying the envelope on the table.

Leo called after him to take the pictures away, but as if on the wings of the wind, Salzman had disappeared.

March came. Leo returned to his regular routine. Although he felt not quite himself yet—lacked energy—he was making plans for a more active social life. Of course it would cost something, but he was an expert in cutting corners; and when there were no corners left he would make circles rounder. All the while Salzman's pictures had lain on the table, gathering dust. Occasionally as Leo sat studying, or enjoying a cup of tea, his eyes fell on the manila envelope, but he never opened it.

The days went by and no social life to speak of developed with a member of the opposite sex—it was difficult, given the circumstances of his situation. One morning Leo toiled up the stairs to his room and stared out the window at the city. Although the day was bright his view of it was dark. For some time he watched the people in the street below hurrying along and then turned with a heavy heart to his little room. On the table was the packet. With a sudden relentless gesture he tore it open. For a half hour he stood by the table in a state of excitement, examining the photographs of the ladies Salzman had included. Finally, with a deep sigh he put them down. There were six, of varying degrees of attractiveness, but look at them long enough and they all became Lily Hirschorn: all past their prime, all starved behind bright smiles, not a true personality in the lot. Life, despite their frantic yoohooings, had passed them by; they were pictures in a briefcase that stank of fish. After a while, however, as Leo attempted to return the photographs into the envelope, he found in it another, a snapshot of the type taken by a machine for a quarter. He gazed at it a moment and let out a low cry.

Her face deeply moved him. Why, he could at first not say. It gave him the impression of youth—spring flowers, yet age—a sense of having been used to the bone, wasted; this came from the eyes, which were hauntingly familiar, yet absolutely strange. He had a vivid impression that he had met her before, but try as he might he could not place her although he could almost recall her name, as if he had read it in her own handwriting. No, this couldn't be; he would have remembered her. It was not, he affirmed, that she had an extraordinary beauty—no, though her face was attractive enough; it was that *something* about her moved him. Feature for feature, even some of the ladies of the photographs could do better; but she leaped forth to his heart—had *lived*, or wanted to—more than just wanted, perhaps regretted how she had lived—had somehow deeply suffered: it could be seen in the depths of those reluctant eyes, and from the way the light enclosed and shone from her, and within her, opening realms of possibility: this was her own. Her he desired. His head ached and eyes narrowed with the intensity of his gazing, then as if an obscure fog had blown up in the mind, he experienced fear of her and was aware that he had received an impression, somehow, of evil. He shuddered, saying softly, it is thus with us all. Leo brewed some tea in a small pot and sat sipping it without sugar, to calm himself. But before he had finished drinking, again with excitement he examined the face and found it good: good for Leo Finkle. Only such a one could understand him and help him seek whatever he was seeking. She might, perhaps, love him. How she had happened to be among the discards in Salzman's barrel he could never guess, but he knew he must urgently go find her.

Leo rushed downstairs, grabbed up the Bronx telephone book, and searched for Salzman's home address. He was not listed, nor was his office. Neither was he in the Manhattan book. But Leo remembered having written down the address on a slip of paper after he had read Salzman's advertisement in the "personals" column of the *Forward*. He ran up to his room and tore through his papers, without luck. It was exasperating. Just when he needed the matchmaker he was nowhere to be found. Fortunately Leo remembered to look in his wallet. There on a card he found his name written and a Bronx address. No phone number was listed, the reason—Leo now recalled—he had originally communicated with Salzman by letter. He got on his coat, put a hat on over his skullcap and hurried to the subway station. All the way to the far end of the Bronx he sat on the edge of his seat. He was more than once tempted to take out the picture and see if the girl's face was as he remembered, but he refrained, allowing the snapshot to remain in his inside coat pocket, content to have her so close. When the train pulled into the station he was waiting at the door and bolted out. He quickly located the street Salzman had advertised.

The building he sought was less than a block from the subway, but it was not an office building, nor even a loft, nor a store in which one could rent office space. It was a very old tenement house. Leo found Salzman's name in pencil on a soiled tag under the bell and climbed three dark flights to his apartment. When he knocked, the door was opened by a thin, asthmatic, gray-haired woman, in felt slippers.

"Yes?" she said, expecting nothing. She listened without listening. He could have sworn he had seen her, too, before but knew it was an illusion.

"Salzman—does he live here? Pinye Salzman," he said, "the matchmaker?"

She stared at him a long minute. "Of course."

He felt embarrassed. "Is he in?"

"No." Her mouth, though left open, offered nothing more.

"The matter is urgent. Can you tell me where his office is?"

"In the air." She pointed upward.

"You mean he has no office?" Leo asked.

"In his socks."

He peered into the apartment. It was sunless and dingy, one large room divided by a half-open curtain, beyond which he could see a sagging metal bed. The near side of the room was crowded with rickety chairs, old bureaus, a three-legged table, racks of cooking utensils, and all the apparatus of a kitchen. But there was no sign of Salzman or his magic barrel, probably also a figment of his imagination. An odor of frying fish made Leo weak to the knees.

"Where is he?" he insisted. "I've got to see your husband."

At length she answered, "So who knows where he is? Every time he thinks a new thought he runs to a different place. Go home, he will find you."

"Tell him Leo Finkle."

She gave no sign she had heard.

He walked downstairs, depressed.

But Salzman, breathless, stood waiting at his door.

Leo was astounded and overjoyed. "How did you get here before me?"

"I rushed."

"Come inside."

They entered. Leo fixed tea, and a sardine sandwich for Salzman. As they were drinking he reached behind him for the packet of pictures and handed them to the marriage broker.

Salzman put down his glass and said expectantly, "You found somebody you like?"

"Not among these."

The marriage broker turned away.

"Here is the one I want." Leo held forth the snapshot.

Salzman slipped on his glasses and took the picture into his trembling hand. He turned ghastly and let out a groan.

"What's the matter?" cried Leo.

"Excuse me. Was an accident this picture. She isn't for you."

Salzman frantically shoved the manila packet into his portfolio. He thrust the snapshot into his pocket and fled down the stairs.

Leo, after momentary paralysis, gave chase and cornered the marriage broker in the vestibule. The landlady made hysterical outcries but neither of them listened.

"Give me back the picture, Salzman."

"No." The pain in his eyes was terrible.

"Tell me who she is then."

"This I can't tell you. Excuse me."

He made to depart, but Leo, forgetting himself, seized the matchmaker by his tight coat and shook him frenziedly.

"Please," sighed Salzman. "*Please.*"

Leo ashamedly let him go. "Tell me who she is," he begged. "It's very important for me to know."

"She is not for you. She is a wild one—wild, without shame. This is not a bride for a rabbi."

"What do you mean wild?"

"Like an animal. Like a dog. For her to be poor was a sin. This is why to me she is dead now."

"In God's name, what do you mean?"

"Her I can't introduce to you," Salzman cried.

"Why are you so excited?"

"Why, he asks," Salzman said, bursting into tears. "This is my baby, my Stella, she should burn in hell."

Leo hurried up to bed and hid under the covers. Under the covers he thought his life through. Although he soon fell asleep he could not sleep her out of his mind. He woke, beating his breast. Though he prayed to be rid of her, his prayers went unanswered. Through days of torment he endlessly struggled not to love her; fearing success, he escaped it. He then concluded to convert her to goodness, himself to God. The idea alternately nauseated and exalted him.

He perhaps did not know that he had come to a final decision until he encountered Salzman in a Broadway cafeteria. He was sitting alone at a rear table, sucking the bony remains of a fish. The marriage broker appeared haggard, and transparent to the point of vanishing.

Salzman looked up at first without recognizing him. Leo had grown a pointed beard and his eyes were weighted with wisdom.

"Salzman," he said, "love has at last come to my heart."

"Who can love from a picture?" mocked the marriage broker.

"It is not impossible."

"If you can love her, then you can love anybody. Let me show you some new clients that they just sent me their photographs. One is a little doll."

"Just her I want," Leo murmured.

"Don't be a fool, doctor. Don't bother with her."

"Put me in touch with her, Salzman," Leo said humbly. "Perhaps I can be of service."

Salzman had stopped eating and Leo understood with emotion that it was now arranged.

Leaving the cafeteria, he was, however, afflicted by a tormenting suspicion that Salzman had planned it all to happen this way.

⌒

Leo was informed by letter that she would meet him on a certain corner, and she was there one spring night, waiting under a street lamp. He appeared, carrying a small bouquet of violets and rosebuds. Stella stood by the lamppost, smoking. She wore white with red shoes, which fitted his expectations, although in a troubled moment he had imagined the dress red, and only the shoes white. She waited uneasily and shyly. From afar he saw that her eyes—clearly her father's—were filled with desperate innocence. He pictured, in her, his own redemption. Violins and lit candles revolved in the sky. Leo ran forward with flowers outthrust.

Around the corner, Salzman, leaning against a wall, chanted prayers for the dead.

(Don't worry about the ending. If you think about it it will come to you.) Now let's go back to the development of the story.

First there is a note in my journal, dated March 8, 1954: It reads: "Go back to the poetic, evocative, singing—often symbolic short story. Use all you've got. Go for more than story—but make story good."

That was a reaction against the short, realistic pieces that I had been writing for a while. In other words, I had the basic feeling for the story, you might call it, long before I got the idea for the story. And I might say that it is that kind of feeling that still conditions some of my most recent stories, though not all.

The idea for the story itself, the donnée, came about through Irving Howe's invitation to me to translate a story from the Yiddish for inclusion in his and Eliezer Greenberg's anthology called *A Treasury of Yiddish Stories.*

My reading in Royte Pomerantzen provided the six marriage anecdotes—two of which were very important.

◆

Love Match

A marriage broker once came to a young man to suggest a match. He said to him, "Look, I have a girl for you who's a regular doll. But really a pretty girl. What do you say?"

The young man answered, "Leave me alone."

"Well, if you're not interested in beauty," said the marriage broker, "then let me tell you about another girl I have, not so pretty but I wouldn't exactly call her ugly. She has five thousand in cash."

"Leave me alone," said the young man.

The marriage broker went on: "Say, if you've really got your mind made up for something extra special, that's fine. I've got another girl for you who has twenty thousand in cash."

"Look," said the young man, "why don't you leave me alone? Money is no consideration."

"Ah, is that so?" said the marriage broker. "Then if you're looking for something extraordinary, I have a girl of the finest quality, descended from twenty generations of rabbis, the best of the very best."

But the young man replied, "Listen, mister, I don't want to hear anything more. I intend strictly a love match."

"Don't say another word," the broker quickly answered. "I can get you that kind too."

◆

It Makes No Difference

A marriage broker once visited a young man to propose a match.

"I have a nice girl for you from a very fine family, only one thing: the girl has no money."

The young man said, "This makes no difference to me."

"And there's just another small disadvantage," said the marriage broker, "she's a bit hard of hearing in the right ear."

"That makes no difference."

"But there's still another little disadvantage: she has one eye that doesn't see so well."

"I'm not worried."

"Listen, I'll tell you the absolute truth, she limps a little too."

"That doesn't make any difference either."

"One other thing," said the marriage broker, "she's a bit of a hunchback."

"Why bother talking about it: it makes no difference whatever."

The marriage broker wasn't sure that he had been hearing right. "What kind of story is this, that nothing makes any difference to you?"

"Why should these things bother me," the young man said, "if I haven't the slightest intention of taking the girl?"

From the first anecdote I got the basic idea for the story. From the second and one or two of the others, enough of the personality of the marriage broker to develop him with comparative ease. In other words, I recognized and understood him; I was able to recognize him in my past, though I had never met a marriage broker.

His name connects him to other stories I wrote and to people I knew in the past.

Salzman, without a first name, appeared in a first novel I wrote, destroyed some time after I finished it. He is a peddler in the book, who appears in the last chapter; and he is related to a character in my first published short story, "The Cost of Living," where he appears as an Italian shoemaker who goes bankrupt and takes to peddling.

Pinye, the first name I gave Salzman, is the true first name of a bulb peddler, something like the person who appears in my novel, *The Assistant*, and in a story called "An Apology," which I did not include in my present collection of short stories because I didn't like the ending.

These people may be called *luftmenschen*—literally they live on air. Perhaps their best prototype is Menachim Mendel from the stories of Sholem Aleichem, the Yiddish humorist; but I was familiar with this kind of person from childhood.

Now I'll read the first note in my journal for this particular short story.

1. *August 21, 1954*

"The Marriage Broker's Daughter." A m.b. tries to interest a young man in a bride. The young man won't hear of it; he wants marriage for love. The m.b. then attempts to dig up a girl he thinks the young man will fall in love with. No go. By accident the young man sees the m.b.'s daughter and goes mad over her. He tries to get her father's permission to court her. The m.b. refuses a) because the daughter is the apple of his eye, b) because he will not be done out of a commission. The young man somehow gets the girl. Not sure what the miracle is but he's got to do something that satisfies everyone but the m.b. He (the m.b.) has to be disappointed yet resigned. Once I work out the meaning of the piece I'll have the ending. Season with Chagall?

We have here the basic idea of the story.

Note the invented element of the introduction of the marriage broker's daughter, and his unwillingness to let the young man have her. Also that the young man is to get the girl.

The Chagall reminder was a challenge to myself to work in a richer, more poetic vein, with more evocative imagery than I previously had.

A week later I wrote another note.

2. *August 28, 1954*

Meaning: Connected with the defeat of the m.b. Despite himself and his profession he gives up a commission. The idealism—or desire—of the young man (Chagallean character) in the end is fulfilled, just when it seemed he would lose. Plot goes something like this: M.b. tries to convince him he ought to get married. Then shows his clientele. Actually brings one around to meet young man, who is embarrassed. He tries to get rid of the m.b. because he believes in love. M.b. pooh-poohs it: love-shmove. Hounds the guy who thinks of moving out of the neighborhood. His view of the m.b. as some sort of avenging angel—or devil—something mercurial and evil. But the m.b. has awakened in him a desire for marriage. Note he lives in a furnished room. Either he is an orphan or parents live far away. (Canada?) Once again the m.b. corners him; he has a fist full of pictures. Among them he has by accident included one of his 16-year-old daughter. Our friend is at once taken by her. Trembles. Begs to meet her. M.b. backs out. Gives various reasons, then admits the girl is his daughter. Departs running. Young man follows him to his house. Begs, will pay a good commission. M.b., in kitchen, half-heartedly tries to sell him someone else. Then tries to get him to leave. But he sees the girl. She is older than sixteen, about twenty. He talks to her, the m.b. making acid comments. Finally the young man asks her to go for a walk with him, to share the beauty of the summer night. The m.b. tries to prevent this: "It's raining; you'll get wet," he says to his daughter. "This young man is a poor man—a substitute teacher, not even a regular." The girl says it's only for a walk. And she goes. They go down the stairs, laughing; the m.b. cursing.

(Maybe he never does get to see the girl?)

In this we have the development of the protagonist, whom I will to some degree connect with myself, mainly because of the teacher reference.

My only connection with a marriage broker is that once, after I became a teacher-in-training in the New York City high school system in 1939, I received a list of prospects from a matrimonial agency. From the long yellow list I remembered the phrases: "well-Americanized," "owns Dodge car," and "her father is a dentist."

With reference to the picture that Leo falls in love with. There are several such scenes in literature; I may have had in mind a scene from *The Idiot*, which I vaguely remember, but more likely it comes from the life of Mark Twain, who, as you know, fell in love with his wife when he saw the picture in her brother's possession. I've carried a romantic liking for that sort of thing for years.

Eleven days later I entered a short note, nothing much new in it.

3. September 9, 1954

(On the same day I made some notes for *The Assistant*, and started a notebook for the novel.)

Short Story: Now the boy is poor; the marriage-broker moved by compassion. Perhaps there is a plain woman in it, and the marriage broker's
daughter. In the end does the student win the girl? Is she, so to speak, presented to him by the m.b.?

I was having trouble with the story; it was not developing into the
sort of thing I wanted.

Then one day my wife and I were having a discussion, in the course
of which she said, "You talk a good deal about love, but you don't
always love."

Later on I admitted to myself that what she had said was true, and
thinking about it I concluded that the problem of not loving, or of not
being able to love, was one of the central problems of our existence; so I
immediately tied it up with the idea for my story. Here was a man who
wanted to marry for love; would it not be dramatic if he wanted to do so
to prove that he could love?

I recalled, too, a recent review of Whittaker Chambers's book,
Witness; one of the reviewers had questioned his love for God, because it
seemed to the reviewer that the book did not give any evidence of love
for man.

I had felt that I needed a religious element to the story and almost at
once the idea came to make the young man of the tale a rabbi. The rest
of the love theme was developed in the writing.

I made the following note:

4. September 14, 1954

The Marriage Broker's Daughter—further development.

The main character is a rabbinical student. He is close to God—weeps for
him at night—but he has difficulty loving his fellow men, hence he is a sad
person. To him comes a m.b. offering a bride. This will help him when he is
looking for a congregation. The student turns down the m.b. on grounds
that he wants to marry for love. The m.b. shrugs. Perhaps the young man
tells his need to love. He believes or has been told this will lead him to love
of others. But the m.b. prevails and the student goes out with two of his
clients: a Miss Hirshorn who has money and even soul but is without beauty;
then there is a beautiful girl who is rather empty. Neither of them suits the
student. The m.b., unwilling to give up, hands him some pictures of girls
and tells him to make a choice. None interest the student. (On the back of
each picture is a legend describing the attributes of the girl in round figures—also "well-Americanized") until he comes to the one who makes him

glow. He calls the m.b. and he comes a'running. When he sees the picture he pooh-poohs—it was included by mistake. The girl is married. The student, after a time, suspects something and demands more information about the girl. Finally the m.b. confesses the girl is his daughter—a *vilder*. She is a bad girl—the bane of his life. The student thinks it over and sees a way of life with her. He can help her to goodness, she can help him to love. Despite the denials of the m.b. the student insists on meeting the girl. He will come that night. He does with a wild song in his heart. Behind the door the m.b. chants a prayer for the dead.

That is pretty much the story; the changes that were made were made in the writing.

The title of the story came from a phrase in the marriage broker's speech. I had at one point listed about a dozen names and then the idea that the barrel was magic came into my head. I did not have that in mind until the story was half written.

Some other autobiographical elements are:

1. the rooming house
2. in a sense, the time of year: between end of winter and spring is to me a very dramatic time
3. the tomato, a detail from childhood

The story has been interpreted in two ways, as realism and as fantasy. I had meant it to be realistic, but two things conditioned some people's reading of it. In the original version Salzman says somewhere, referring to his daughter, "For her to be poor was a sin. This is why she is dead now." And the Chagallean imagery of the ending convinces some that it was meant to be fantasy. Either interpretation suits me, I thought, but then in the ms I sent to the publisher I altered Salzman's speech so that it now reads, "This is why to me she is dead now."

The Chagallean imagery, at least the Chagallean idea was very helpful to me in the writing of the story, but its disadvantage is that now almost anything I write is Chagallean, something I hope to live down before too very long.

The daughter of the marriage broker came into my head full grown; I can't account for her; and I've forgotten some other details of source, but there is quite a good deal of invention in the story.

The one other lesson from experience I would like to leave with young short story writers was that the story was almost all thought out before it was written, usual with me.

7

◆

After completing my first novel, *The Natural*, in essence mythic, I wanted to do a more serious, deeper perhaps, realistic piece of work. The apprentice character interested me, as he has in much of my fiction, the man, who, as much as he can in the modern world, is in the process of changing his fate, his life. This sort of person, not at all complicated, appears for the first time in my writing in the short story, "The First Seven Years" (included in my first story collection, *The Magic Barrel*), and I thought I would like to develop the possibilities of his type. The refugee shoemaker in the story becomes the Italo-American assistant, Frank Alpine, whose way of achieving his spiritual freedom is to adopt the burdens of a Jew. The grocery story background came from "The Cost of Living," another short story written in the early fifties, and now reprinted in my most recent story collection, *Idiots First*. Morris Bober resembles Sam Thomashevsky, though his fate, I should think, is more moving, because he helps call it down upon himself, whereas Sam is the victim mostly of economic circumstances. Thus from these two stories came the store background, and characters, who were to become Frank Alpine, Morris Bober, and Ida and Helen Bober.

What sort of Jew is Frank? Not much of one, I am sometimes told, because his beliefs are not explicitly stated; certainly they do not seem to be Orthodox beliefs. I admit that Frank sees the Jew a good deal as a symbol, and that there is perhaps an element of Christianity in his Judaism. However, I doubt that his view of the Jew is limited only to the man who has suffered. I think he has begun to understand the mean-

ing of the Law, and since he is engaged, at the end of the book, in reading the Old Testament, perhaps he will appreciate the Prophetic quality
of the Jewish religion. As for the Christian elements in Judaism, ideas
flow backwards and forwards, and it is ridiculous to define love, charity,
endurance, as the particular quality or province of one religion over
another. I would want Frank to continue to love St. Francis as much as
he may love Isaiah. If it is possible to wish a fate upon a character one
has created, I would hope that his making a Jew of himself, however
envisioned or achieved, will lead him into a richer humanity.

8

◆

After my last novel I was sniffing for
an idea in the direction of injustice on the American scene, partly for
obvious reasons—this was a time of revolutionary advances in Negro
rights—and because I became involved with this theme in a way that
sets off my imagination in terms of art. I had hoped to portray an
American experience, possibly concerned with a Negro protagonist, but
that didn't work out into a usable plan for a long fiction. Searching in a
similar direction, I thought of the Sacco and Vanzetti case, but after I
had read a few books about them I realized that for me the legend was
beyond further invention. And simply retelling their lives and history
didn't interest me. By this time a theme, perhaps as a residue of what I
had read, had materialized around a man (not necessarily a moral man)
who is arrested for a crime he didn't commit and spends years in prison.
The suffering and rage he undergoes cause him to examine his life and
values. The story would be about what he becomes in prison: whatever
else it had to be about it had to be about how the idea of freedom grows
in the mind of a man subjected to a grave injustice.

I was now looking for a story that had happened in the past and perhaps would happen again. I wanted the historical tie-up so I could
invent it into myth. In other words, I wanted to show how recurrent,
almost without thought, almost ritualistic, some of our unfortunate historical experiences are. I considered basing a fiction on the life of Caryl
Chessman, and then on the Dreyfus case, but for different reasons neither idea suited me. Then I remembered—I had never forgotten—the

name of Mendel Beilis, whom my father had told me about when I was a boy; and I remember being moved and frightened by the story. Beilis, an office manager in a Kiev brick factory in tsarist times, was a Jew accused of committing a ritual murder; he was charged with killing a Christian boy and stealing his blood for the making of Passover matzos. This superstition, in an early form directed against the first Christians, was turned against the Jews and persisted in Europe throughout the Middle Ages. In modern times it was rife among many of the masses of prerevolutionary Russia; and even nowadays, from time to time, the accusation is revived in the Soviet Union.

Beilis, when arrested for killing a boy and hiding his body in a cave, was a man of thirty-nine. For almost two-and-a-half years he was kept in prison without an indictment. He suffered greatly but was finally brought to trial and acquitted. In *The Fixer* I use some of his experiences, though not, basically, the man, partly because his life came to less than he had paid for by his suffering and endurance, and because I had to have room to invent. To his trials in prison I added something of Dreyfus's and Vanzetti's, shaping the whole to suggest the quality of the afflictions of the Jews under Hitler. These I dumped on the head of poor Yakov Bok, thirty, the fixer, or handyman, of the novel, a poor man seeking a better future and at once falling into a trap. He comes to Kiev on his father-in-law's horse, saves an anti-Semite from suffocating in the snow, is rewarded with a job in a brickyard, and is there arrested for the murder of a twelve-year-old boy he had one day chased from the brick kilns. Yakov had a lot to learn and maybe he learned it. His experiences in prison lead to a change in him that is the drama of the book.

So a novel that began as an idea concerned with injustice in America today has become one set in Russia fifty years ago, dealing with anti-Semitism there. Injustice is injustice.

Part **3**

**THE WRITER AND
HIS CRAFT**

◆

◆

In the previous section we found
Malamud speaking of one writer's approach to his work. In the section
that follows, "The Writer and His Craft," the subject becomes more
general, but no less specific about how to make good fiction and how
to read it. Here are teaching lectures: notes on the art and craft of the
story and the novel; a question-and-answer session following a reading
at the University of Tennessee in the early 1980s; an additional such
session ("Jewishness in American Fiction") that takes its title from the
first topic addressed; the notes that Malamud worked up (for a discussion group in Manhattan) after his careful reading in literary biography
and psychoanalysis; ruminations on the relation of subject matter and
craft; and, finally, a brief selection from his much more extensive notes
on his novel-in-progress, *The People*, unfinished at his death. Here the
reader and writer will find Malamud drawing some important and useful general examples out of the specific problems and successes in his
own workshop.

None of this material has been published before, although the questions Malamud addresses make up the core of the writer's wondering in
his own imagination: how to make a novel work, what lies at the center
of short fiction, how to live at ease with one's own questing and ques-
tioning imagination, what it is about what we know about ourselves
that we may translate into our own work, and much more that pertains
to the art and craft of fiction. As Malamud moves out from his own magical corpus and shows us how to think about these matters in our own

art and lives, his own spare but nourishing voice comes alive for the reader who may never have known him in the flesh.

Of the unnumbered evenings I recall spending in his company, one stands out among all the others. A dinner party in my Bennington College apartment, many other writers present, including our dear old late friend John Gardner, who was very drunk and his usual intellectually pugnacious self that evening—as on so many others. After our meal, Gardner went around the room and addressed each of the writers, giving them little writing lessons about their own work. "If you had only done thus and so in that middle scene in your wonderful chapter, you could have made it so much better than its already wonderful state, etc." After about an hour of this, throughout which Malamud, at the far end of the room, watched in fascination, Gardner approached him, flopping down on the floor and saying, as he gazed up at Malamud, "Now, Master, you teach me."

Malamud declined. He made some characteristically gnomic response and said nothing more. But now we all have a chance to sit at his feet and listen. —*Alan Cheuse*

9

BEGINNING THE NOVEL

◆

I would like to begin by saying a few words about good and bad ideas for novels: ideas, which as ideas may be worthwhile or impoverished. By "idea," I may mean a theme-idea or plot-idea or character-idea or some combination of these and others. In whatever shape or form the idea comes, it is something which may be developed—lends itself to this development—into a story, a series of arranged events that contain the lives or reveal the lives of certain human beings.

Is there anything such as a worthwhile theme per se? I will try to say something about that a little later.

At this point I would like to say that some people seem to take it for granted that an idea for a novel is an idea for a novel—good in itself; but many novels of beginners and others fail before they even get started, because the ideas do not lend themselves to imaginative development. By this I mean that the ideas, to begin with, are such that trivialize experience. In such ideas possibility does not, even in defeat, exist. The possibility of an esthetic and moral development, the two becoming one. I am not arguing that worthwhile ideas are necessarily what we call affirmative experience. The test, however, is that man will be important whether he fails or succeeds; his life will have value for us; the reader will know this value and will feel it.

Granted that there are weak ideas, one would think that a writer would discover and discard his before he is too long involved in them, but such is not always the case. When one has learned the discipline of completing his stories (one of the signs of the professional writer is that he won't abandon a story if he can possibly help it) he will go on with a trivial idea to the very end.

Perhaps we have here a misunderstanding of what will is. The writer may think he is exercising his will by completing the story, but he is not exercising it by abandoning the idea as trivial. This is what may have occurred in some of the later work of Mark Twain, of Steinbeck, Dos Passos, Hemingway, and others. At this point one may ask: isn't it possible that the ideas of these writers are good but that there is a deficiency of some sort in carrying out the conception, a failure of taste or talent? That is always a danger with any writer, but I think that we may say that even when a man's creative powers, for one reason or another, are on the wane, he can still deal with good ideas—for instance, Tolstoy in *Resurrection* and Faulkner in some of his latest pieces. Compare with Steinbeck's *Sweet Thursday* and Hemingway's *Across the River and Into the Trees*.

It seems to me that the most important thing a writer can do to help himself to a good book is first to help himself to a significant idea, a worthwhile theme. To create a mighty book, said Melville, one must have a mighty theme. By theme is meant idea or concept, perhaps argument; it can of course mean both.

It may also mean "material," "subject," "plot." Ortega y Gassett uses all of the foregoing expressions, including "theme," to mean mostly plot. I will say more about his theories in a few minutes.

Right now I want to make an obvious statement: that a significant idea (a mighty theme) is not easy to come by. That in order to come by it the author must strive, must strain; he must enlarge himself and his experience. He must obviously not grab at the first thought that flies through his head, no matter how strongly it appeals to him. One says, look into yourself and write, but that is often not enough, because the self may be shallow, even a talented writer's self. I would say, look into the world and write; look into your brother's heart and write. Often if we make the attempt to understand others we begin to understand ourselves. At this point look into your heart and write.

I mentioned Ortega y Gassett. To him ideas as ideas are not significant for the novel if they lack novelty. They have been used too often; the major themes have been used up—think of the work of the nineteenth century American, British, French, Italian, and Russian novelists and then add the finest writers of the first half of the twentieth century. Ortega argues that because of the lack of novelty in plot and theme the novel is more or less depleted as a genre. It may be impossible to write an important novel again. "To be a gifted writer is no longer a guarantee for producing a good novel."

I quote him:

> It is erroneous to think of the novel—and I refer to the modern novel in particular—as an endless field capable of rendering ever new forms. Rather it may be compared to a vast but finite quarry. There exist a definite number of possible themes for a novel. The workman of the primal hour had no trouble finding new blocks—new characters, new themes. But present-day writers face the fact that only narrow and concealed veins are left them.

Elsewhere in his "Notes on the Novel" he states that since present-day novelists are at a loss to invent "great new plots . . . we must dispense with them as Proust did, and concentrate on great new characters." That is the burden of his argument, that plots must give way to characters.

There is something to this question of novelty, but it is one that does not basically worry me. I am not seriously concerned that the emphasis has shifted (if it has) from the plot to the characters, or vice versa, or upon the theme for all three are part of the fiction. The artist is always working against concealed veins, and it is his business to unconceal them. The good novel has always been about man (not backgrounds or things) and will always be about man. I'm not disturbed that I'm working with this stuff—the same man they were writing about thousands of years ago, and it doesn't bother me that plots are scarce. If they are, that condition is the one that excites the writer, that makes him when he is good, better. The question then becomes: What can he do with his resources to create a work of art? Moreover, I believe, as many others do, that when a good writer comes along he brings with him his own novelty, his own distinction, either by unearthing new, unexpected themes (for which one may read plots or characters) or by using old ones in such a way as to make them seem new. He draws truth from present experience—makes the life and the times meaningful to the reader. He tells what the reality of the appearance is.

Art has as many possibilities as life—the creation of great characters can cause the invention of great plots. The two interact. I feel that a meaningful enough plot can cause the creation of characters worthy of living the events that are created.

Another reason I am not concerned with this whole death of the novel propaganda, and I ask you not to be, is that if one accepts this idea as true, he may just as well give up writing, which no dedicated writer will do. He will seek for what he needs to be effective, original, successful as a novelist.

Lastly—and this may sound a bit like a joke—Ortega states in the very essay that I have been quoting from (towards the end) the following: "Today, in the great hour of the decline of the genre, good novels and poor ones differ very much indeed. Hence, the opportunity of achieving the perfect work is excellent though extremely precarious. . . . The decline of an artistic genre, like that of a race, affects but the average specimen." He goes on: "the novel is one of the few fields that may still yield illustrious fruits, more exquisite ones than were ever garnered in previous harvests. . . . But that is for minds of rare distinction."

From which we may conclude the following: Don't be average if you want to be a good writer. The novel, rather than dead, is full of promises. To write a good one you have to be good. Those conditions that have always made the novel great are: minds of distinction working with ideas of rare distinction; I should say that is how it has always been.

I am quoting Ortega y Gassett again: "This possibility of constructing human souls is perhaps the major asset of future novelists."

That's enough for me. This "possibility" is all we need.

The question of novelty having been exhausted, we return to that of the search for worthy ideas. Perhaps this is the place to define one (admitting that it is impossible to make the ultimate definition) a bit further than I already have by implication, and thus to answer the question I asked in the beginning: Is there such a thing as a worthwhile idea for a novel, per se? Someone may justly ask: Mayn't it be said that writers working with, let us say, Melville's mighty theme: "the mystery of iniquity" and Faulkner's "the human heart in conflict with itself," can fail with them, come to artistic disaster? Obviously they can, and have. A child who chances upon these themes may fail with them, and so may a writer who doesn't understand them, who can't see farther than the length of his arm. But mayn't it be said that a writer who alights upon these ideas, who discovers them through his own searching, his experience and meditation, who is moved by them, by a vision of the drama inherent in them, by their enormous possibilities of imaginative development, who senses the concealed veins in them, will he not, given the fact that he is as talented as the next man, have far greater opportunities to produce something of importance than he who doesn't have such ideas and can't seem to acquire them?

Let me define a significant idea for a writer as one that is basically dramatic and will therefore lend itself to the uses of imagination. It will have a strong ideational content and compel the writer, in one way or another to deal with ideas as ideas. It will in the end, whether it is affirmatively handled or not, in the sense of an affirmative philosophy of life, so long as it achieves its necessary form, make man seem important, even great, his life of extraordinary importance; and in having these possibilities the idea may be said to possess moral content. At the very least we can say that a writer, good or bad, working with themes that have throughout history been considered to be worthy, important, significant, has a better opportunity for true intellectual and esthetic achievement than he working with ideas that yield little or nothing in the way of insights about man and his condition to the reader. I could now endlessly qualify what I have just said but I shall leave it as it stands.

Why are significant ideas so hard to come by and half-baked ones so easy?

1. There are times when society itself conceals the traditionally valuable ideas.
2. The writer may not be able to recognize the valuable ideas because he has had no education to speak of: no knowledge of himself; no knowledge of the ideals of Western Civilization; no mature philosophy of life.
3. He may not be serious as a writer, a trickster, immature, dishonest so that he will settle for the first thing that looks good. Anything goes if he can possibly sell it and too often he can.
4. He may have a false idea of what drama is, will equate it with trauma or sickness or sensationalism.
5. He may be afraid to take a chance with material that is not to a large extent autobiographical: he may rely too strongly on memory and not enough on invention.
6. He may be led astray by attempting to write what his contemporaries, as contemporaries, are writing. In too many cases he knows modern writing but hasn't read anything before 1900.
7. He may have no love for anyone but himself.

I think it is now clear what I meant when I said before that it was necessary to *strive* for the significant theme, to enlarge the self to encompass it. I might add that I am one of those who feel—despite a good deal of evidence to the contrary—that the enlargement of one's character as a person, his wisdom, knowledge, power to love, will not hurt him as an artist.

I won't attempt to spell out for you what I think is trivial subject matter in contemporary writing. I have an idea that you already know. Nor will I say what I think may be the significant theme for this age. There is no such theme; there are many themes for these sad times, some old, perhaps some new. I think you will discover what they are if you give yourself to the task, keeping in mind, perhaps, some things Albert Camus expressed in his Nobel Prize acceptance speech.

He says that the task of his generation, and I would say that it takes in yours, "consists in keeping the world from destroying itself." One should feel a certain quantity of horror that such a task is necessary. However, it states the problem that confronts us in a nutshell. It is easy to remember as we hunt around for themes.

On the other hand, Camus asks, who can expect of the writer "ready-made solutions and fine moral codes? Truth is mysterious, elusive, ever to be won anew. Liberty is dangerous, as hard to get along with as it is exciting. We must progress toward those two objectives painfully but resolutely, sure in advance that we shall weaken and flinch on such a long road. Consequently what writer would dare, with a clear conscience, to become a preacher of virtue?"

Preaching virtue, propagating moral ideas is exactly what the writer must not dare. Once he begins sermonizing, poking his head through the fabric of the fiction and addressing his countrymen, or the world at large, he has given up being an artist. I have heard some people predict a time when the preachment may be more necessary than the art, but if that time comes our doom is near, too near for preachments to do much good. The writer must not preach, but he must write to the best of his ability in a way that ultimately dignifies man and fights the forces of dehumanization in our society. The artist's function, John Wain puts it, is "always to humanize the society he is living in, to assert the importance of humanity in the teeth of whatever is currently trying to annihilate that importance."

If we are concerned with the preservation of the human, we are concerned with morality whether we write in sunshine or gloom, about good men or evil men. There are some who don't understand this: that a writer can be deliciously describing what is evil, yet at the same time defining what is good. And some do not understand that one can be concerned with morality without in the least preaching it. I would like to make clear how this is done. Ortega says:

Within the novel almost anything fits: science, religion, sociology, aesthetic criticism—if only it is ultimately derealized and confined within the inner world of the novel; e.g., if it remains without actual and effective validity. . . . The dose of alien elements a book can bear . . . depends on the author's capability of dissolving them in the atmosphere of the novel as such.

I say it is done by making the moral esthetic; that is, by creating the total fiction that the moral is locked into. It is not visible, it is itself the fabric. It is expectedly hidden; the artist defeats our expectations of its appearance until we realize it has long since appeared, has in a sense always been present. That man is unique; that his existence is extraordinary; that if he realizes his highest self he will prevail. When the reader understands this he understands that he has in a sense been telling the same thing to the artist; he has compelled the meaning to be present.

We can make the moral esthetic, because it is in a sense esthetic to begin with. It has an emotional quality, is in itself a form of drama. It is man-invented and has man-value. It moves us because it gives us purpose. It permits us to love ourselves. We sense that if morality did not exist for us, as it has throughout the history of our civilization, we would have invented it, just as we have invented poetry. Not all are poets—but many respond to poetry once they bring themselves to read it; similarly, not all men know the moving beauty of morality, but those who do have in a variety of ways—through act, teaching and art, caused countless others to know it for what it is and also be moved. Art purges us and we are opened to the moral insight.

I have entitled this little talk, "Beginning the Novel," and I think it will be clear to you why I have given so much time to idea, theme, material, but now I would like to say a few words about several technical problems as one begins the novel. However, I will tie up the two parts of my talk by beginning this section with the problem of technique in general—as it pertains, let's say, to the first novelist.

In general our young writers tend to be very proficient in their technique. There is speculation that they are developed as technicians by courses in college, by writers' conferences, and their own awareness of the emphasis on form in contemporary criticism. Our young writers seem to be very much aware of critics.

I'd like to say a word about how far a novelist should go with "courses." Cowley's proposals. I disagree in principle.

However, the effect of this emphasis on technique seems to be the well-wrought novel par excellance. Fiedler says that many first novels are as rigid and conventional as icons. And Ralph Ellison points out that this great emphasis on what he calls "formula and neat theme" "evoke a response much like that we extend to those miniaturists who work in ivory."

In general I am for the well-formed novel, but not at the expense of spirit, of life in the world, of breadth of characterization. I would like to see the young writer take a chance with form. This means, once more, working with ideas that will lead him perhaps into the picaresque, or something resembling it. Of course there is the question of how much the beginning writer can chew off of experience and still control; but perhaps he may do well to perform his experiments in form in connection with the short story. I'll try to say a little more about this subject at some other occasion.

Perhaps I can add to your understanding of the point I am developing by quoting from a recent article by Norman Podhoretz on this season's crop of first novelists, almost all excellent technicians whom he describes as enormously talented and devoted to serious fiction. He feels they are somewhat abstract, not fully realistic because concerned largely, in an abstract fashion, with the effects of imagination and love upon the lives of their characters. He criticizes them for the refusal to "make social generalizations" and goes on:

> The truth is . . . that a novelist achieves significance by taking thought about the world he lives in, by trying to understand what it is that most matters to himself and his contemporaries from day to day and from decade to decade; by trying to determine what constitutes the uniqueness of his own period (and therefore of his own experience).

He continues, "I am suggesting that (the novelist) use his intelligence, that he put his mind and his critical faculties at the service of his imagination. And I am suggesting that he attempt to reassert the traditional office of the novelist, which was to tell men most fully and concretely what manner of life they were living." I am in sympathy with most of these remarks.

I would also like to see the first novelist take more of a chance with comedy. "American humor," says Constance O'Rourke, "has the function of defining and consolidating the diverse elements—racial, cultural and otherwise—which go into the American character." There's a need for a more fruitful satire of society, a laughing at the wrong things instead of conforming to them.

There are certain advantages of handling comedy that seem to me to be of importance to the writer.

A strong attitude of objectivity is developed in the taking the comic attitude.

The opportunities for inventive manipulation are increased; and there is an enormous imaginative stimulation that comes from trying to make things funny.

Comedy implies a seriousness and develops a critical attitude towards man and society at a time when there is a need for it.

Don't forget that comedy may reveal the human predicament as well as tragedy. Man may be uplifted by laughter.

1. THE GROWTH OF AN IDEA

A. The use of journal notes and outlines as a means of developing, focusing and consolidating an idea; of achieving a hint or prefiguration of its form.

B. In one way or another a writer should shift his characters and ideas and set up every sort of combination to test their dramatic strength. To test an idea he must have ideas; he should test his drama against other dramas.

C. When the ideas are really flowing and it looks as though the story may be achieved, the writer might try a more elaborate synopsis. From it he may derive certain necessary parts that he has not yet come by; he may derive the ending or the theme from several times reworking the synopsis. John Brooks wrote recently in *The Living Novel*, that "as for the theme—well, it's best to let that take care of itself. Start with the theme, and you find you have created a lecture." There is some possibility of that danger, but I think the writer can control it as he creates the fiction. He has to, anyway, once he does have the theme. I think it is almost ridiculous to attempt to write a story and not at once be concerned with its meaning. Knowledge of the theme will help the writer to fit his material into form; it will exclude what isn't necessary. Having the ending in mind also helps a great deal in channelizing the action and achieving form.

D. I would say that the more fully the story idea is thought out, the better off the writer is as he sits down to write. In saying this I should say that some allowance should be made for individual differences; but in general I will stick by my point. The writer is, of course, not necessarily bound by the ideas he has outlined. As he begins to write, his concept of the short story or novel may develop beyond the limits he has conceived for it, and he will change many things that he once thought were adequate or necessary.

2. THE PLOT

Having the theme often helps in developing the plot. You know what you intend to mean, and events occur to illustrate your meaning. Some writers nowadays are discouraged from plotting because they feel that plots are as a rule unoriginal, thus passé; they are content to work with what is called the plot-germ, and as Ortega y Gassett suggests, place most of their emphasis upon the characters; often they seem to be more concerned with background than anything else. I would urge the writer not to give up on a plot before he has really worked at it. Plot, if handled well, can be sheer poetry. It will help create the sense of the mystery of human life, the unknown, almost unknowable things that enter into our lives. Walk into the next room and your destiny may be changed. You can achieve some of that feeling from characterization, but plot intensifies it. And of course characters spring from plot. If something can be done, or has to be done, obviously someone may do it. Not everyone, but someone. Anything is possible in life, or should be, the writer must feel. Once you understand that, you will be less afraid to handle a plot, whose events are at their most interesting when they spring out of a person's character.

3. POINT OF VIEW

Point of view—or angle of vision—should not be such a great problem as some beginning writers make it. I would suggest, for the most part, the use of that point of view that elicits one's strongest powers.

A. Don't be worried about stream of consciousness or interior monologue just because it is modern and in a way the thing to do. You don't have to do what Joyce and Faulkner did to be a good or even a surpassing novelist.

B. Avoid entrapment in the "objective" point of view before you have experimented with the others. Hemingway is enormously seductive with his point of view, but it is also responsible for his greatest weaknesses, or at least it attempts to conceal those weaknesses: an inability to develop ideas as ideas, to permit drama to spring from thought, or to broaden human personality. Hemingway is an unusual craftsman, but for a young writer to be seduced by his method may lead to disaster.

C. I repeat, try all points of view, then stick with the one or two, or combinations of one with another that give your writing the widest range of opportunity; that makes you as strong as you can be. Don't worry about subtlety. If your imagination is subtle, your work will be. If it isn't you can't invent it.

D. A word about experimentation in the novel, which seems, in this century at least to center about the problem of point of view, time, myth, symbol. Auden, I think, speaks of the experimenters as "colonizers" and those who come after and work in the new tradition as "settlers." I would urge everyone to experiment to some degree, not to be satisfied with a style and a subject matter, but not to worry about revolutionizing point of view, or hunting for new domains of time and myth. If a genius comes along he may be compelled in those directions. However, my own interest is in that genius who can reveal the great breadth of realistic life at the same time as he increases the scope of art. Most often the two go together, but, I think, not always. Technique for the sake of technique is not too terribly important.

4. CHARACTERIZATION

A. Think out what your characters represent—in terms of the meaning as a whole, and then try to make them richer than the meaning they may represent.

B. Don't be satisfied with a character as a flat. Try to give every human being some depth.

C. Endow your character with an unconscious, and if possible put him in conflict with himself. Let him find things in the self that he did not expect to find. Don't tell all you know about your character. Hold part of him in reserve to surprise the reader: as in Dostoyevsky, not Thomas Hardy.

D. Use the self, the person as substance—art demands this. Be aware of the past self and that the self changes. Permit him to think; increase his ability to feel, or not feel. Give your character imagination, give him wit.

E. Understand the necessity of mystery in the human being. Don't think that modern psychology or psychiatry has discovered everything worth knowing about the person. Science has not yet, nor will it ever is my guess—unlock the secret of the soul. The writer should try to do this through art. In a sense that is the highest purpose of art.

5. STYLE

A. Style is the truest expression of yourself. Read what you write, strengthen what is honest and beautiful, throw out what is weak or false. As one's hunger for artistic complexity or depth develops, so will his style.

B. Avoid too much fact: of description or data of sensation. Keep your writing as free as possible for emotions, ideas, insights.

C. For style one needs a good ear. A lot can be learned from poetry. Remember especially wit and interior music, also rhythm. Work for economy and precision, as in Faulkner at his simple best. Even when he is literary his precision is unerring. His great fault is that his style sometimes gets in the way of the emotions.

D. Note the difference between his style and Hemingway's, the latter's a style almost of conversation, mood, overtone, a style of rhythms often.

6. SYMBOLISM

Fiedler is right when he says, "for us the reality, the value of a work of art lies in its symbolic depth and resonance, not in the exhaustiveness of its data." However, the symbolic as such should not be a major concern of the beginning novelist, except as the recognition of the metaphorical meaning of his story will help him to achieve its truest and fullest form. If he develops his material in its truest form that resonance that Fiedler speaks of will be there; the writer will not have to hunt for the symbol; he will not be able to escape it.

Symbol is less complicated a phenomenon than many people think. The mind, if encouraged to, will bring discrete things together and increase their dimensions and meanings, achieving at the same time the ultimate in simplicity and depth. Present time flows into the past, the particular into the universal, the image into archetype. If one doesn't understand this, he ought to read more poetry, more of the very greatest novels.

One ought to say here that there is often more to a book or short story than the writer himself knows. When he works to the deepest depths he may create patterns, forms, meanings, qualities, possibilities, symbols, undertones—more than he knows.

My last word is for the writer to strive to make the next thing he does more artistically complex, more interesting, more important, more courageous, more worthwhile, in sum, than whatever he has just completed. The writer must grow; he must never be satisfied. He must strive always to be an artist.

10

◆

The author finds his voice: the fusion of form, meaning, his own unique quality, so that his writing becomes recognizable even when his name is not there to identify it.

It is impossible to say exactly how this comes about. There are many ways:

A. It may occur as a result of certain changes in his life, emotional, intellectual, a progression of understanding.
B. More likely (or just as likely) it will occur as a result of a recognition (conscious or unconscious) of the growth or progression of his work. He is completing his stories; they show more variety and depth. At a certain point the writer recognizes that he is with authority and confidence.
C. It may occur as a result of the favorable reception of his work.

It may occur in all these ways. It may also occur—especially in a beginning or apprentice writer—at a moment when he becomes seriously aware of what he is saying. Or to put it another way: when the writer recognizes that he has a subject and it is his to use in order to give meaning to the experiences of his life, and to give order, unity, form to his fiction.

One of the most difficult things in writing when you first set out to write—and this may hold for some writers long into their apprenticeship years—is to understand what you are saying in your stories, and to make your writing conform to what it is about.

I've used the expression—the writer's subject. Now as I define it, it is not just so much raw experience, though I suppose some people think of it as just that. I don't think of it, either, as a place to write about, for example, Faulkner's South or James Farrell's Chicago. It isn't necessarily a subject matter. It is not, therefore, Negroes, or Jews, or homosexuality, or frank heterosexual experience, or childhood, or an endless variety of such material. It is something more than a body of fact or data; it is what the author uses his facts to say. It is what the author extracts from these facts as the meaning of his fiction; or to put it another way it's what he organizes his facts, subject matter, experiences to say. It's what he feels he must say in his fiction that life means to him. Life may mean—and does mean—many things, but it is the thing he wants, or has, most to say. Of course that doesn't mean he can't change his subject, or express it more consciously and with greater control as he develops as a writer.

Let me give you an example of one writer's subject matter. I recently read a review by Marius Bewley of some books about the work of F. Scott Fitzgerald. According to Bewley, Fitzgerald's subject was grounded in his feeling of the transience and mortality of life, and he gave it a romantic cast so that it became a tragedy of the American hero who must die of a love for which there was no worthy object. Of course that says something about America, or he made it say something about America. "If the American Dream seems delusively to carry a suggestion of infinite possibilities, it tolerates no fresh perfections beyond its own material boundaries. If it engenders heroic desires in the hearts of its advocates, it can only offer unheroic fulfillments. This is the loss, the waste of life."

In the writing of Thomas Wolfe the subject is closer to the subject matter: a gargantuan eating of experience to produce the energy and matter or art. There is a Faustian motif therein—power through total experience, if possible—a consumption of space, food, women, and words. Wolfe was so concerned with experience and the remembrance of it that he almost never did find a subject, and he needed Maxwell Perkins, his editor, to help him dig through his experiences to find it.

Hemingway's subject might be described as the testing of man through his experience with death. All his heroes were concerned with death, and to face it with grace was their often self-imposed trial.

The subject matter of some contemporary writers is that life as we live it, or have lived it, is sheer disaster. Obviously present society is disaster, and since they are not revolutionaries, perhaps only rebels, in various ways they deny the society that distorts our natures. Unfortunately their denial often comes in trivial ways: a return to the good life of the instinctual, what may also be called polymorphous perverse; or the deepening but not, I am afraid, broadening of consciousness through psychedelic and drug experiences. Some of them feel that if you merely record such interesting experiences you have drama, fiction. Some assert that revealing the depths of the mind through free associative means is necessary in art.

Norman Mailer seems to have a special problem with his subject. He has promulgated a doctrine of certain acts, or subject matter, as necessary to his fiction: murder, incest, suicide, black magic. In other words he says this is what fiction should be about. The result is *An American Dream*, which to me seems an attempt to disguise the fact, that for one reason or another, he has no subject. He has substituted a certain sort of esthetic of evil for the true evil of life. *An American Dream* is a substitute for a true novel.

Perhaps I ought now to come to the point I intend to make in this short talk, and it is addressed to the beginning writer—the one who is producing his first stories and wants to go on writing. How does one go about finding his subject, or as some call it, his particular theme?

A. Some don't have to look. They are like Fitzgerald, born with it. Once they begin to write they say at once what they will want to say, with increasing understanding, wit, power, all their writing lives. These are the happy few.

B. Some find it in their own writing after years of writing. They read what their writing says until they understand the message.

C. Some, if they are lucky, find it in desperation, when they are not writing—when they can't; and they ask themselves over and over why they have talent and can't write. However, this is a complex matter and may never be solved even if they presumably come to a subject. Perhaps the point I'm really making is that some do it between unsuccessful pieces of work.

D. Some find it by hitting some sort of technique or form in fiction that suddenly opens possibility for them. They have a way to say it and almost at once what they want to say occurs to them.

E. One can find it by reading a great writer, who acts inspirationally, and gives rise in the reader to a desire to say something similar or related to; or the very opposite of what he has read.

F. There is no one way to find one's subject and one's voice. It comes as a result of one's education, not necessarily formal education; but obviously it can come as a result of that. Education is a way of exploring the world and coming to terms with it.

The writer must learn who he is. He must reflect on his experience and the experience of others. He must learn to reason. He must understand that he is more than a passive being, or an animal. He must learn that art is hard to come by, and the more strength of character he has, and the more true education, the stronger his art.

There are many ways to find one's own voice in fiction.

11

ON SUBJECT MATTER

◆

INTRODUCTION

Every writer's problem is different, perhaps by degree of difference. In a class of this kind it might be best to speak informally on any subject that comes up—to compare experiences, to induce insights.

Question and answer—as best I can answer—might be best, but I would like to start by making some observations about the writer's subject matter that may be helpful to you. I do not pretend to solve anything in this little talk, I just mean to raise questions. After I finish we can talk about what I've said or anything else you may care to bring up.

It is difficult to say, why, after a period of softness, stress, and comparative formlessness, the stories of certain writers suddenly begin to coalesce, achieve form, come to life.

Sometimes the process is unexplainable. No doubt there are many reasons, some personal—conscious or unconscious. Sometimes the stories of those I shall call student writers seem to come to life when they hit a certain subject matter (perhaps as place or people, perhaps as narrative or theme—or a combination of these things that might show itself, for instance, as the realization of the pleasure value of being a student, a hippy, a Negro or a Jew), a subject matter that excites their imagination in a way that produces a fruitful written response. What I am saying, in other words is that not every writer is able quickly to discover what he can do best—write best—what most moves him and suits him to write.

This isn't, of course, limited to student writers. It can be a problem of a professional anytime during his career. It's usually at the outset; it is at any time when he seems to use up a certain kind of material and has to go seeking another. Some professional writers give the impression—from their work—of seeming to spend a large portion of their writing lives searching for a fruitful subject matter. (Some people distinguish between subject matter and the more limited subject of a book.) Until they do they go from matter to matter without achieving their most effective stories or novels—they are good but not good enough. As I said before, this can be caused by unknown quantities, but for my purposes, I continue to relate it to the writer's subject matter. More than one talented and sometimes "successful" writer spends years looking for material, or an aspect of it, that will help them produce their best strength as writers—make their breakthroughs. One seeks what lights up his vision.

A case in point is Norman Mailer, a greatly talented writer who, after writing three of his early novels and somewhere along the line walking into a severe case of writer's block, came forth with a theory that the true stuff of fiction (at least for him) was the stuff of evil, suicide, incest, murder—I forget exactly how he stated it in an essay. This isn't a greatly original idea for fiction, but apparently it was for him at that moment, perhaps an attempt to destroy in himself the remnants of any middle-class image. At any rate, it indicated that he was dissatisfied with what he had been writing about—let's say to *Deer Park*—and wanted more effective material to deal with. Effective in the sense that it excited him to think of the imaginative possibilities. Since that time he's tried this kind of material in *An American Dream*, which did not come off well. *Why Are We In Vietnam?* was closer to an experiment in style, so is obviously a seeking for new subject matter.

Here I will interrupt my remarks on Mailer to make a point I should perhaps have made before. That is to say that no subject matter, no material—narrative, thematic or otherwise, is in itself more valuable than any other. The important thing is that the writer must feel that it is for him. He may respond to "the mighty theme" or to the life of the flea—despite Melville, both are potentially useful. (John Barth with his sense of comedy and profusion of metaphor might easily handle the flea, nonhuman or otherwise.) When vision is inflamed, possibilities proliferate, which is perhaps another way of saying that when one is moved deeply, strangely, by what he contemplates writing, sometimes there is a mysterious response that I shan't try to describe even if I could; out of which comes, to put it mildly, better work.

We go back to Mailer. Shortly after publishing his new theory of fiction—that for him it must be steeped in evil, concerned with evil—he stabbed his wife at a party. This may have been simply an unfortunate irrational act (it is no explanation to say he was drunk), but I could not help interpreting it as a further seeking, however lamentable . . . of a new material, as though he were trying to make a drama happen so that he could write it more easily. He would not be the first writer who had done this.

It can't really be said that he produced a distinguished novel after he had developed his theory, or resolve, or whatever you may call it, to deal more thickly with evil. I've mentioned *An American Dream* and *Why Are We In Vietnam?*, although I should add it has been rumored for years that Mailer is from time to time slowly at work on a novel he hopes will be his masterpiece, no doubt concerned with evil in one massive form or another.

However, as we all know, he has come (perhaps willy-nilly, though I doubt it) upon a new subject-matter deriving both from the fiction and his journalism: Norman Mailer, protagonist, engaged in an act-with-analysis of personal and political defiance of the Establishment—in *The Armies of the Night*, and to a degree, in the convention book, *Miami and the Siege of Chicago*. In these books (one of which he calls "the novel as history," which seems to be a redefinition of position), he has done his best sustained para-imaginative writing, and some think that *The Armies of the Night* may be considered his best book to date, including those he formally calls novels. In the Pentagon and Convention books we have Mailer, writer, confessor, celebrator of self, acute political observer-commentator, enjoying the extended role of dualist. The protagonist of his new books combines wise man with narcissistic self and makes an unusual construction. The point is that this change of material, so far as it goes, seems to suit Mailer and has been helpful to him in his writing.

Recently Philip Roth told me in jest that he had found his "true" subject matter—not the Jews but sex. The id in Yid. See *Portnoy's Complaint*. The book does show a new emphasis of concerns. That Roth was searching for something different to write about was obvious from his last book, *When She Was Good*.

And John Updike has a material problem, too, which runs through his recent work like a repetition compulsion. How much more can he do with adultery and divorce? I know he wants to break away from this subject matter, and is actively wrestling with the problem.

Now what does all this mean to you as young writers who want to be professional writers, and some who hope to be true artists? Some of you may indeed have come upon the material that you will be mining for many years, but are presently unable to do as much as you like with, for reasons I can only guess at.

It may be that some of you haven't seriously investigated this particular problem. Mostly you write about anything that pops into your mind, and when between stories, you spend a good deal of time scrounging around for story ideas. Frequently these ideas are vastly different from one another and have no thematic similarities or even relationships. The stories that are written are discrete pieces of work. Except for superficial similarities it is hard to recognize that the same person wrote them.

Where does one find the sort of material that will move him to more fruitful, more effective writing? How does he do it? The answer is anticlimactic—the way differs for each writer. The trick is to try anything—everything, to experiment within the limits of one's capabilities, to learn what those capabilities are. Talents differ. Some writers are more gifted stylists; some handle ideas more effectively—ideas as drama; some have and convey greater feeling; some create more complex characters. Some are enormously inventive; some are more technically proficient. Talents lie within talents; you must learn the geography and archaeology of yours.

Let me conclude with a few general remarks—a few thoughts that come to mind to convey to those of you who are consciously on the hunt for something worthwhile to say. Finding it may become the work of a lifetime—a true seeking always is—but even as one seeks he must say what he knows presently as though it were worth saying, although some writers would warn you, "There's nothing to write about. Amuse yourself. It's all words and nothing but words." Others translate "something worthwhile to say" into "something new." But I'm sure you understand that novelty—being à la mode—at the heart of the scene, is not necessarily being where a writer ought to be. On the other hand, to experiment implies concern with newness, though best as originality. That means it is your business to try to present your material, if you possibly can—we are back to talents within talents—to present it in new forms.

Obviously the major source of fiction ideas is the self's experience, your lives, individual to collective. I want to say a word about the collective, but first let me qualify what I said about originality by adding that one ought to say what he can say—although it has been said, written, untold times before. To throw out experience because it isn't unique (theoretically individual experience always is) is to throw out the baby with the water. One has to begin at the beginning—with what one is and knows.

As for collective experience as a subject matter, there are sometimes advantages of great inspiration, as well as scope, if one is committed to a cause he wants to write about. For instance, if one has talent, and is committed, it is for obvious reasons an advantage to be black now, as it was to be Jewish (and is diminishingly) when I began to write. I say "if one has talent" because I am told by some editors that too many manuscripts by young blacks are little more than agit-propaganda. Thus far there is only one Ralph Ellison. Not all blacks, merely because they are black, can write well about the racial and political problems of blacks. Consider the divided loyalties and mixed accomplishment of James Baldwin. Some black writers would do best to write simple love stories. (Recently I met an Israeli novelist who hungered to write a love story but almost didn't dare.) A social novel or story may not be your thing, but the only way to find out is to try, keeping in mind that writing about the social scene sometimes reduces dense texture, and abstracts, if one is not careful, from human quality. The ideal is, of course, to make art of the message.

Can one derive a subject matter from a critical theory? I'm not for writing from theory, prescription, or manifesto. Some critics (Fiedler, for one) say such and such a thing is "incumbent" on the writer. Nothing is incumbent on the writer except to write well. However you ought to be familiar with the new theories of fiction such as Robbe-Grillet's, for instance, which tells us: "To tell a story has become strictly impossible." And: "The exclusive cult of the 'human' has given way to a larger consciousness." In this country Susan Sontag, Richard Poirier, and others who seem to have been influenced by the theory of the "new novel" are also convinced that traditional forms of fiction are démodé, and the novel must go "beyond signification"—beyond meaning, hence beyond interpretation "to express new relations between man and the world." The argument becomes this: Style can be content, as it attempts to be in modernist painting.

If this theory appeals to you and you have a strong language gift (think of Updike and Barth), you may want to experiment in this direction. Incidentally, I have nothing against the pop novel, or pop poetry, except that it seems a bore. Still, I would not advise you not to write it if you feel you must. One might try and, with luck, find himself doing something more unexpected and interesting. One of the most wonderful things that can happen to a writer of fiction is that he might write himself into something unexpectedly original. That of course can happen even if you start out to write traditional narrative. Among contemporary writers, John Barth, William Gass, and Donald Barthelme are original writers of varying degrees of accomplishment. Barth I genuinely admire, though I like the *Fun House* book more than *Giles Goat Boy*.

One last word in summary: Mastering material—achieving something worthwhile to say—implies that you have taught yourself to weigh experience, you intend to understand life's meaning or unmeaning. The scale of weighing or measuring is knowledge, of self as well as the world. To achieve it is very hard work. That's why psychedelic experience is no substitute for this knowledge. And it is hard work to be an artist. If you become one you become less a coward; conversely you become braver and even less ignorant.

12

THE SHORT STORY

♦

The short story has many entice-
ments. One is that the satisfaction in completing a good short fiction is
as sure as that which comes from finishing a good longer work. I refer to
the feeling at the end when it has turned out right; one has achieved a
meaning in a form. Art is adventure, and whether the adventure is short
and perilous, or long and perilous, a satisfying accomplishment means a
satisfying adventure. When you are done with the short story, you
breathe, whereas the novel is a long underwater job. And a happy payoff of the short story, one that attests to an inherent magical quality of
the form, is that when you put a dozen good ones together you should
have a good book, one which gives the reader all the pleasure of a novel
and sells for the same price.

Another enticement of the short story is that it offers the complex of
much in little, more intensely of course than the novel. Like a poem, it
contains multitudes. There is a wonderful tension created in letting few
words say much—God forbid the other way—at the same time achieving quickly what Poe described as "the immense force derivable from
totality." The opportunities, the possibilities of the short story excite the
writer's imagination. Within a dozen or few more pages, whole lives are
implied and even understood. Every effective story—think of Chekhov,
Joyce, Babel, Hemingway, Faulkner—is a revelation, in essence a confession of what a person, in his deepest heart, is, even when he pretends
he is not; and what is confessed to the reader is nothing less than a man's
mystery. Though events are endless, lives aren't, yet there is a tempta-

tion in telling of lives to spin them endlessly. But the short story, though it reconceives lives, must limit itself to the sweeping realization of its meaning, which is to say it quickly runs its course because that's its nature, its fate. And that relates it more fittingly to our short lives.

Though short stories tend not to deal with long periods of time, even when they do, through the judicious use of synoptic passages, the effect is of the fleeting quality of life. Time flies because so much happens so quickly, good and bad, sad and comic. A single event, experience, moment may discharge a new fate, better or worse. In a sense the short story tells us, time and again, how vulnerable human lives are to the human condition. It arranges experience so that we understand, at least for a moment, how events combine, sometimes to lengthen, too often to shorten our days, our joys, or, happily, our illusions; or to say how suddenly we fall into error and how irrevocably we are judged, as though for all time for a single mistake, and *that* though it takes a thousand errors to make a moral man. Short stories, perhaps better than other forms of fiction, point up the haste and heaviness of the odds against us, and our million daily miraculous escapes from the worst of fates and the best of insights.

Frank O'Connor argues there is a particular subject matter of the short story, the little man's intense awareness of his loneliness. I have used this lonely man in my novels, and so have others in theirs. Many of the experimental playwrights of these times have featured him in their dramas. It seems to me that where all subject matters meet is in theme, that which converts action into meaning. The themes of the short story are, of course, the themes of literature, but perhaps one of the distinctive qualities of a short story, still another enticement for me, is that it runs at once to the defense of the disadvantaged; it runs to moral causes. The writer is better off aroused; in the short story he may strike first, before the novel lumbers into action. Much that is happening nowadays, although it has, in one or another form, happened before, incites to stories of rage, nausea, love, understanding—in a word, arouses the humanity of the writer, even when he pretends he has none. I speak of those who can go beyond themselves. It's as if one says, I must write this story before it is forgotten. I must preserve the passion. So he will say who suffers and why, and he will write it sad or he may write it comic. But he will treat whatever it is he is concerned with—misery, joy, or no feeling—as though it were a vase on a potter's wheel, for he has learned, perhaps from the failure of some of the fiction of the thirties, not to treat it as ideology. He will keep in mind that his strongest defense against the evils of the world is to tell his stories as works of art.

13

◆

Telling tales is a way of putting together what life means. It's a way of dipping your fingertips into experience, or dipping your fingertips and coming up with some substance—some mysterious writing on the tips of your experience that say this is what you've done and this is what it's all about.

If you're not a teller of tales . . . you spend a good deal of your life trying to contemplate what you've been through and you're lucky because not all are lucky enough to know where life directs you. You are lucky to know that life directs you to know yourself.

In a way, experience is for knowledge. That is to say, experience is for experience. Experience is for knowing. So that you can tune it up, so that in the end, when it comes—or not even, let's say—so that your earnings of wisdom begin to show themselves.

What you say the first time is generally off the top of the head, comes quickly, and you can't necessarily get too accurate a focus. . . . This is why you write second drafts. . . . For example, if I could reinvent myself, I would re-invent myself with more thought between what I say and what I think. I tend to speak very quickly, and one writes the same way. Once you begin writing. And it is only in the reflection of afterwards that you put in place and in focus and in proportion those thoughts that you have that are necessary to the argument.

And the argument is whatever issue you are addressing yourself to, without necessarily arguing about it. And so, therefore, if you are the kind of thoughtful person who really weighs experience and weighs the self and weighs language, then ultimately you come pretty much to where the story comes from.

The storyteller does it in a different way. He invents someone, a tale, an animal, a human being in a situation and then he tries to say what these thoughts I've been describing to you turn into in the way of what we would call a fiction or what we would call a story.

And therefore, there is a gift, and the gift is the gift of fiction. Those who have the gift spend half their lives determining whether they have the gift, the one-half of their lives determining how to use the gift, and a third half of their lives using the gift. (I say that advisedly—that makes three halves.)

So therefore telling stories is using what you have, which is known as a talent for fiction. I'm calling it a gift, here. I like the word which takes on this kind of significance in life and when you use it well, you don't use it only for self-knowledge.

I'm not intending to go on to a lecture. You know there are times when I will take a few minutes to talk at larger length. I answered a question and I'm open to other questions.

I'm going back to another question that was asked, and that's this business of the man and his relation to fiction. The man who has obviously a life, a plain, ordinary, human life, with some expressive privileges, so that it is not necessarily every man's life—it is the life of a writer, life of a painter, life of a composer—but whose workaday life is workaday life like you and me and whose history, therefore, is going to be pretty much like any other human being.

One of the ways in which we learn, one of the ways in which we excite ourselves by sheer life is our empathy with other human beings and part of the excitement of having an artist around is to measure yourself with—and sometimes against—the artist. What has he got that I haven't got? It's a good question and it's the right thing to ask.

A question I get almost every time I read these days is "Are you Dubin?"

I am an inventor, I am an imaginative writer. Some of my writing is creation from the word go. . . . That's the way I like to work.

Biography—how writers use it. I am much more interested in the imaginative, the inventive, what I can put together, what I can remember. That holds true to a different degree in different writers.

For example, Bellow has sections that are biographical scenes in almost all of his novels. Roth has this same woman in from *Letting Go* to *Professor of Desire* who represents Maggie, his former wife, who was an enormously difficult handful of spinach, who made his life rough for him for quite a while. I'm giving you biographical details to tell you why biographical details exist—he could not exorcise her except through his books.

Some cannot even invent anyone over and above autobiographical. What I'm saying is, if Roth gives you this much, and John Updike gives you this much—particularly in the short stories—I think one of the best things he's done is *The Coup*, an invention based on a great deal of reading of African myth, African history, African geography, plus the original idea. But in short stories, he doesn't do the difficult kind of imagined—and what he calls "engineered"—kind of fiction that he did in *The Coup*.

What he does is remember and more. In Updike's case, there is not enough invention in the short fiction, for example. What I'm trying to say, since he does remember as much as he does, he holds so tight to it, he works so quickly from memory, I feel some of the short stories are thinner than they need be, from a writer as good as he is.

He doesn't miss a thing. His training was to be an artist, he thought he was going to be a painter, and he went to the Ruskin Institute and he sees everything, remembers more.

That comes back to what I need and what I need is not biographical history. I need biographical essence. In other words, I may take an essential self, let's say, that may or may not be close to me. In essence, going from book to book, I will change. Sometimes nothing, sometimes a fairly decent amount of biographical detail so that I can recognize, myself, a person I might have used as a biographical outline or adumbration of a character.

I don't use these adumbrations to make character development easy for myself. A good way to do it is to invent it by putting in details one by one and making them spring to life *mostly* by a dialogue.

Person talks and you see a fused human being. And of course, through certain actions, particularly symbolical actions. Therefore, where the biographical is concerned, I more or less told you how I would work, and I would say, yes—in Dubin, perhaps, I have taken more from autobiographical history than I have in, let's say, any other book.

On the other hand, it is not autobiographical. Anybody who expects to find that is interested, it seems to me, basically in gossip. Did he? Didn't he? I leave it for you to guess.

Q: *Did you ever keep a diary?*
No. Time problem. First, I spend a lot of time reading. I love to read.
Secondly, if you're a writer, you need the time you have left over for

reading. . . . Thirdly, all my working life I have a family, and before the kids grew up and disappeared—obviously, when they were children, I enjoyed their company and wanted to give them a little more time. Not as much as, ideally, one ought to give kids.

A writer has to face the fact that he goes inside a room—and that he'd *better* go in that room and he'd *better* close the door and he'd *better* stay there and he'd *better* write—and let come will come, never talk to people.

Q: *Would it be hard to write, say the snow scene, if you'd lived in Knoxville all your life?*

Yes. Experience of snow, experience of being afraid of being lost. I know snow. I know fear, fear of being lost.

Fanny. That kind of obsession is easily possible. When you ask me how do I know, I can tick off lives of people whom I know and whom I've taught, who have filled me in, among other things. I think one of the most wonderful parts of an education in a non-state institution—namely, Bennington College, which has six hundred students—was that we had so many counselees who were bright, beautiful, and wanting to talk about their lives.

Now, not everybody can listen; we had teachers who were dispirited, wouldn't have anything to do with anybody who wanted to talk about her life—particularly her sex life.

In one case, one young woman disturbed me to the point where I actually talked her into going to the school psychologist, accompanied her down. I felt her life was an absolute shambles and if someone didn't help her turn to immediate assistance, I thought possibly schizophrenia. Happy to say she is a married woman now, living in Alaska.

I was not afraid to listen to them talk about anything. In other words, if they were willing to talk, I was willing to listen. When Bennington became coeducational, I was willing to listen to men, even though they are not as confiding, and not as personal as women are. That's the nature of the beast. Of course, in the course of your college life, you hear the most outlandish tales. Some of the most interesting ones. Some of course, of the nature of love, the obsession of love.

Q: *Why fiction over other forms? What do you try to do in a short story that you don't do in a novel? How do you approach writing? Do you sit down and say, "I'm going to write a short story"?*

I have a kind of mind that wants to complete something. Feels an architectural form. Once I get it that way, if I have to revise, it's usually pretty much the same architecture, but with different stresses, and the stresses change and so on and so forth. Not a great deal of re-working.

To get back, I just have a trick of sticking to whatever I'm working on. That is to say, if I'm working on a novel, I don't think about a short story. I simply write down in a notebook what a short story should be, if I get an idea about a short story.

Now, sometimes I may lose it, sometimes I outgrow it. Sometimes I work this same idea in a fiction and I don't need the short story. Other times, after I finish a novel, I say I deserve a year of being able to leave the fiction and travel for a week somewhere or to visit another country or to do something like that, so I've ignored the short story for a year and ultimately feel I'm building another book, because once you have a dozen of them, you have the background, you have the material in front of you, a book to be published.

Not all writers work on the shorter stories, and those who don't fully build up a reputation in it want to keep it going. So, therefore, I come to the short story in that particular way.

And now as for the first part of the question on why do I write fiction? Because fiction wants me to. Poetry doesn't want me to.

Writing poetic sentences in response to other sentences is one thing. And of course you know, there is a good deal of not calling it poetic prose, but I'm calling it versism prose from a number of good writers you have probably read, and why it gets into your fiction and not some other writer's fiction—they were born with a natural gift.

That is to say, if you have versism in you, you can use it. If there is no versism in you, you can't use it. If you are poetic, you have poetry in you, even if you use it through the medium of prose.

One of the things I've tried to do in my novels, one of the reasons I go from one different kind of novel to another is that I want to see what I have that I don't know about. It isn't always on anguish, as someone suggested by implication, gloom. It isn't always sad endings. There's a great deal of love for life in my fiction. If you haven't found it, you haven't read me well.

If you want to read a good article on what I have done in *Dubin*, in essence, one that I think shows a good deal of perspicacity, right down the line that I was aiming at, read the *Virginia Quarterly*, I think April, by David Rabinov, a review of *Dubin's Lives*. About six or eight pages long, but it gives a love-of-life theme more than anything, and you see this is why, in a sense, the obsession theme is less important in

that particular work. A love-of-life theme which is expressed because
Dubin is compelled to face his relationship with Fanny, and do it by
the invention of biography. Dubin is a biographer.

What I do with biography is part of the fiction and that which gives the
book its richness. In other words, there's the thing that's taking a
chance. It's the story of an older man and a young woman. My god,
how many millions of stories are there like that? Okay, so it's taking a chance right off to write that kind of fiction. What are you
going to do to make it different?

Two things that I did that really have made it the kind of invention that
I could work with:

One, was to invent Dubin's walk, so he walks, in his four- to five-mile
circle, after he does his day's writing for an hour, hour-and-a-half,
or two hours, and this gave me the opportunity of creating the
somewhat picturesque inventions or some fantastic inventions that
occurred on the road.

The second invention that opened that book was that, instead of making Dubin a cellist (which was my first idea), I made him a biographer, so that his tampering on the lives of others could be found in
the books that he loved, books that he read, lives that he lived, and
therefore becomes a life book—a book about lives.

Q: *Folk tale—oral tale. You draw heavily on the folklore about Judaism,
which I find very interesting. I would like to hear whatever you care to say
about it.*

I know what the oral tale is, I try to hear something of the human voice
in my ear as I write. Sometimes, when a story won't come off, it's
because I'm not hearing a voice.

My connection with Jewish literature is secondary. That is to say, my
connection with American literature is primary. I was a reader of
English fiction before, in my youth, I went to the Jewish writers
like Sholem Asch, who came out of Russia, writers whom I knew
before I knew the Jewish writers.

I have had no orthodoxy in my life and very little Jewish living. That is
to say, that my father was not a religious man. Our lives were the
lives of an immigrant family. I had, obviously, Jewish friends. I
know very little of the synagogue life from experience. So the
Jewish experience is both primary and tertiary.

Literature experience is primary. It is literature that has led me up and
what you see in that way in Jewish experience is important to me,

out of which I have made many good fictions, and this has come not as a result of primary experiences but as a result of thinking back to what I saw in my parents' life and my parents' people. I also am thinking of what I learned when I read the Jewish short stories, and therefore in my contemplation . . . on what Jewish life really meant after I had lived through the experience of the refugees and at the same time, the experience which is called the Holocaust.

In other words, I had to face myself with the question, "Are you a Jew?" and at that particular time it meant a lot to me to be able to say that I am. And that is why, from time to time, I go back to my experience related to Jews and Jewish life.

If you look through my short fiction, and you look through my novels, you'll see that I have not devoted myself entirely to that. I define myself, as I hope you would define me, as an American writer, who writes sometimes stories of Jewish subjects.

Q: *Is this serious practicing writer—like you—is he too busy writing about life to live it, or does he experience it more thoroughly through writing about it?*

Biographical request? Both. Let's put it this way: You cut out things because you had to enter that room with only a table and chair, paper and a pen. Obviously, you're cutting out leisure activities, cutting out warmth, you're cutting out emotion, you're cutting out lack of emotion, you're cutting out boredom, you're cutting out— what shall I say—anything that can happen in life!

On the other hand, as you write, you make decisions as to what is important in life that you have to give your life to. Somewhere along the line—I don't know, part of it may be a genetic gift, because my father was a gregarious person, and my people—but I felt along the line, unless I were related to human beings quite strongly, that I would be missing . . . what life means.

That is to say, there are people who are loners. I can't say that I love every human being I've ever met, but I get a good deal of pleasure out of human beings, and my relationship to them. That's one of the things that my fiction taught me that I had better do if I wanted more than to be a writer.

You can't deny the fact that you are a living human being, and no matter if you're the greatest writer in the world, if you haven't had the experience—in the fullest sense of the term—of human intercourse, you're lost.

Q: *You're nothing like the two characters in* The Tenants.?
Oh, no!

Q: *When you started, did you know how it would end? Or did it sort of work itself out as you go along?*

Well, sometimes I have had the assumption of what an ending is going to be and I head towards it.

Q: *Putting characters in a room, throwing the window open and seeing what will happen. To what extent do you pre-block, and to what extent do you free-flow development?*

Q: *How do you work best? How do you work most comfortably? How do you work without anxiety? Do you work best by opening the window, as it were, and letting the characters do as they please? Or do you have to have a line on what the characters are going to do, so that you achieve that kind of comfort that permits you to sit at the desk anguishing over every word?*

Again, it's self-knowledge, and this is why I keep on saying that anybody who is interested in writing had better explore himself pretty well, to find out how he works. Otherwise, he's going to work up a good deal of anguish for himself where it is not necessarily called for. There's a lot of anguish in writing but there can be less than some people experience *if* you have discovered how you work best, and then work in that particular way.

That doesn't mean to say to give up taking chances. Obviously, I take chances in any book I write.

I don't mind saying that I do plan in advance where I'm going. Right now, for example, for the book I'm working on—a kind of fable, will be two hundred pages—I have six envelopes in which I put notes, headings on each envelope saying what's happening. The envelopes are arranged in order and when I get an idea, I put it in an envelope—envelope two which is chapter two, etc.

So you can see it's pretty well thought out and now the invention lies within the confines of the idea. One character has entered whom I didn't think of. So freedom does exist, but on the other hand, I do feel that I have mapped the city or the island and now whoever appears is not going to surprise me that much. . . .

Someone said, "Dissipated genius will not produce a great work of art." That's absolutely true. Concentrated talent will produce a great work of art. And I like to think of myself in that second category. Where talent ends and where genius begins is beyond me, except to say that genius seems to me a quality of mind that goes with certain kinds of

experiences of a number of categories, including use of languages. Talent will give you an especially strong ability to use language well.
As far as compressionism, and why I do the compressed sentence, compressed thought may have a lot to do with the fact that the metaphor seems to be part of itself for me and the abstract thinking, the conceptual thought, I find much more difficult for *me* than ultimately appearing with the image and the action and the narrative instead of the conceptual idea as it appears in Thomas Mann. I come forth to the metaphoric and the symbolic ideas. . . . And I would say that one of my gifts is a symbolic gift.

Q: *To what extent have you found that the time you spend teaching takes away from the time that you're able to spend writing?*

Obviously, it does take away time. About fifteen years ago, I was able to drop to half-time; about ten years ago, I was able to drop to quarter-time; and now that I have been retired, I'm still teaching, I've worked it out that I teach a month in the spring and a month in the fall. The reason I want to do that, obviously, is to keep my finger on it, because it means something to me. . . .

I don't legislate the total meanings of my novel. I hope that as you read them you continue to find meanings I didn't know exist, because of the way words prevail, create their own fabric, own coloration, own design. I'm not saying an idiot can read my books and say, "Oh, this means such and such." Obviously, it implies a mind, a sensitivity, an awareness of language, an awareness of what fiction is, and so on.

Some people are gifted as readers, they read more. Mr. [Jon Manchip] White and I were talking about one of the things that a writing course will do, even if it doesn't teach you how to write. It may teach some of you how to read fiction, and that puts you a way ahead of the game.

When they say to me in England, "How do you Americans teach these courses? How can you teach the people who pretend that you can make a writer in a creative writing course. We don't have any such pretense."

If a person's talented, you can help them realize themself, but if he's not talented you can't do a damned thing. If you sometimes have someone who loves fiction and thinks he can be a writer and then he can't, because in essence the talent of invention and language are missing, then at least if he loves writing you can teach him to read it a little better.

Q: *How long do you wait between the first rough draft before you read it again, and are you ever struck with despair when you reread it?*

I despair in reading almost any first draft. First draft is the time of the hypothesis—you try to make it into a life or a representation of a life. Therefore, you are making mistakes, sometimes doing it well, sometimes too thin, sometimes overdoing it, as you do the fiction.

And on reading it over, you can see all the mistakes at once, and the idea is not to be overcome by it. Say, okay, I'm going at it again, and I don't recoil at it.

Another thing about a writer that represents sparkles, important experience, is the ability to see where he's gone wrong. Not to kid himself that he's done the right thing because, "Baby, he's mine and I love him."

That exists! Even to this day, I remember the wife of a talented friend of mine, many, many years ago, when we were young men and my wife and I were living in Greenwich Village, New York, and some friends who were writers came to see us. One began a book and his wife said, "He wrote ten thousand wonderful words." I didn't sink through the floor but I should have. Those "ten thousand wonderful words" came to not very much.

The romance of writing! I really shouldn't belittle that. God knows, there's enough anguish and pain out of writing.

Hemingway wouldn't talk about a story because if you talked about them, you told them and therefore they came apart. Which meant to me, there were times when they came apart.

He had devices. For example, if you don't finish an idea, but leave it, so sort of semi-completed, with more to go for the next day, then you start with a bang and you're into your fiction. Therefore, you did not bang your head against the table, when no ideas would come.

Now, why ideas come more quickly at one time than another, I can't say. But that is a fact. On the other hand, if you are a professional writer . . . you're wearing a certain kind of equanimity, the equanimity of working every day, equanimity of being sure the inspiration evolves from the work, not from whoever you happened to meet last night at a party. That's the way it works.

Q: *How did you realize you had this gift for writing and how can other people realize they have this gift?*

That's a hard question. What can I tell people about getting organized to be a writer? How can you discover it? You discover it pretty early. I was a storyteller when I was a kid. I'd go to movies, tell about them; tell ghost stories around a campfire. One thing is, the story apparatus appears early. Then I began to write stories in grammar school. . . . You find it because it's there.

Q: *Why is there anguish in writing?*

Because it doesn't always come and it gets to mean a lot to you and the minute you write a good book, you want to write another good book and if you can't, you are anguished. You set up the ideal by yourself, as a human being, and as your book, as a book, is a work of art, you want to repeat. But it's not that easy.

Q: *In a book of short stories, do you arrange them according to some order that suits you?*

Yes. It might be a rhythm of form, might be a rhythm of: one or two short stories not as good as four or five short stories. Might have to do with subject matter, have to do with your best fiction—I can't give you one answer.

Q: *When do you stop revising?*

When the page proofs are in. I have the bad habit of revising page proofs and you should see the bills that come out! It's nothing at all to be charged over a thousand dollars!

Q: *How much do you consider your audience? Do you let them dictate at all? Would you still write if you did not have a following?*

I think so. I think if you have the gift of writing, you have to.

Q: *In writing the first draft of a novel or short story, how particular should a writer be? Should he spend time on every word, or inspect his writing generally?*

I have to have a perfect first paragraph, at the start—this is my way of thinking. Then, the second paragraph, and so on. And I will rewrite the first paragraph thirty or forty times, because I can't stand looking at the first draft. If, on the other hand, you can stand it, then it might pay you to write one very, very quickly, get the form, then go back and do it slowly and obviously, much better. How can you do it? Do it! And if you can't do it, do what I do.

Q: *How do you feel about comparisons with Nathaniel Hawthorne, etc.*

It is an extraordinary compliment. I'm absolutely delighted. I have been mentioned with him in comparison with *The Magic Barrel*. I have also been mentioned as one who derives from Isaac Singer. I wrote most of my stories before I read any of his stories, which I find most inspiring. People see relationships—that's up to them. Now, if you ask me, have I read Nathaniel West, yes, ages ago. Have you been moved by Nathaniel West? You can't not be moved by his particular genius. Has he affected me? Yes, but very little.

14

PSYCHOANALYSIS AND

LITERARY CRITICISM

◆

I.

Before describing how psychoanalysis is now being used for research and criticism in literature, I'd like, briefly, to say a few things in explanation of how it fits into the scheme of literary criticism in its broadest sense. In order to do that, I shall have to speak first about meaning in a work of literary art.

By meaning I refer quite simply to the point the author of a short story, novel, or poem has in mind for the reader to understand by the time he has come to the end of his reading. If the work has form it will, to a lesser or greater degree, contain a meaning, which the writer desires the reader to comprehend. If the reader doesn't, or can't, the writer is disappointed, even though the reader may confess to an admiration of the characters, plot, or style of the work.

However, it should be pointed out that not all writers present their meaning in the same way—or to the same degree. So far as I can see there are at present three possible ways—the future may contain others—of presenting a meaning to the reader, and all three are determined by the writer. *The first* is to unfold a story and say with it, as many a writer has done: this is my meaning—that villainy, for instance, never succeeds

While at work on *Dubin's Lives*, Malamud joined a New York group of psychoanalysts and biographers who presented informal papers to each other on matters of shared interest.

and good triumphs in the end; *the second* is to present a story, or narrative, without comment of any kind—as a matter of fact with great restraint—and expect the reader to dig under all that is said and done in order to discover its signification. If after reading Hemingway's "A Clean, Well-Lighted Place," you think that the writer is saying something like, "Values have ceased to exist; the world is nothing," you probably have discovered the primary meaning of the story. (Here it should be said that you have not exhausted all meanings of this short story. More will be said on this subject later.) *The third* method of presenting meanings is to do so in terms of symbolism, which is a technique closer to the second method than to the first. To come by symbolic meaning the reader must learn to read signs. For instance, in Thomas Mann's *Joseph* story, the well into which Joseph is thrown by his brothers is of course a well, but it must also be read as a womb; and the point of the incident is that Joseph will be reborn—he will be a different kind of person—when he emerges from the well. In the first way of presenting a meaning the writer says "this is it"; in the second he says "come and get it"; in the third he says "look into the well, if it is a well."

Let us examine each of these means or methods of presenting meanings a little further.

In the first method described above, we can include practically every Victorian novelist, even those difficult to understand. In our own time we can include novelists like Somerset Maugham, Scott Fitzgerald for the most part, Thomas Wolfe, Theodore Dreiser, Farrell, Dos Passos, and others. They differ among themselves stylistically and in other ways, but on the whole they write clearly and strive to make their meanings understood. That is not to say that everybody understands their meanings; or understands them to the same depth and breadth. There are, after all, individual differences in all intelligence and apperception; and sometimes people will try to read some extrinsic meaning into a book which the book cannot possibly contain. On the whole, though, most people will agree that they get similar meanings from these books.

Using the second method, the writer writes so as to compel the reader to join with him in elucidating meanings. This writer often tries to make poems of his stories. He has a high opinion of imagination and he probably knows psychology; he also experiments with style. He may be Chekhov, Joyce, Katherine Mansfield, Virginia Woolf, Faulkner, Eudora Welty, Katherine Ann Porter, or, in selected stories, Ernest Hemingway. "Experimental writers," Frederick Hoffman tells us, "expect their readers to participate in the creative act in an ingenious way. . . . If a writer is not merely capricious—that is, if his images (and *I* may add, his ideas) are not so remote that only he knows what they mean—then the reader may discover the meanings himself."

If the reader fails to discover these meanings, and they are not remote, in the sense of private to the writer or his coterie, it may be then that the reader has difficulty interpreting the author's complex style or subtle ideas (I don't say the author's profundity); or perhaps because he has not had much experience, and therefore insight, into this kind of writing; or because he refuses to work for the meaning—as he must in most of the poetry he reads—for the reason that it is hard work, and he would prefer to be more passively entertained.

Even good critics disagree about the meanings of some of the stories written by the authors just mentioned. Or they may disagree concerning the depth and breadth of the meanings. Both Mark Schorer and Robert Heilmann agree on the central meaning of "A Clean, Well-Lighted Place," but Heilmann calls the story symbolic and Schorer has no such thought in mind. The same is true in their interpretation of "The Use of Force" by William Carlos Williams. Heilmann considers it to be a symbolic story, which means that it has a level of meaning that Schorer, who describes it as simply a story built from an anecdote, does not see. Here it should be said that it is sometimes possible to follow the implications of a story far beyond the meaning the author intended it to have. In regard to this, Eudora Welty says:

I have been baffled by analysis and criticism of some of my stories. When I see them analyzed—most usually "reduced to elements"—sometimes I think, "This is none of me." Not that I am too proud to like being reduced, especially; but that I do not remember *starting* with those elements—with anything that I could so label. The fact that a story will reduce to elements, can be analyzed, does not necessarily mean it started with them—certainly not consciously.

That, by the way, is an important word—consciously. And we shall soon see what critical meanings are valid in a story—what meanings are there.

In the third method, symbolism, where the author encloses the meaning within objects, or signs, which when juxtaposed with other objects or signs may sometimes alter the original meanings, as they are altered in dreams, the reader is compelled to translate the meanings out of these objects and juxtapositions, and he may, because such is intended by the writer, come up with more than one meaning of equal validity. There is more than one way to interpret Mann's *Joseph* story, his *Magic Mountain*, Kafka's *The Trial* and *The Castle*, and, to include a poet, T. S. Eliot's "The Waste Land" and "Four Quartets." Mr. Eliot doesn't care how many meanings you come up with. He expects you, within his universe, and subject to his architecture, his language, to find whatever meanings you can.

Now, before I leave the subject of symbolism, I should like to point out—there is not time to develop the idea—that there are degrees of symbolism. I mean then that some writers will write a story with only one symbolic object or person in it; others will include many symbolic objects and persons; and some will try to make the entire texture of their creation symbolic. Think, for example, of the difference between *The Robe* and *Moby Dick*.

II.

Though one can train himself to derive meanings from each of the three above mentioned categories of instilled meanings in fiction, it can readily be seen—life and art being as complex as they are—that not all meanings, particularly in the hidden and symbolic levels, will necessarily yield to a first or second reading. Since that is so, people will be dissatisfied by the continuing mysteries—everything is a mystery that is unknown—and will wish, so to speak, to crack them. Moreover, they will want to come by another category of meanings—those implied by Miss Welty in her use of the term "consciously" (i.e., the unconscious meanings). These are meanings which exist in the work, and which the author, for a variety of reasons may not be aware of; just as in conversation, though one thinks he knows what he is saying, he may, in his choice of words and manner of saying things, reveal more than he thinks. I am merely saying here that the author does not always know how much he is saying, either because he is working symbolically or close to symbol, and he himself cannot estimate the number of ripples he has set into motion, or because he does not understand himself in relation to his art, usually because the strongest tie of this relationship is unconscious, and therefore he does not or cannot see all he has created, or sometimes what for that matter, he has omitted from his creation.

If there are then, these unread meanings, or conscious and unconscious planes, it will be seen that it is the function of literary criticism to clarify them, to bring them up whole and close to the eye. I think this function belongs, essentially, and to the farthest possible extent, to literary criticism in the formal sense of the term, as differentiated from biographical and historical criticism. First the literary critic must comb the text to elucidate the meaning, the writer's intention, if possible, and the meaning despite the intention. (Parenthetically it can be said he must also weigh the success of the achievement of the intention.) I say that literary criticism should make the first attempt to seek out all possible meanings, because a work of art, besides being a *Ding an Sich*, is also a collection of possibilities. It will usually yield up its meaning or meanings within its own terrain—that is, when worked from within.

After literary criticism has done its work of exploration, explication, and evaluation, and not before, so as to leave alone the pattern of the wholeness of the art work—the experience of elucidating the whole intrinsically—then biographical and historical criticism, which are all-extrinsic to the work and amplificatory, may contribute what they can. Usually biographical and historical criticism elicit details that are more useful to writers than readers: to wit, the author's relation to his time and society, details of causation, and the source of the values he commends in his art—in other words, the influences and conditions of his art. In a sense this is a means of sounding for meanings without the work. Much of it is hit or miss. The biographical critic will get an idea or theory first and then try to prove it from the work. He will aim to relate the writer to events, other writers, books, experiences to build evidence for his hypotheses and thus to collect meanings. He will, by taking so many pot shots, make a certain number of hits, ties, new relationships, possible meanings, but it will remain for the formal literary critic to sift through these meanings and parts of meanings, to indicate the relative importance of the acceptable ones and to say how they fit without diminishing the form or stature of the work.

At this point, perhaps as an adjunct to biographical criticism, psychoanalysis or depth psychology—or that body of psychological lore which is derived from Freud—may make its appearance. Let us remember that there may be symbolic meanings in a work of art, and that the whole science of psychoanalysis is set up to interpret these meanings as it does dream symbols, just as it is set up to arrange and interpret biographical data, especially the writer's relation and attitude to his mother and father, in terms of unconscious psychic patterns which are evident in neurosis. Through biographical and cultural details that are extrinsically elucidated by biographical critics, psychoanalysis reveals, according to its theories, the unconscious motivations of the writer in the choice of his subject matter and perhaps his treatment of it. It explains, in so far as it is possible to explain this, how the artist turns his biography into art (Freud confessed himself pretty much licked by the imaginative process) and analyzes whatever unconscious—or Freudian, if you will—meanings there are in any given art work. Sometimes it will relate the work of art—a work that reveals no apparent mythic quality—to myth itself, and hence to what Jung calls, somewhat too mystically for the Freudians, "the collective unconscious."

In summary, as a rule, psychoanalysis deepens the work of the biographical and historical critics. It does not by itself enhance the appreciation of the work—and may have the opposite effect; however, a work of art may make sense in terms of Freud and still be subject to appreciation on other levels, as we shall see soon. Remember that psychoanalysis does not—cannot—in itself alter the meaning of the work as the author conceived it, though it may reveal a room—or two—and a basement in the house he built, that he didn't know were there.

15

◆

I'm not so sure I see a "school" of
Jewish writers in contemporary American writing. Obviously there are
a number of American Jewish writers of diverse backgrounds who may,
to various degrees, share a common fund of Jewish experience in their
fiction—let's say what inspires it is the emotionalization of Jewish experience after their history in Germany under Hitler—and possibly they
share an interest in ethicality which may have a Jewish source, and perhaps a similarity of manner or style, centered around their handling of
people in their fiction; but apart from these elements I don't find a common ideology. This is a diverse group of writers we are talking about:
Salinger, Mailer, Roth, Bellow, Stern, Blechman, Markfield, among others—whose works may or may not influence one another, and who perform in many different ways. There's nothing cohesive about the group.
Some say yes to Jewish life and tradition, some say no; some largely
overlook it though they may, for a variety of reasons, call themselves
Jews. I would say they are a group of American Jewish writers handling
basically American themes sometimes in terms of Jewish subject mat-

These are a series of answers to questions that were not recorded. This conversation, however, is much less improvisational and more clearly "worked" than
was the session in Knoxville, Tennessee. It antedates that one by nearly fifteen
years, since *The Fixer* ("my new book") appeared in 1966—and here also editorial emendations have been made for the sake of clarity.

ter, sometimes not, as in the case of Mailer, Salinger, and various individual works by other Jews: *Henderson the Rain King, The Natural, Stations, Golk*, etc.

As for "denying" Jewish experience, I doubt I'd call it that. It doesn't bother me that Salinger, for instance, is not concerned with a Jewish subject matter so-called. If there are Jews who have no meaningful relation to Jewish experience, they would be fools to try to write about it. I don't consider this, in the true sense of the word, a denial. What they don't know they aren't writing about.

I feel that indeed I try to represent in my fiction the Jew as universal man. It isn't a hard thing to do because of the historical dispersion of the Jews and the fact that they have picked up their lives and cultures in various countries, intertwining theirs with others; we therefore have the historical conversion of the Jews to a kind of universal man, and at the same time it is a symbolic one. Now what I said was really, "Every man is a Jew though he may not know it," and that last part is not usually quoted. What I mean, I'm sure you understand, is that the Jewish drama is prototypic, "formed," and symbolically understandable. If you understand it you realize it is your own, whether you are a Jew or not; and I suppose what I hope by saying that is that recognition of this drama should ally human beings to one another, should ally them, even strangers, to those who have as a people for historical reasons lived through it recurrently, and that's what I mean.

Jewish self-hatred is a personal psychological problem: I don't think it will keep anybody from becoming an important artist. The opposite is possible. I don't care what an artist feels about his religion or culture, or what he chooses as subject matter from these sources, if anything— ultimately he has to make a choice in terms of his vision of life and in terms of his art. And to get back to the point whether this is going to create a fragmentation of his art because of broken roots or whatever, that's impossible to say. So much depends on the particular élan of the individual. What he gets out of his perverse philosophy or his healthy philosophy is what most moves him; it isn't necessarily the validity of the attitude or belief itself. It is what you feel your belief is worth that produces the fiction.

A NEW LIFE

Yes, I still think of it as a good book though I see now how I could have made it better. Perhaps I should have balanced Levin better, maybe explained him more, ducked away from the objectivity implied in the point of view I used. It isn't true that the book is a great departure from *The Assistant*. First of all, there is some relationship in themes and persons; there is a similarity of spiritual quest; and if you must hunt for an element of Jewish subject matter (this is all that concerns some critics, even non-Jews) it's there though indirectly, in that I asked myself what it is that a man who has been brought up among Jews, in a Jewish ambient—which may be ethical or symbolic rather than theological—what is it that such a man does or represents when he walks into a strange country, or has an adventure in a place other than his own, other than where he has been brought up—what can he bring to the American experience? May it be, to some degree, a high spiritual intensity, a certain inspirational quality of even indirect Jewish experience? In other words, what stays with the Jew who is not steeped in Jewishness? And to my mind this is shown—though this isn't the only way—in the ideal of responsibility in love and service in love, and the idea of making moral use of oneself in the community, despite personal weaknesses—to seize the weakness and squeeze out strength—the idea of representing as best he could the forces of good. In other words, to make a human use of the self in two main ways: his personal relationship to Pauline Gilley; and his communal responsibility—to bring the college to some awareness of its purpose, hence to some kind of improvement.

So far as my heroes are concerned the battle, the true battle, is of the spirit. My feeling about Levin is that perhaps I was a little too hard on him. I'm sorry if he comes out to some people as a bit of a schlemiel. I respect him more than that; I don't want him to be an automaton, always reacting to experience six degrees left of ordinary, with less success than others. I wanted him to have more possibility. I wanted him to take advantage of possibilities, as I think he ultimately does, in some way that would satisfy his spirit, if not now then in the future; and even though at the end of the book, because he is coming out of a state of temporary depersonalization, he may not know he has won a victory over his past, hence over himself—my feeling was that Levin had won, not that Levin had lost.

One interesting thing is that few American commentators on the book emphasize the fact that the action occurs in America at the time of Senator McCarthy's malign influence. I was also saying that the sickness of Cascadia was an almost universal sickness in the United States at that time, and the kind of timidity and dishonesty that occur in the story, the lack of responsibility, even of understanding, was heightened by the general political and moral malaise. Levin was in a sense challenging

McCarthy—the man who almost ruined the nation—possibly because for a long time no one else was, certainly not Eisenhower. It is interesting to me that some European reviews of the book come at once to the nature of the political theme.

SUBJECT MATTER AND IMAGINATION

I feel that a writer must continue to take chances with subject matter—attempt now and then dangerous things, even if it may mean the failure of a book, or a temporary attenuation of powers. It is important to see how far one can go in the sheer grasp and understanding of his subject matter. It is important to take chances. For example, after doing some apprentice stories about Jewish life, I wanted to see what happened if I took off into a story like *The Natural*. I asked myself—what do I have imaginatively, what can I do that I haven't tried, what can I get away with, how good will I be? I have used the short story to probe for new powers. It was in the short story that I found I could handle fantasy with good effect. And after I wrote "The German Refugee" I was determined to do a novel using political or social experience as the basis of the fiction. I've done that in *The Fixer*, my new novel. For the first time I am using historical material, though with a largely invented set of characters, to create what I hope is a more powerful imaginative experience with the same major ideas about life. As for the future, what interests me is how can I continue to produce as an artist, how can I continue to grow, how can I continue to discover those realms of experience that will bring me always a subject to deal with seriously on the highest terms? Subject interests me more than experimenting with technique. I appreciate what Robbe-Grillet, Sarraute, and others are doing, but I think I know where my strength lies and I intend to use it.

Suppose I were to decide, after this book, that I wanted my next to deal with new problems of American youth, particularly concerning love, a vision of oneness in the world, a belief in life, and all that's so hard to come by in youth and I began to explore that. I don't much care, since you make so much of this, if it has any relation to Jewishness. I would want to do it in some unique way. I am one of those writers who takes imaginative chances, as I said, who believes in the uses of the extraordinary, in inventiveness of the highest kind. I prefer to invent a world rather than remember it. I use autobiography exceedingly sparingly. I like to deal with people who are born and start running as the pen moves.

FIDELMAN

Now that I am finished with *The Fixer* I may pick up Fidelman again, who has appeared in three short stories as an artist manqué, and through a continuing series of stories (possibly four) try to find out why he has come to this false art and so on. Basically, he too is a man seeking himself at the edge of disaster, and perhaps keeping his finger in art is what prevents him from going over the cliff. He doesn't know, though he may think he does, why he is "involved" in art, as many on the fringes are involved, and sooner or later he has to learn he hasn't got it. And sooner or later I am hoping he will find out what he does have that may be of some use. Some readers call him schmuck, stupid, other names; others think he is very funny, but of course nobody knows where he is going for the simple reason that his story is in progress. Long ago I decided I would let him go on and write about him just when I felt like it and see what effect writing a book of related short stories would have on the character and style and the quality of the fiction if the writing went on at intervals during a ten- or fifteen-year period. I wrote the first story in Rome in 1956, and there are three now: "The Last Mohican," "Still Life," and "Naked Nude." I hope to do the fourth sometime in 1966. Perhaps I'll finish up in 1968 or 1969.

THE JEWBIRD

The story came to me after I had read "Digressions on a Crow" by Howard Nemerov. He had written a short story based on the adventures of a crow his son had enticed into the orchard at Bennington, where we live. Ultimately the crow disappeared and might have been killed. The thought of having a crow in a story amused me. I tried him in imagination as a Jewish crow and almost without thought, when I sat down to write, the story came as it did. Schwartz is Nemerov's crow once removed, made into something that expressed a thought I had about anti-Semitism. What is anti-Semitism, basically, and could you sometimes call it something else, and is it that if a Jew hates a Jew? So the fact that it took on, as you say, the quality of *The Assistant* is not entirely explainable, it seems to me, by its Jewish subject matter. It partly depends on how an idea hits you, how it fulfills, or becomes a metaphor for certain ideas you may have, the excitement you get out of having a Jewish bird and seeing what he will stir up simply by appearing on the scene.

JEWISH ANXIETY

I don't connect . . . anxiety . . . to the Jewish experience of necessity. I don't know there is anything like national anxiety, though there certainly are anxious Jews. I look at anxiety as not all of a piece and think of it as personal in origin. Not every Jew has the same experience obviously. I doubt that, if anyone were to make a statistical study of all Jews in all countries, that he would find an identifiable Jewish anxiety. You would have to prove this to me, and I don't think social psychology has been able to prove it up to now. There is such a thing, I understand, as national character, but I'm not so sure of national, or in the case of the Jews, international anxiety. As for myself, if there is anxiety in my work it comes out of my personal life and may have nothing whatever to do with Jewishness. I'm not denying there is a possibility of "Jewish anxiety," but if I search for evidence of it through my experiences in childhood and youth I rarely find that specifically. I was never seriously the victim of anti-Semitism: I never had problems of this sort that I was conscious of. Of course my father spoke of these things but he spoke of them as a safe man. I became deeply aware of what it could mean to be a Jew during the time of the Nazis. Naturally I was disturbed, but was that Jewish anxiety or the concern of a man?

THE LUCK OF BEING IN A MINORITY GROUP

If you want to know how I feel about it, I feel that being Jew is a lucky break for a writer. It's a lucky break to be a member of a minority group, since you put it that way, in this particular way in this particular time in America. It helps you define your world and gather your themes. It endows you with a usable and perhaps more easily handleable ethos. But there's more to it than that, obviously. Joyce came out of a minority group, but he was always more than a minority man. In the end he had of necessity to be a minority out of a minority, and so must we all be. Universality comes out of one's response to the totality of his experience. The Jewish and Negro novelists in America are lucky in that they are born with a vivid past and cause to write out of, an orientation. However there are other ways to be a minority if one wants that advantage. And I won't tie up achieving art with having been born Jewish.

THE NEGRO WRITERS

As for the Negro writers, I admire Ellison most. I suppose you can tie up the rise of a group of Negro writers with this quickening of their history, but it's not a one-for-one relationship. These things are so complicated. What has been happening in the United States that they are faced with is the great change in Negro experience—Negro attitudes—since the 1954 Supreme Court decision, and that has been so drastic, so much a drama of the highest importance that it is bound to affect the Negro writer and, of course, has. It brings him into action. It inspires him to write, to bear witness. If you insist on a parallel between the Negro and Jewish writers, it may indeed be the historical accident—that the subject matter that is available to them becomes "hot," surcharged—call it the emotionalization of history; the writer is moved by what is happening with such intensity to him personally, to his group, and to the country. What's more, this isn't only a Negro revolution, it is a revolution for whites too. The Negro victory—since it is political, moral—is good for the victors and good—whether they know it or not—for those who yield it up. My feeling is that the Negro revolution now is a middle-class revolution. And of course each writer sees it his own way. Ellison responds to it as more than only the drama of the Negro man. His view is broad, he doesn't treat experience reductively. Baldwin translates the cause into basically religious and sexual drama. And LeRoi Jones, given a certain amount of talent, what has he accomplished by hating half the human race?

THE HUMAN SPIRIT

What I really often try to say is what is the value of human experience, how may it affect the spirit, what can you do with what you are endowed with? I think of the self, the self's spirit, as material for shaping, reshaping, in much the way a sculptor may do it, and what if he can do it for himself? Sometimes I ask myself what in particular happens to those who become conscious of their lives as stuff that can be shaped. Not everybody thinks of life in this way. Now if you want to call that attitude Jewish, you can, but I think I got it out of literature—or at least affirmed it in literature—my sense of what people, over and beyond the necessities of existence, are trying to do with themselves, particularly as you come across it in Russian literature. Through the major Russian novels of the nineteenth century perhaps more than others, you meet unforgettable human beings trying to understand why they are what they are, trying to find some experience that will open the doors of possibility and give them the kind of satisfaction they want out of life. They are self-conscious, erratic, self-exploratory, and the fascination this produces is endless, life-sustaining because necessary to life. I don't tie this up to Jewishness alone.

SUFFERING

Suffering? I'm not for it. The less we have, the better. We will always have as much as we need to make us think we are human.

As for the uses of suffering—if you have it what can you do with it? If you have the wool you might as well weave the rug. I ask myself as a writer what can be made of suffering—what as a result of it can you have that you didn't have, and perhaps give that you couldn't give? You may say that this is romantic, and perhaps it is, but it's a way of using experience to one's advantage.

Levin goes through a period of intense suffering, in *A New Life*, when he cuts himself off from Pauline and lives through a time of trying to purge his love, which he is never able to do; that is to say, the intense emotional experience that occurs as a result of this produces a stasis—of being unable to respond to any kind of . . . a kind of half-deadness, depersonalization, if you will, that he begins to show signs of losing at the end of the book. What good will it do? What he doesn't eat he will wear.

And let's not talk of Jewish suffering.

LOVE

Love enlarges beauty. It enlarges life. It isn't always comfortable but it is an extraordinary experience. Yet, living with love forever—wanting to, with the same intensity of love—is a somewhat useless state; it centers love on enjoyment. It is so varied and has so many forms, so many ways of expressing itself that I can't see it as an enduring state of a certain intensity. It must grow, diminish, be involved, inspired, self-questioning. Even when love is cruel, painful, it enlarges the person who is not afraid of self-understanding, is capable of it; who is not afraid of pain—I am not saying wants pain, just is not afraid of it. Lear learns at eighty.

The fulfillment of love, perhaps, is knowing that love must become responsibility, service, that love can't simply stay as love for the beloved. It is love for her, and self, and then it loses some of that and is a quality of being that one works out of in the direction of compassion and charity. In other words, it must go beyond two, become a way of life: perhaps it must be propelled into use, made active. Now you may think this is idealistic or puritanical, but what I am trying to say is that I don't think much is made of the possibilities of love. I think that love isn't much understood in American life, perhaps partly because of our puritan background, and partly because our country is so much moved by its youth, who have incomplete notions of love. Love, as you know, is deeper, more complex, less satisfying, more satisfying, more intense, impossible, possible than most people know or imagine. Too many are afraid to take their chances with love. It could stand a little more exploration in American fiction.

WOMAN-HATRED IN AMERICA

So far as some playwrights are concerned, when you are dealing with Tennessee Williams and Edward Albee and perhaps some others you are dealing with homosexuals, and as a result of this naturally the whole syndrome is a running away from the real woman into an identification with a woman they can live with within themselves; usually in some way (if my psychology is right) a revolt against the mother for whatever she has imposed in the way of nervous distress upon them. And perhaps this is just the accident of the times. This is a subject matter that has become very important in our drama and in our writing generally.

Then another thing would be, in our society so much is made of the superficiality of women on TV—women's hair, clothing, brassiéres and underwear, and that kind of thing—that obviously young men will find themselves reacting against what they find to be the necessity of confronting the woman in person and it may produce a sense of panic and possibly even disgust to find that a woman, despite all the libidinization of her that occurs in our civilization from advertising and magazines and everything, has to be replaced by ultimately a personalization of her and a dealing, a confronting of a person with a person. And it may be that this is causing it. I am merely hazarding a guess.

Why this doesn't occur in my work? Who knows in the long run? I'm not afraid of women—I feel a great love for them. They've always meant much to me. I find all sorts of wonderful excitement—esthetic, spiritual, other, in women and I can't think of them as objects. Experience is too complicated for that.

I wasn't satisfied with Bellow's treatment of Madeline in *Herzog*. I would like the old boy to show a little of the humanity I presume he has learned in the end, to let a moment of mercy creep into his contemplation of Madeline, or wife number one.

The quality of reverence for life must enter into it—the fertility of women, creativity, earth quality. I can't conceive of a mature man responding to women habitually with disgust or hatred. . . . Shall I summarize it by saying that where love for life exists, so does love for woman.

CLOWNS AND SAINTS

Any categorizing of this kind shrinks or reduces the variety of the fiction. When people categorize my heroes as schlemiels I lose interest in what they're saying because it obscures the truth of the people. For instance, one thing to note about the protagonists in my books is their hidden strength. The man may look or act like a schlemiel but isn't one.

I use comedy obviously because I have it in me. The laugh rolls off the pen. When I first began to write short stories the dialogue made me laugh. Comedy was something I could do, therefore I did it; there was no literary theory or ideology about it. I think my first truly successful comedy was "The Magic Barrel." My new book, *The Fixer*, is basically not comic; the experience certainly isn't, but the protagonist sometimes has wit, and even some of the moments of horror have a certain weird comedy. The drama of existence is tragic but if you have a laugh you might as well give it.

JEWISH WIT

Of course the joke is against the self; and the point is made that Jewish wit and humor lighten the Jewish misery with a sort of ironic self-deliverance, by seeing themselves objectively in life, yet often in relation to God, though they didn't always see him as a kindly member of the confraternity. To believe in God you have to have a sense of humor. I suppose Jewish wit is, in essence, used in self-defense.

There is something ironic in my work. I think irony is a wonderful quality for fiction and of course it is used enormously beautifully in Stendhal, for example, and with many writers who have this quality and since it is another kind of good fiction, if I have it to use, then I use it. I don't make a study but I mean it is there, economy is there, irony is there, tragedy is there, pathos is there, tears are there, laughter is there. You have to get in as much as you can of the whole of the human comedy.

A NEW FERMENT AMONG INTELLECTUALS

A new spirit on the campus? I see it, though my personal contacts with students are limited; but from them and from what I've read, and my discussion with people who have taught in various parts of the country, I would say that they are restless and want to be treated more sanely; they're not afraid of politics, as the so-called "silent generation" was. They are seeking drastic changes not only in their immediate environment but in society. I think this is all to the good.

Part of it has, of course, to do with the Negro civil rights movement; the whole business of what we are using our affluence for—is it to preserve the power of the buck?; the continuation of the Cold War exacerbated by Vietnam, itself a serious misery and reason for uneasiness and indignation. There is an overwhelming desire to live in some state other than anxiety, and to do something about it. This is showing among students, teachers, artists—a ferment is on.

ROBERT LOWELL

I was one of the twenty or so people who signed the telegram in Lowell's support when he withdrew from the White House reading. His position happened to be close to mine. I want to see writers in the midst of political issues. Whether they are writing social novels or works of "interiority and transcendence" makes no difference. I want to see those in power challenged by those with other ideas and that's why I welcomed Lowell's letter. Similarly, I protested for Sinyavsky and Daniel.

THE SIXTIES

It has been said that these are times without ideology, though there are those who say no historical era is without its ideology. I am sure the motives of the students in the Berkeley crisis were mixed. But on the other hand there was a group of, shall we call them, "idealists of the best kind" who want a better life for themselves and the American people. And I think they made themselves heard. This sort of protest occurs in various periods of American life. It's said we are always divided between the practical and idealistic, and that makes for one of our primary indigenous battles. The country that is based on a Constitution that is basically an ideal will always have people who will say, "Let's remember the ideal. Let's improve the ideal." And I'm glad that we have that among us. I'm glad that we are, in a sense, an invented country, that we invented ourselves, and that there are among us those who are trying, in a variety of ways, to perfect the invention.

16

NOTES ON *The People*

◆

NOTES FOR CHAPTER 15, 16

Where is the action and where are we going?

What is the drama of the wanderers?

Is Jozip showing off when he can't be caught?

The NP (Nez Perces) flight to Canada: a zigzag 1,700-mile flight

The NP are attacked by govt forces they repeatedly defeat.

Jozip is a member of the Council of Leaders.

Jozip's authority derives from his rocklike dignity and calm, his devotion to duty and to principle.

The tribe as a whole consists of perhaps 3,000 people (divided into many small autonomous bands) (each with chiefs)

Want only peace with the white man from first contact (1806) on.

An advanced & enterprising tribe, masters of selective horsebreeding.

Old Joseph was a convert to Protestantism (Spalding's mission in 1840's)

Joseph and his brother Ollikut (Frog) spent much of their early childhood at the mission

The following are representative notes from a much larger series of folders on Malamud's final work-in-progress, *The People*. We include them here in the conviction that they stand for his working method throughout. Some are marginalia, some are transcribed passages, some are lists of data copied from his research texts.

But late in the 1840's (Joseph is about 10 yrs old) Old Joseph moves his band
to the southern part of their homeland, the ancestral home. Wallowa (Valley of
the Winding Waters)

Old J. signs the treaty (with other NP bands) in 1855 with US govt, establish-
ing a reservation of 10,000 square miles

But in 1860's (early years) there's a Gold Rush in NP country (in spite of treaty
forbidding prospecting by whites)

Dissension increases because miners who leave steal the good NP horses and
many stay on to become farmers & stockmen

Trouble over fences.

Indian Bureau of the time: characterized by prejudice, inequities

Council of 1863: whites reduce NP holdings to fraction of former (from 10,000
square miles down to *1,000 square miles*)

("Lawyer" had been appointed by whites head chief of all NP, which of course
the other NP didn't recognize. A Christian, he signed the new treaty because
his own band's homeland near Lapwai wouldn't be affected. But Joseph and
neighboring bands in the "lower" part split permanently and refused to sign or
recognize Lawyer's right to sign away their lands. Thus the tribe became divided
{margin note: Where? When?} into treaty and non-treaty bands.)

The non-treaty bands revert to ancestral religion. The chiefs split. Joseph for
example doesn't sign, tears up "The Book of Heaven."

{margin note: Jozip} Indian lands are gift of the great spirit. Inalienable rights.

Old Joseph fails in health steadily in troubled years after 1863.

{margin note: The father?} His 2 sons take over his duties: Ollikut (popular) as war chief, Joseph as *civil chief*.

Whites argue that 1863 treaty (not signed by Joseph's band) obligates *all* NP
to move to reservation at Lapwai.

Old Joseph, dying, tells young J:

"Your father never sold his country. You are chief of our people.

"My son, my body is returning to my mother earth, and my spirit is going
very soon to see the Great Spirit. When I am gone, think of your country. You
are the chief of these people. They look to you to guide them. Always remember that your father never sold his country. You must stop your ears whenever
you are asked to sign a treaty selling your home."

Young Joseph says of Wallowa Valley, where he buried his father: "I love that
land more than all the rest of the world."

But General Sherman insists the non-treaty bands be put on the reservation,
where there wasn't room for them all.

(The army made a legal study of the question and declared the non-treaty bands
were *not* bound by the treaty)

Though legal rights were on the Indians' side, the non-treaty bands were given 30 days to move people, possessions, herds to the reservation. Not possible without abandoning many animals to the white invaders. And the spring run-off made crossing the rivers in flood dangerous for people and stock.

Joseph gives in to avoid a suicidal confrontation. Convinces the young resisters to comply.

The members of the Dreamer cult taunt Joseph as a coward. He insists war with the whites would be foolhardy.

Dismantle the village. Say goodbye to Wallowa.

Go north. Ford Snake & Salmon rivers swollen with snow.

But get to point just outside Lapwai with week to spare. J's band (few hundred people) camp with 4 other non-treaty bands.

At this crucial point, Joseph leaves with brother & small party to butcher some cattle left behind (to fulfill funeral obligation to a tribesman who'd died some time before. Man had asked for his cattle to be killed and distributed after death)

While J & brother are gone, young hothead Wallaitits set out with 2 friends to avenge death of his father (killed in brawl with a white *3 years before.*) Couldn't find culprit. Killed 4 whites instead—all guilty of some brutality to NP in past.

After this "success," 21 others make second foray. Kill at least 14 whites, including some women & children.

Farmers & ranchers throughout region flee in fright to small towns.

Many NP are afraid, too, of punishment (indiscriminate) by whites.

Joseph returns, finds them striking tipis & preparing to flee away from reservation they were supposed to enter.

Joseph resigns himself to fighting if people attacked.

J. preaches humane rules of conduct for the war:

- Stop young men from killing women or children
- No scalping of dead
- No slaying of wounded soldiers
- No savagery in conflict. (Gets chiefs to agree to try to keep headstrong young warriors under control.)

General Howard marshals formidable forces to crush rebels. (Courier & telegraph messages to *seven* Army posts in his dept. Plus troops shipped from San Fran, artillery units from Alaska, infantry regiment from Georgia.)

Some 2,000 soldiers (plus countless local volunteers, Indian auxiliaries from other bands & tribes, many supply workers).

NP didn't even have *one-tenth* of the fighting strength. Less.

Howard wires his superiors: "Think we shall make short work of it."

{margin note: Dreamers —use later?}

{margin note: Chap. 14? Exodus. A few hundred people. Camp with other non-treaty bands.}

{margin note: Attack.}

{margin note: Can I make anything with this? A sudden cause?}

149

{*margin
note:
Jozip as
paci-
fist—
work out
carefully
from
begin-
ning.*}

SOME WARMED-OVER REFLECTIONS ON JOZIP AS LAPSED PACIFIST

- The book spins on the necessary axis of Jozip's pacifism.
- The irony of the NP scouts kidnapping him, rather than another, is a vital one. They want their law & order man, who will draw a tough line with the whites. And of course he is exactly that, but a man of the higher law, the higher order.

  The hotheads of the tribe, eager to prove their valor in a just war, lust for conflict and vindication. But the Old Chief, pacifist to the core, knows he has by indirection chosen his only possible heir. He marks him as the man for the impossible job long before Jozip himself knows it. Only Jozip can delay the suicidal conflict until it shapes itself as a noble (if vain) act of defense instead of vengeful aggression. And only he can conduct the necessary resistance, when it comes, with tactics smacking of honor instead of savagery.
- That he doubts, often, his place, is necessary too. The wrong man in the wrong place at the wrong time, he thinks. As he must.
- And in the moment when his feeling for One Blossom erupts in that deadly compromising of his principles, the reader can believe fully in his dedication to compassion and peace—because the "oracle" for such a stance is capable of its opposite and knows through his own life how necessary his position is. That he kills under duress, under anguish, from a part of himself his pacifism exists to acknowledge and control, marks Jozip with our trust. That he kills the wrong man is the exact and ironic punishment the universe demands to temper any attempt at self-justification. (I believe the text could bring out this crucial irony more strongly. It is easy for the reader to just read "soldier" and not realize the distinction between the two as J. shoots.) Jozip has in fact murdered, and unjustly, too. That moment of truth can't be denied him if we are to go with him the rest of the way.

{*margin
note: But
I am a
pacifist.*}

- The decision to fight, and to urge his people to do so, is no vitiation of his beliefs. Few pacifists have ever interpreted their creed as an obligation to submit to slaughter or permit the destruction of the innocent lives around them they have tried to nourish with their vision of peace. And few have willingly moved toward the executioner's bullet or blade.
- Jozip and the tribe's dilemma (and it must be one if the book is to live) is familiar to all the Quakers and other pacifists who chose to fight when pressed to the sticking place. Especially in World War II. At times such apparent contradiction of belief and former action has been the only way to object conscientiously. To remain passive under such circumstances would be a tacit condoning of, and direct complicity in, a larger and far

more pervasive act of violence—not only against the bodies of men but against the very traits that give us our only traction in the muck we must crawl through.

- And it is Jozip's pacifism that allows the book to proceed to its proper end. Only he can extricate the tribe from total destruction by resisting the "honorable" impulse to fight to the end. His compassion for his adopted people (who in turn adopted him) leads him to resist the warrior code with its inevitable samurai-kamikaze overtones. Jozip understands the brutal law of diminishing returns. He surrenders, as he must, having fought the good fight he would have given anything to avert, knowing his responsibility in saving what is left. And he makes that gesture worthy of its cost rather than a cheap caving in to superior force. That is his victory—he and his people have been the superior force the whites can't recognize.

- The tentative chapter outline suggests Jozip will be imprisoned after the surrender. That seems exactly right. The whites can't allow another white, even an immigrant, to live on a government-sustained reservation as chief of an Indian tribe. Nor can they set him free as if he hadn't committed treason. He must be imprisoned. But neither prison nor reservation can hold the peddler's heart. Out he must get, by his own wit and tactics so amply displayed before, rather than through any gesture of largess on the part of the conquering whites. But of course he slips away peaceably, as is his nature.

- And it is Jozip's pacifist core that allows for his life—and that of his tribe—beyond the dismal injustice of the reservation. Instead of thinking himself well out of it all, and embarking on the American ladder of Upward Mobility that so often proves a treadmill, he transmutes the impulse in a way that honors all he's come through, that restates the old bargain forced on him by both Old Chief J. and the whites. After all, he's not a mercenary, he's not merchandise (as a fragment of conversation with Gump at the surrendered insisted). So he goes to Chicago to peddle his mind and his energies in school, education being the ultimate way to fill that wagon of his—and for the ultimate benefit of his tribesmen, the victims he has had to leave behind in order to continue to serve them. He works to peddle what justice and relief he can to those too decimated by malnutrition and disease to help themselves.

Jozip's lapse from grace has been a double one: the first internal (the killing) and the second external (being forced to fight the whites). Both are critical exceptions that prove his rule over himself and his beliefs— and thus of the reader's acceptance and confirmation of them as our own.

(AUGUST 13, 1985)

A new view and deepening of material that has become very complicated.

One issue revolves around the question of Jozip's loyalty to the United States of America—the American Government.

{margin note: Traitors?} One might say that he owes this land his loyalty but gives it instead to the Indian people—especially those who are mistreated by the whites—particularly because the whites mistreat them.

Perhaps he thinks of them as his Indians; as though he has taken over the tribe. It is his tribe but he is torn by the struggle to be loyal to them, and at the same time be loyal to the United States government which has accepted him as a citizen. This issue should be sharpened as he gives it thought.

Does the Colonel-General call him a traitor?

Do they ask him whose side he is on?

Do the Indians call him a traitor because they suspect he is not entirely pledged to them?

Every so often he is reminded that he is a Jew?

Indian Head becomes one of those who regard him as a traitor and actually try to kill him because he is, in their minds, disaffected with the tribe, the cause, the People.

{margin note: The duel.} They say that they do not trust him.

He and Jozip fight a duel between them, but by this time Jozip has given up the battle with the whites, and at the end is seeking for another way out.

Jozip's compromise at the end is in taking over the legal side of the Indians' cause. His purpose is to win freedom and justice for them and their cause.

At the beginning he is punished by both forces—the whites and the Indians.—How?

THE NP FLIGHT 1877

STAGES & EVENTS: SUMMARY

1. Indians *win first round.*

   (Troops try to do surprise attack but NP know. *Truce incident.* Wipe out troops in second-worst defeat for army in Indian wars. Only Custer worse. *White Bird Creek* & Canyon battle. Victory)

   (NP chase survivors all way to town, 18 miles from battlefield)

2. The wild goose chase.

   (NP lead Gen. Howard in week-long futile trek across rivers & through mts.)

3. The draw: NP surprised by Howard at *Clearwater* camp at noon. Howitzer & Gatling guns. But recover, small force outflank much larger enemy. NP adopt white military tactics: build barricades, dig

rifle pits. Surround troops. Hold at bay until can get non-combatants to safety & withdraw.

4. Trek over Lolo trail. The incredible forced march.
5. NP outwit barricade since known as Fort Fizzle.
6. NP politely pay exorbitant prices to white storekeepers for supplies at Stevensville in Bitterroot Valley. Assure whites no molesting.
7. Surprise attack at Big Hole Camp. Slaughter of NP. But rally. In spite of great losses, retreat and escape with survivors.
8. Retreat of wounded and pursuit through buffalo country.
9. Ollikut's pack mule coup on Camas Prairie. Soldiers lose week hunting the countryside for replacements of *200 mules lost* in brilliant raid at night by Joseph's brother.
10. NP capture a tourist sight-seeing party in Yellowstone. Released unharmed, but kill white non-combatants for first time after Joseph's band violates his humanitarian rules.
11. Refusal of Crows to give NP shelter or help on Plains.
12. Final push towards Canada (but must go south & roundabout before north).
13. Skirmish at Cow Island.
14. Final battle at Bear Paw Mountain Camp. Stalemate. No help from Sitting Bull in Canada because all six messengers killed.
15. Conditional surrender arranged with Miles.
16. Betrayal of Chief Joseph, his tribe, and terms of surrender.
17. The sorry aftermath: moved from reservation to reservation in Kansas & Indian Territory. Death by disease, malnutrition, despair.

Possible details to add to the battle (surprise attack)

- Soldiers splashing through the waist-deep stream to attack
- Running through the camp, firing directly into the teepees (and low, where they knew the Indians were sleeping)
- Indians coming out of their tepees in panic
- Soldiers shooting them, and *clubbing them* to death (because rifles were single-shots, not pausing to reload)
- Old men and the ones dazed by alarm, sleep, and firewater the night before shot down before they could flee
- Women shot down, and children
- Skulls of babies crushed by soldiers' rifles or boots to save ammunition
- Soldiers to bloody work efficiently. No taking of prisoners. The wounded killed off

{margin note: Note details on this page.}

- Many Indians sold their lives as dearly as they could: a captain shoots a warrior; his wife grabs his rifle from his dead hand, shoots the murderer in the head, keeps on firing until she's a sieve of bullets
- Indians at first disorganized, in panic & desperate
- but begin counterattack from east end of camp, rallied by the chiefs ("You can kill right and left! Now is our time to fight!")
- Ragged line of warriors advances against the troops
- Troops caught in deadly crossfire from NP *snipers* across the river
- Colonel breaks off the battle at 8 AM, orders troops to withdraw to a wooded hill
- During battle, *what does Jozip hear* as he holds One Blossom's body? *What is going on around him*:
- Indians fronting the soldiers or galloping by them, firing from horse-back
- The musketry all around the soldiers' position going off like 4th of July firecrackers
- Howitzers booming & the tat-tat of Gatling guns
- Indians whooping. Soldiers cheering.
- Mules of the pack train braying so loud they drown all other sounds
- Soldiers' horses in panic, uncontrollable, not trained like NP ones
- Sun burning down, the need for water. Soldiers can't get it.
- After soldiers withdraw, the NP return to camp to bury dead & pack to flee again
- The soldiers hear the unearthly wail of grief mixed with rage & horror as NP recognize slaughtered relatives.

POSSIBLE OUTLINE OF CHAPTERS:

Chapter 15: On the Road
(A few pages on the way Jozip operates)
Chapter 16: The Defeat as Military leader
Surrender

{margin note: What about fight with Indian head?}

Chapter 17: Back to the reservation.
Imprisonment of Jozip
Chapter 18: The Ghostdancers
Chapter 19: Back to the Wagon? On the Road
Chapter 20: In Chicago?

THE NEZ PERCE CALENDAR

There were twelve months in the year according to the ancient calendar. But authorities have not been able to determine which of these *began* the year.

So the following list corresponds to our own calendar's order.

January 1st: Wilu'pup. Translation not certain. Some say it means *The middle of cold weather*

February 2nd: Alatama'l. *The month of swelling buds*

March 3rd: Lati'tal. *The month of flowers* ("latis" means flowers)

April 4th: Kakital.' *The month of kakit* ("kakit" was a favorite root used for food—much like kouse)

May 5th: Apaal.' *The month of kouse bread* (kouse bread was made from the fresh roots gathered at this time. I have the "recipe" or process)

June 6th: Hil'lal. *The month of the first run of the salmon*

July 7th: Hasoal.' *The month of eels* OR

Qoiiktsal. *The month of the blue-backed salmon*

August 8th: Taiyaal. Meaning uncertain. Since "taiyam" means "summer," possibly *the month of hot weather*

September 9th: Wauwama aiakal. *The month of salmon spawning at the heads of creeks*

October 10th: Aiakal Pikun'me. *The month of spawning salmon on Snake River*

November 11th: Hoplal. *The month when tamarack (larch) trees lose their needles*

December 12th: Saxliwali. *The beginning of cold weather* OR *The time of the fall deer hunt*

The NP named the four seasons as follows:

Spring: etaiyam
Summer: taiyam
Fall: saxnim'
Winter: enim

THE NEZ PERCE INDIANS: NAMES

The NP call themselves *NUMIPU* or Nimípu ("we people") but outsiders chose other names. The NP applied the name to the *tribe as a whole* & gave other names to geographical divisions and bands. (But it is *not* a stock name. Doesn't include neighboring tribes speaking a related language. We use a Salish word, Shahaptin. That word was used by the earliest fur-traders, however, to designate both the NP nation and the Snake River. The Spokan Indians called the NP by this name, and it has taken many different forms: Saptin, Sapetins, Shawpatins, Chohoptins, Shawhaptins, etc.)

Choppunish: much used by Lewis and Clark as name for NP. Perhaps
derives from eastern Salish language or corrupted from Indian word
"Tsupnitpelun." Few others use this name for the tribe except in reference to Lewis and Clark.

The Nez Perces: the French translation of an Indian name for NP, perhaps
from their enemies the Sioux. Possibly "Tsupnitpelun." Refers to an
early custom (not practiced for years before Chief Joseph's time) of wearing a *dentalium shell* (imported through Indian trade with West Coast
tribes) through septum of nose.

Pierced Noses: Lewis and Clark sometimes call the tribe this & mention
that the NP *occasionally* (1806) wear the shell.

Ross, an early fur-trader, also explains this name as coming from the
custom "of having their noses bored to hold a certain white shell like
the fluke of an anchor."

NAMES GIVEN BY OTHER TRIBES

Each tribe had its own name for the NP. I have the transliterated Indian forms
of these from 18 tribes, but only have a few translations:

Crow: "Aupupe": "to paddle" or "paddles" (The Paddle People?)
Kiowa: "people with hair cut across the forehead" (see early portraits)
Osage: "plaited hair over the forehead"
Shoshoni: (Thoigarikkah) "kouse eaters"
Tenaino: "strangers from up the river"

THE NEZ PERCES: NAMES OF INDIVIDUALS FROM EARLY 19TH C ON.

Cut Nose	Bobtail Horse
Broken Arm	Buffalo Horn
Sparkling Horn	Buffalo Hump
Speaking Eagle	Old Man Chief
Rabbit Skin Leggings	Yellow Buffalo Bull
No Horns on His Head	Daytime Smoke
Horns Worn Down Like Those Of	Eagle From the Light
An Old Buffalo	Eagle Robe
Man of the Morning	Fair Land
Dawn Light	Feathercap
Flint Necklace	Frog (Joseph's brother, Ollokot)
Looking Glass	Geese Three Times Lighting
	on Water
Red Wolf	Going Out
Red Head	Grey Eagle

Red Heart

Rotten Belly

Red Crow/Raven

High Bear

Bull's Head

Thunder Strikes

Thunder Eyes

Red Grizzly
Mountain Heights

Many Wounds

Blue Cloak

The Hat

Green Cap

Twisted Hair

No Feet

Vicious Weasel

Fire Body

Two Moons

Rainbow

Five Wounds

Bird Alighting

Red Spy

Strong Eagle

Wounded Mouth

No Heart

Three Feathers

Eagle Heart

Spotted Eagle

Big Thunder

Yellow Bird

Five Crows

Young Chief

Chapped Lips

Bear on Top

Big Head

Bighorn Bow

Black Feather

Black Hair

Bloody Chief

Grizzly Bear Boy

Grizzly Bear Ferocious

Red Echo

Halfmoon

Sound of Running Feet

Little Baldhead

Little Chief

Thunder Traveling to Loftier

(1 trans. of Chief J's name—
young J)

Loose bark on trees

Bark Scrapings

Know Nothing

Red Owl

Lean Elk

Left Hand

Little Tobacco

Lone Bird

Man With A Rope In His Mouth

Baby (same as Know Nothing)

White Bird

Plenty Bears

Roaring Bull

Red Moccasin Tops

Shore Crossing

Show-Away

Ice

Speaking Owl

Springtime

Stabbing Man

Swan Necklace

Meadow

Whisk-tasket

White Goose

Wind Blowing

Wolf Calf

Part 4

THE WRITER IN THE
MODERN WORLD

◆

EDITOR'S NOTE

As suggested in the headnote to Part One, my wife and I often attended movies with the Malamuds. Indeed, the four of us went to his first viewing of "The Natural" when it arrived in Bennington. (What other contemporary writer would turn down the chance to hobnob with the likes of Robert Redford, Robert Duvall, Glenn Close and Kim Basinger? Not for Malamud, however, the lure and distraction of Hollywood; he sold the rights, they made the film, and that was that.) So he had known no more than did the rest of us about the thing we drove off to see in a half-empty hall.

Bern sat to my right, I remember, and was palpably pleased at the start—the baseball scenes came to vivid cinematic life, the dialogue was more or less similar to that which he'd composed. As the movie veered increasingly away from his own story line, however, he grew restive; his fingers tapped the armrest, he elbowed my ribs. What he muttered is best summarized by the Yiddish exclamation of disgust: *feh, feh.* By movie's end, (when Robert Redford triumphs and lives happily ever after—as opposed to the novel's ending, which describes Roy Hobbs's collapse) he had come to terms with and distanced himself from the spectacle, saying, "Well, this may or may not be a good picture but it isn't what I wrote. It certainly isn't *my* book."

I tell this story since it seems representative: no one could have been less worldly nor more scrupulous about his personal relation to the publicity mill. There's a quasi-comic irony in the commercial fact that his name has been kept largely alive since his death—for the reading public at large—by paperback sales of *The Natural*. Though Malamud's occupation demanded privacy, and problems of the craft preoccupied him constantly, he was nonetheless a citizen of the *comitas*.

Here we include an unpublished series of "occasional" speeches and undated essays aptly subsumed by the title for entry # 24—a grab-bag of opinions as to "The Writer in the Modern World." [In committee or town meeting or he registered his vote.] Social injustice, economic imperatives, racial and religious prejudice, political inequities are the "stuff" of *The Tenants* and *The Fixer*, after all, and the newspaper was part of the writer's daily reading. That hunt for Melville's "mighty theme" of which he speaks in his 1967 NBA address proved constant, as did his intention there declared: "What a fool I'd be not to say what I think of the world!"

"The Modern World," it goes without saying, is a various and complicated place. And these speeches and essays make no claim to absolute authority, nor do they stake out positions that will astonish the reader. In this regard it's notable how often here—and elsewhere—he quoted from himself in public, using his fiction to buttress a point. He did so, I'm certain, neither from vainglory nor laziness but more nearly for opposite reasons: he was modestly unwilling to improvise an attitude, and he worked very hard to get the language right. This brave premonitory caution, as it were, is a hallmark of the whole.

Malamud's stance was liberal, his sympathy with the downtrodden, his anxiety for the future of the planet and its population real. Whether predicting the result of nuclear catastrophe in a Bennington College commencement address, or discussing "Imaginative Writing and the Jewish Experience," the common denominator is humane concern— that the individual may function fruitfully within the commonweal, and that the latter not muzzle the former. His commitment to PEN, and his willingness to serve as president of American PEN derived from the conviction that censorship is evil, that the banning of books is a prelude to burning and that the artist must speak out against constraint.

The Holocaust haunted him always. To my knowledge he was not the direct or particular victim of prejudice, nor was he orthodox in faith, but "the Jewish experience" was manifestly crucial to his "imaginative writing." It provided an emblem, in effect, or a paradigmatic instance of the commonweal at risk—and his various parables (the Jew as Crusoe, the Jew as prisoner, as cowboy) all speak to the condition of the outcast in a threatful and violent world. There is always someone poised to take advantage of a weaker someone else in Malamud's pages, and often the intricacy of his plotting has to do with the question of who's the oppressor and who the actual oppressed.

Yet he was proudly an American citizen, proud of this created nation and its love of freedom. He tried, in his prose, to provide "a serious examination of the social structure and certain significant ideas and issues of our times." This last phrase comes from the first sentence of his untitled rumination on critiques by Alfred Kazin and Stephen Marcus, and the force of his conclusion is palpable: "An artist can tell the truth in any language and by any means. . . . His business is to stay free and, through art, create freedom." Malamud's inventiveness was in the service, always, of that ongoing attempt.   —*Nicholas Delbanco*

17

◆

PEN Address—Installation

Here I am surprising myself: my presence here, now, being formally installed as president of PEN American Center, though I have no trouble justifying to myself my acceptance of the office. Yet surprise prevails: I live most of the year miles away, in a small town in Vermont, where I write full-time and teach in the spring. Who wants to come running to New York City, leaving a world of fields and flowers, to chair institutional meetings in Manhattan? I have a book to begin and stay with until it says what it must. You know the feeling. I was not, therefore, thinking of assuming a task of communal responsibility two hundred miles from home. To assure me that it could be done without seriously getting in the way of my work, a former PEN president told me on the telephone, "Malamud, I guarantee you, we will not interfere with a single paragraph of your prose." But we agreed to wait until I had finished a long book. That was about four years ago.

The novel is at last launched; someone called me up to remind me of that. I agreed to serve and here I am because I want to be. I may lose a paragraph here, a paragraph there—without regret in a good cause. On my return I will say, "Good morning, paragraph, I have not abandoned you. Good morning, comrade, I have lost weight but not faith."

I am willing to serve because I have been here, at various times, as a member of the Board of Directors and have seen and admired the force of commitment with which many of you work for PEN.

I am willing because I am past sixty and have long reflected on what being a writer is and entails. I believe in a fellowship of writers, more or less informally constituted, aware of how deeply and complexly we are concerned with, and foster, literature as a civilizing force in an unstable world; a literature that gives flesh, bones, and perhaps a brain to the politics that assail us; a literature that entices us to understand and value life, and act as though we value it, before it is gone. I approve the idea and endeavor of PEN and feel I owe it a more active service than I've given it in the past.

We are part of a world association of writers. We are united to protect and defend our freedom to write. We deal with any government to free imprisoned men and women who write. We oppose those who oppose the rights and duties that make a human being free. As we write for ourselves we write for others. We encourage the arts of translation. Literature has never been, nor can be, only a national endeavor. We instruct the imprisoned who write. We assist sick and indigent writers. We give awards in recognition of accomplishment in literature. We stand, therefore, for humanity. We champion their right to live in peace in a difficult and sometimes desperate world.

Auden, in "Voltaire in Ferney" says this:

> He would write
> "Nothing is better than life." But was it? Yes, the fight
> Against the false and the unfair
> Was always worth it. So was gardening. Civilize.

Civilize: That's still what it's mainly about.

18

◆

PEN Address—Valedictory

After serving for two years as president
of PEN American Center, I am more than ever convinced that one of our
most serious obligations as writers, in a democracy whose history and
meaning too many of our people can't describe or comprehend, is to preserve and defend our Constitutional right to freedom of expression. I
think you know that many writers shy away from this kind of issue or
activity because they think it interferes with the pure act of writing; and
perhaps with the free life of the writer. I think they are wrong. I think
that they will have to commit themselves to a defense of their right to
express themselves as free minds, or they may soon have to contend with
a much diminished freedom of expression.

I will affirm this later, but now let me say why I think the matter has
become so serious. Let me begin by citing a censorship experience of my
own—namely the banning of my novel *The Fixer* by the Island Trees
(Long Island) School Board in 1977. It is still banned, along with nine
other books by contemporary writers—Vonnegut, Piri Thomas, and
others—five of whom are or were PEN members. I think one died. The
nine books (one has been restricted) have been removed from the junior
and senior high school library shelves, despite the fact that they were
chosen and purchased by responsible teachers and librarians for the use
of their students. One of the students, *et aliis*, filed a case against the
school board and it is presently awaiting judgment in the U.S. Supreme
Court, concerning a decision of the Court of Appeals for the Second
Circuit overturning a District Court decision upholding the Island Trees

School Board. The board is hoping to prevent the case from being retried in the District Court. If it is retried, they will have to testify why they banned the books.

They may have to explain, for instance, why they characterized *The Fixer* as an anti-Semitic book. If that characterization astonishes you, reflect for a moment on the color of blindness, self-induced or otherwise. The astonishment I feel in one sense gratifies me because I love fantasy. On the other hand, what sobers and disturbs me about the board's characterization of my book is that it wasn't made by Dr. Goebbels, but by a group of well-meaning, ordinary American citizens (albeit, I imagine, frightened people, who either can't or won't read the novel; won't, for various reasons, struggle with a work of fiction to learn what it really says). In essence, therefore, they have lied about the book.

If they hadn't read *The Fixer* (possibly some of them now have since the case went to court), what brought them to the book and their accusation of its anti-Semitism? It boils down to the fact that they heard from others that the book was a bad one; and they have—perhaps were given—excerpts to prove it.

From reading the brief of *amici curiae*, submitted by attorney Henry Kaufman on behalf of the American Association of Publishers, PEN American Center, Writers Guild of America, etc., to the U.S. Court of Appeals, I have learned that the indictments of the ten books by the board was "prompted by a small group of parents from outside its district representing a narrow band of interests." (Elsewhere, in a footnote on page 10, this group is referred to as "PONY-U, the 'conservative' organization whose ideology the board sought to impose in Island Trees"). The brief (pp. 31–32) goes on as follows:

> The sole criteria against which the books were judged were the personal views, reactions and biases of the Board members to brief passages wrenched out of the context of the works as a whole. So unrelated to educational objectives or potential curricular value were the Board's decisions that the Board ignored the recommendations of its own review committee . . . charged by the Board with assessing the educational significance of the works.

How that worked out with *The Fixer* would be something like this: I don't know whether the excerpt I am about to read you is one of those they considered, but I imagine it would have to be, and certainly the process of reaching their judgment of anti-Semitism can easily be deduced from it, or from any other excerpt from the book that has pretty much the same effect, and is, according to the school board, "of potential offense to Jews" (p. 7).

Let me read you a short scene from pp. 27–28 of *The Fixer*, published in 1966 by Farrar, Straus and Giroux:

"At first I thought you were a goddam Pole. Pan whosis, Pani whatsis." The boatman laughed, then snickered. "Or maybe a motherfucking Jew. But though you're dressed like a Russian you look more like a German, may the devil destroy them all, excepting yourself and yours of course."

"Latvian," said Yakov.

"Anyway, God save us all from the bloody Jews," the boatman said as he rowed, "those long-nosed, pock-marked, cheating, bloodsucking parasites. They'd rob us of daylight if they could. They foul up earth and air with their body stink and garlic breaths, and Russia will be done to death by the diseases they spread unless we make an end to it. A Jew's a devil—it's a known fact—and if you ever watch one peel off his stinking boot you'll see a split hoof, it's true, I know, for as the Lord is my witness, I saw one with my own eyes. He thought nobody was looking, but I saw his hoof as plain as day."

He stared at Yakov with the bloody eye. The fixer's foot itched but he didn't touch it.

Let him talk, he thought, yet he shivered.

"Day after day they crap up the Motherland," the boatman went on monotonously, "and the only way to save ourselves is to wipe them out. I don't mean kill a Zhid now and then with a blow of the fist or kick in the head, but wipe them all out, which we've sometimes tried but never done as it should be done. I say we ought to call our menfolk together, armed with guns, knives, pitchforks, clubs—anything that will kill a Jew—and when the church bells begin to ring we move on the Zhidy quarter, which you can tell by the stink, routing them out of wherever they're hiding—in attics, cellars, or ratholes—bashing in their brains, stabbing their herring-filled guts, shooting off their snotty noses, no exceptions made for young or old, because if you spare any they breed like rats and then the job's to do all over again.

"And then when we've slaughtered the whole cursed tribe of them—and the same is done in every province throughout Russia, wherever we can smoke them out—though we've got most of them nice and bunched up in the Pale—we'll pile up the corpses and soak them with benzine and light fires that people will enjoy all over the world. Then when that's done we hose the stinking ashes away and divide the rubles and jewels and silver and furs and all the other loot they stole, or give it back to the poor who it rightfully belongs to anyway. You can take my word—the time's not far off when

everything I say, we will do, because our Lord, who they crucified, wants his
rightful revenge."

He dropped an oar and crossed himself.

Yakov fought an impulse to do the same. His bag of prayer things fell
with a plop into the Dnieper and sank like lead.

If the school board made their judgment that the book was anti-
Semitic after reading this excerpt, or one like it that they either came
upon by themselves or were given to read by a neighboring community
group, or a national organization—wherever the condemnation of the
book ultimately originated—it is not hard to see how their thinking
might have gone:

> This is a shocking expression of anti-Semitism by the Russian ferryman, and
> contains words, expressions, statements they think would cause fear in
> friends who are Jews—or in Jews who are members of the school board or
> related groups—who not only don't care to hear this sort of thing, because
> it makes them uncomfortable, but don't want gentiles to read it, because it
> will cause anti-Semitism. How could it not—giving such a dreadful picture
> of Jews? That being the case, the passage, and others like it, are anti-Semitic
> in effect, whatever else the author may have thought he was doing.
>
> Besides that there are some dirty words in the book and some explicitly
> sexual scenes. Therefore for all these reasons the book ought to be banned
> from the school library shelves. It stands to reason.

The brief of the *amici curiae* I have referred to states that the banning
of the nine or ten books is "irrational," "political," "ideological." That
may be, but what I would point out is that one is dealing with people
who are afraid of certain books and want their children to be. Some of
them are nonreaders. But if, for instance, some have read *The Fixer* or
Slaughterhouse Five or any of the other novels among the banned books,
their act of banning them reflects on their ability to understand serious
fiction—to discover a theme; to translate symbol and metaphor; to identify with one or another character; to empathize with another human life
and, as a result, grow in their insight of it. The sad thing therefore is that
they are unmoved, unaffected, by literature. It is also obvious that they
can't seem to understand the relation of freedom of expression to the
health of a constitutional democracy.

The same may be said about the Moral Majority, the Eagle Forum,
and the Christian Broadcasting Network, among other Fundamentalist-

related groups, those who assert that only the Bible and books derived from Fundamentalist teaching can speak the truth. These organizations, via television, have enlisted multitudes in their cause, collect millions of dollars, and have gone political. Abortion, women's rights, homosexuality, evolution, and every concept they can subsume under "secular humanism" are hateful to them. Therefore they attack and manage to purge from public schools—which they would rather were private schools—books they call "anti-American," "unchristian," "unpatriotic." They even manage to close schools in order to keep books they don't approve of from being read by their children. This isn't the time to go further into their fears or modes of operation, nor to say more on the subject than that the present administration in Washington—because of its meagerness of human compassion, comprehension, and imagination—is sympathetic to these forces of restriction and censorship.

I do, however, want to remind this audience in particular that there is another form of censorship, seriously harmful, that writers—particularly young writers—have to contend with; that dreadful kind of surrender we call self-censorship. One of the reasons it occurs is that some publishers, obsequious to conglomerate support and economic goals, are more interested in books that sell in great numbers than in moderately selling works of literature. Subtly or unsubtly, they bring pressure on writers to write what sells in the mass market and goes at the highest prices in paperback auctions. Good writers who find it hard to be published, or if published, promoted, may be tempted to write books for the marketplace, thereby failing to address their best ideas and feelings in order to tempt publishers to buy their works.

My advice to them is to be who they are—to stay with what is best in themselves, not to compromise. My advice is to write what you must and circulate manuscripts as long as you can before you lock them away in the drawer. If a book is good, well-imagined, -formed, and -written, it will, by some heavenly justice, ultimately be published. Many small publishers are on the rise. Publication with small presses, once they appear, won't make the writer wealthy, or even feed his children, but it will permit him to feel the dignity of completion. On the other hand a lifetime may have gone by. Still, one writes because he must. These are difficult times for those who write seriously.

I spoke at the beginning about those writers who shy away from involvement in issues and activity—even in defense of freedom of expression. The "itch of creativity" I heard someone call it. They say this "interferes" with the private act of writing. "I don't want to get into a defense of civil rights," one of them might say. "I want my books, because they dignify man, because they, too, reach for freedom—I want them to do it for me. I want them to influence others. Art is the only activity I can reasonably and happily engage in. My books will defend my rights."

To him I must say that *The Fixer*, off the library shelves by command of the school board, does not defend me. I must defend it. And PEN supports me in that defense. I must, with other writers, support PEN.

19

◆

June 12, 1981

I thought that if I was ever called on to give a commencement address at Bennington College, it would be a memoir of my experiences here, to some degree confessional, principally on the subject of how excitingly one may grow here, provided that he or she is inspired to grow. Not all are; therefore the enterprise of education for some is compromised to begin with. Yet opportunity abounds.

I might also say that, on the whole, the best thing about the college has been some of the extraordinary people on its faculty and, of course, a good many of its gifted students. Richness comes from richness; people are the gift—those who give and those who keep on giving. I might also shake a stick at the college and say that given its freedom, its uniqueness, it ought to be better than it is.

But that's for another time, when I'm older and wiser. Now I'll begin by reading you a few pages of the opening of a new novel, a fable called *God's Grace.* That may not sound like a commencement address, but I'll get around to that before we part. *(Reads)*

This is that story

The heaving high seas were laden with scum
The dull sky glowed red
Dust and ashes drifted in the wind circling the earth
The burdened seas slanted this way, and that, flooding the scorched land under a daylight moon

A black oily rain rained
No one was there

At the end, after the thermonuclear war between the Djanks
and Druzhkies, in consequence of that they had destroyed themselves, and, madly, all other inhabitants of the earth, God spoke
through a glowing crack in a bulbous black cloud to Calvin Cohn,
the paleologist, who of all men had miraculously survived in a battered oceanography vessel with sails, as the swollen seas tilted this
way and that;

Saying this:

"Don't presume on Me a visible face, Mr. Cohn, I am not that
kind, but if you can, imagine Me. I regret to say it was through a
minuscule error that you escaped destruction. Though mine, it
was not a serious one; a serious mistake might have jammed the
universe. The cosmos is so conceived that I myself don't know
what goes on everywhere. It is not perfection although I, of course,
am perfect. That's how I arranged my mind.

"And that you, Mr. Cohn, happen to exist when nothing else
does, though embarrassing to Me, has nothing to do with your
once having studied for the rabbinate, or for that matter, having
given it up.

"That was your concern, but I don't want you to conceive any
false expectations. Inevitably, my purpose is to rectify the error I
conceived.

"I have no wish to torment you, only once more affirm cause
and effect. It is no more than a system within a system, yet I
depend on it to maintain a certain order. Man, after failing to use
to a sufficient purpose his possibilities, and my good will, has
destroyed himself; therefore, in truth, so have you."

Cohn, shivering in his dripping rubber diving suit, complained bitterly:

"After Your first Holocaust You promised no further Floods.
'Never again shall there be a Flood to destroy the earth.' That was
Your Covenant with Noah and all living creatures. Instead, You
turned the water on again. Everyone who wasn't consumed in fire
is drowned in bitter water, and a Second Flood covers the earth."

God said this: "All that was pre-Torah. There was no such
thing as Holocaust, only cause and effect. But after I had created
man I did not know how he would fail Me next, in what manner

of violence, corruption, blasphemy, beastliness, sin beyond belief. Thus he defiled himself. I had not foreseen the extent of it.

"The present Devastation, ending in smoke and dust, comes as a consequence of man's self-betrayal. From the beginning, when I gave them the gift of life, they were perversely greedy for death. At last I thought, I will give them death because they are engrossed in evil.

"They have destroyed my handiwork, the conditions of their survival: the sweet air I gave them to breathe; the fresh water I blessed them with, to drink and bathe in; the fertile green earth. They tore apart my ozone, carbonized my oxygen, acidified my refreshing rain. Now they affront my cosmos. How much shall the Lord endure?

"I made man to be free, but his freedom, badly used, destroyed him. In sum, the evil overwhelmed the good. The Second Flood, this that now subsides on the broken earth, they brought on themselves. They had not lived according to the Covenant.

"Therefore I let them do away with themselves. They invented the manner; I turned my head. That you went on living, Mr. Cohn, I regret to say, was no more than a marginal error. Such things may happen."

"Lord," begged Calvin Cohn, a five-foot-six man in his late thirties, on his wet knees. "It wasn't as though I had a choice. I was at the bottom of the ocean attending to my work when the Devastation struck. Since I am still alive it would only be fair if You let me live. A new fact is a new condition. Though I deeply regret man's insult to a more worthy fate, still I would consider it a favor if You permit me to live."

"That cannot be my intent, Mr. Cohn. My anger has diminished but my patience is not endless. In the past I often forgave them their evil; but I shall not now. No Noah this time, no exceptions, righteous or otherwise. Though it hurts Me to say it, I must slay you; it is just. Yet because of my error, I will grant you time to compose yourself, make your peace. Therefore live quickly—a few deep breaths and go your way. Beyond that lies nothing for you. These are my words."

"It says in Sanhedrin," Cohn attempted to say, " 'He who saves one life, it is as if he saved the world.' " He begged for another such favor.

"Although the world was saved it could not save itself. I will not save it again. I am not a tribal God; I am Master of the

Universe. That means more interrelated responsibilities than you can imagine."

Cohn then asked for a miracle.

"Miracles," God answered, "go only so far. Once you proclaim it, a miracle is limited. Man would need more than a miracle."

The Lord snapped the crack in the cloud shut. He had been invisible, light from which a voice extruded; no sign of Godcrown, silverbeard, peering eye—the image in which man had sought his own. The bulbous cloud sailed imperiously away, vanishing.

A dark coldness descended. Either the dust had thickened or night had fallen. Calvin Cohn was alone, forlorn. When he raised his head the silence all but cracked his neck.

As he struggled to stand, he lifted his fist at the darkened sky. "God made us who we are."

He danced in a shower of rocks; but that may have been his imagining. Yet those that hit the head hurt.

Cohn fell to his knees, fearing God's wrath. His teeth chattered; he shivered as though touched on the neck by icy fingers. Taking back his angry words, he spoke these: "I am not a secularist although I have doubts. Einstein said God doesn't dice with the universe; if he could believe it maybe I can. I accept Your conditions, but please don't cut my time too short."

The rusty, battered vessel with one broken mast drifted on slanted seas. Of all men only Calvin Cohn lived on, passionate to survive.

I shan't comment on the fiction I've read and you won't really know what it means until you've read the whole fable. But some of you will recognize the nature of the argument between God and Calvin Cohn and suspect what I'm up to.

I'd like now to comment generally on the process of putting a fiction together—how one goes about working out a novel such as the one I am attempting. And how the book ultimately gets done. I shall keep in mind that this is a commencement address.

All novels are touched by autobiography, some more than others. Sometimes one begins to understand himself as he reads his own work. Writing fiction, as Arturo Vivante reminds us, is cognitive. One reflects, one discovers, one knows. My last novel, *Dubin's Lives*, though in no sense an autobiography, has more autobiographical details than most of my books. What makes it a work of imagination, however, is that I love invention. George Painter, a biographer of Proust, wrote that a reader could not fully understand *Remembrance of Things Past* without a knowledge of Proust's life. That is not true. Proust had invented his own life into a pure fiction.

My new book, the one I just read the opening scene of, began not with autobiographical details but as an idea, or hypothesis—perhaps an assumption I caught in my hand—that in this fable of a man, some apes, and a God who talks like a man, I shall be able to say something of serious interest about man's condition in these very difficult times; and perhaps something revelatory about man's fate. I had previously written two short stories as fables: "The Jewbird" and "Talking Horse," which Claude Fredericks printed as a book, to help me feel, when I had doubts about the almost unreal enterprise I was about to embark on, that I had already taken the first step and could not fail to take the second.

In a work of fiction the hypothesis is obviously an idea the writer feels he can bring to fruition—that is, invent into its apparent wholeness. Invariably the hypothesis changes as one writes. It changes because the incomplete form makes demands of completion. The logic of the narrative makes demands of resolution. The writer makes many demands upon imagination, upon himself.

Let me put it this way: the moment one sets something down in words, or brushstrokes, or musical notation, an element of approaching form subtly changes the original matter or substance or hypothesis. In a sense, therefore, the hypothesis recedes and the representation of it—not an objective correlative—comes into being. Obviously no completed form can be achieved without the original idea inherent, but it is not bound to the concept that incited it. It is possible to start justifying the ways of God to man, and end justifying the ways of Satan. I am not saying that one is the other or contains the other, though it becomes an interesting question as to who invented evil. I am speaking of temptations necessary to the mind of the writer to make his work various and magical; to bring to it more than he originally conceived. Even if there is no comprehensive completion in art, it must seem complete; much depends on seeming.

As one works towards an end he may or may not have guessed at— some writers say they know the end from the beginning, but it is not the same end that comes at the seeming-end—at any rate, as he works he does so in uncertainty. Working in uncertainty is not easy—it drives some writers wild; it drove Conrad, for instance, wild, but that may be a condition of creativity in certain writers. For them nothing comes easy or can come easy. That wildness, that anxiety, that painful hunger to know what he thinks he already knows sends the artist seeking for that fact, concept, bold idea, that was in him all the time, and which, when he recognizes it, will momentarily destroy the fog and let him see to the opposite shore where the bridge already stands. As he looks it disappears and he may wonder if this was the bridge he saw.

One, therefore, must learn to function in uncertainty. In one of his wonderful letters John Keats uses the term "negative capability," which he defines as the state of "being in uncertainties, mysteries, doubts, without an irritable reaching after fact and reason," or "of remaining content with half knowledge." I would add "remaining content" as one seeks beyond "half knowledge" for that knowing which is needed. Keats may be saying life is uncertain because we can't see the next minute of the future; but one must have faith in his talent to foresee. Although his hand and the ground are shaking the artist goes on working. A certain courage is called for.

Negative capability: the ability to deal with, handle, operate what is not yet there; to function as an artist without knowing final answers, therefore temporarily remaining content with partial knowledge and still being able to work in the dark until something is thought out, flashes on, or thinks itself out and communicates itself to the artist.

After first drafts one may revise endlessly. There is more than one way to revise. Some things come to you serendipitously; other demand hard rethinking. Revision is the constant creation of afterthoughts. One learns the best way to milk his mind. The first draft of anything is suspect unless one is a genius. But if you're a genius like Joyce you revise for years. Once in an interview I said, "First drafts are for learning what your novel or story is about. Revision is working with that knowledge, to enlarge and enhance an idea, to re-form it, so that it says more and says it better." D. H. Lawrence wrote seven or eight drafts of *The Rainbow*. The first draft of a book is the most uncertain—the most vulnerable—where one needs courage to accept the imperfect until it approaches the perfectible, an idea of perfection. Fortunately, revision is one of the true pleasures of creating. "The men and things of today are wont to lie fairer and truer in tomorrow's meadow," Thoreau once said.

As revision goes on the hypothesis is fleshed, fulfilled—fulfilled as possibility. The first draft becomes the second and may become the third. One must be patient with the demands of the work; for perfecting within the limits of one's goods. As he works one finds out what he owns. You use your goods as best you can. You know what is best because you have read—you know how good good art can be; and if you respect yourself you make the work in competition with the best. You must offer the reader, or listener, or observer, more than a dozen prunes if you own two apple trees.

Paul Valéry once said a work of imagination is never completed (*achevé*) but is abandoned. In a sense we abandon whatever we create. Every poor sentence that remains, every failed thought, or imperfect image is abandonment. The writer parts with the work partly because he must prepare for the next work. He also knows that the work ends, if it ends at all, in the reader's mind.

I said I would tell you how this talk about an aspect of the artistic process relates to a commencement address. Let me remind you that I have talked of fulfilling a hypothesis, a thought that a certain idea can be turned into a formed work of art; that there is a way to do it despite the difficulties it entails, the fears of the unknown it incites.

I've spoken of working in uncertainty, revising, completing. In art as in living life one achieves results through purpose, daring, discipline, respect for one's own work, knowledge of the work of others, respect for oneself. Self-respect can't be divorced from the ultimate quality of art.

Members of the graduating class, parents, friends, my message is clear. It is my commencement address. I thank you all.

20

Though I had planned to teach at Bennington this summer, I was unable to for reasons of health. I've heard all sorts of rumors about what I've been through, but I can honestly assure you that I wasn't kidnapped by relatives of E.T. and carried off to a mysterious planet.

I'm not entirely myself yet, but I've come here to meet you and say a few serious words about what we can do to make ourselves more effective writers, and then invite you to ask questions. I'll try to answer them, but if you think I'm not please ask your question again.

Much is made of the mystery of art. It is created as it is revealed. Its effect is ultimately enlightenment. The reader is enlightened as the writer is. If the writer is not enlightened, his work has taught him nothing. It must teach him to understand his work, as it will if he is listening; teach him—ultimately—to understand himself. Young writers find that an especially difficult lesson to learn. Some almost seem to feel

Together with the late John Gardner, Nicholas Delbanco cofounded the Bennington Writing Workshops in 1977; Alan Cheuse joined the workshop faculty in 1978. Malamud addressed our students and joined us routinely in each of the years thereafter; this is the written component, before the question and answer session, of a talk delivered in the summer of 1983.

that if they were to understand themselves, they might have nothing to write about.

Perhaps the point I am making is that for some writers there is more mystery in writing than the experienced writer knows there is. For the experienced, writing is a craft that ultimately explains itself.

However, no writer knows everything about his craft.

For me the true mystery in art is the nature of the individual talent, which is all but to say—the nature of the man himself. Your talent defines you. It says there are certain things one is capable of in fiction, and it is heartbreaking to try to go farther. The talent—your gift—means there are things you can do better than others; and there are certain things you can't do no matter how hard you try. With some writers that does not mean dead-end, because there are some elements that by transmogrification of self one can learn to achieve. But basically the conditions are set by the nature of the life. Thomas Wolfe could never be Proust; for all his desire to be a great writer, he could never do what Proust could. It was not in the nature of his gift.

Some writers are endowed with genius. Some think they are geniuses but can never prove it sufficiently to convince others.

However gifted a writer is, the key to his accomplishment is how much he can teach himself to do with his gift. How well can he listen? How much can he learn? What will he know in the end?

Perhaps the basic means of determining the extent and quality of the talent is determining how honest the writer can be. Some men and women achieve true honesty. The key may be self-knowledge, that is to say, the artist has a large and insightful sense of what he can do and sets out to do it, though he often fails. But he doesn't lie to himself. Some writers lie with their talent—thus they destroy it. Some never achieve enough honesty to write effectively. To lie in writing is to make a pact with deceit, to become part of deceit.

Yeats said: A man can embody truth but he cannot know it. I say— if a man can embody truth he will know it. It will make him look where he has never looked before. It will make him see what he has never seen.

21

Sunday, February 20, 1977

Ladies and gentlemen, here's a passage from an old book of mine: a rabbi speaks at a funeral. He says:

When a Jew dies, who asks if he is a Jew? He is a Jew, we don't ask. There are many ways to be a Jew. So if somebody comes to me and says, "Rabbi, shall we call such a man Jewish who lived and worked among the gentiles and sold them pig meat, trayfe, that we don't eat it, and not once in twenty years come inside a synagogue, is such a man a Jew, rabbi?" To him I will say, "Yes, Morris Bober was to me a true Jew because he lived in the Jewish heart." Maybe not to our formal tradition—for this I don't excuse him—but he was true to the spirit of our life—to want for others that which he wants also for himself. He followed the Law which God gave to Moses on Sinai and told him to bring to the people. He suffered, he endured, but with hope. Who told me this? I know. He asked for himself little—nothing, but he wanted for his beloved child a better existence than he had. For such reasons he was a Jew. What more does our sweet God ask his poor people? So let Him now take care of the widow, to comfort and protect her and give to the fatherless child what her father wanted her to have.

It's not Sholem Aleichem or I. J. Peretz, but I'm sure they'd feel familiar with it—the scene itself and sentiments expressed.

Now here's another passage, from a book I'm presently writing: A man named Dubin, who lives in upstate New York at the edge of New England, has been waiting, through a long slow winter, for spring.

March he had given up to winter—who claimed choice?—but a wintry April tormented him. Yet the frozen dancer invisibly danced. One day he discovered snowdrops amid traces of snow in the woods. The snow vanished in the sun; earth dried or tried to; it got to be mud season later than last year. The sun grew stronger daily. On the long walk Dubin saw a darkly plowed field that shone with a greenish cast to its turned soil. Birds appeared in clusters on Kitty's feeder—jays, robins, house sparrows, starlings Dubin recognized; now and then a purple finch. And when they had flown off a mysterious black-masked loner, a crested red cardinal who had been in and out all winter, popped its beak at grains of corn, stopping as it ate to stare at invisible presences. When a sudden shower struck the earth the birds burst off the ground, flying in crazy arcs. Minutes later they were pecking in greener grass in a soft rain. Then from nowhere—from its grave—a mournful dark wind arose trailing bleak streamers of snow. Moments later the sun flared in the bright blue sky. Dubin, on Thoreau's advice, stopped loitering in winter and called the season spring. (p. 176)

It's not Hawthorne, or Henry David Thoreau, despite the borrowed reference to "loitering in winter," but they were easily familiar with the locale and specific details of the experience I describe, the coming of a late spring in the Northeast, and its metaphoric meaning to one man; in this case my protagonist, William Dubin. I'm sure you are familiar with the experience, the details of which would be somewhat different from the account of a delayed spring in New York after this hard winter. I don't have to explain the setting, or tell you where the subject originates, because you know it as Americans. And the metaphor of new season as new life is universal. Nor do I have to say to those of you who know my work that the human experience, generally as lived by one or another American who is usually a Jew, provides the basic subject matter of my fiction.

And what of the rabbi's funeral sermon in the first passage I read, from my novel *The Assistant?* Its quality originates in my own past in relation to my father and mother and the Jews in our lives—family and others—when I was a child. I came to knowledge of Jewish life mostly through people, not formal education. I learned about Jews by living among them, and by reading their books, often in English translations from Yiddish and Hebrew, of works of literature, history, religion, mores, beliefs. The rabbi in my book says there are many ways to be a Jew. By definition, it helps to have had a Jewish mother, but I'm a Jew pretty much because at a certain point in my youth I felt the need to define myself as one. I had consciously related to the Jewish experience.

In my time, I've lived in that experience when it became particularly perilous, in and during the years of World War II, when a million refugees wandered on thousands of constricted hard dark roads, and sailed on closed seas to closed ports; and when multitudes of Jews were imprisoned and destroyed, without mercy by men or heavenly intervention, in the concentration camps. I did not live the experience in day-to-day terror as some of you here did, but in imagination was affected by it, how deeply, and how imaginatively, and by what other experiences, Jewish or not Jewish, is apparent in my writing.

Ladies and gentlemen, I am grateful for the Jewish Heritage Award for Excellence in Literature. I thank you.

22

IMAGINATIVE WRITING AND

THE JEWISH EXPERIENCE

◆

Assuming that a writer has a choice of subject matter—which may be debatable, because for each writer of fiction there is *his* subject matter (sometimes exceedingly hard to come by), his realm of experience from which he evolves his fictional world; yet within certain limitations there is a choice (I mean of the true material, not the easy choice between one brand of fakery and another); and if a choice exists why should an American writer write about people who are so obviously Jewish rather than obviously American? There are certain disadvantages to doing this: in limitation of market and, to some degree, limitation of the possibility of becoming fashionable, as some writers are in certain magazines. But if there are disadvantages, it is my contention that there are certain more-than-compensating advantages for the artist, the chiefest being that writing about Jews, for me at least, extends the area of imagination. I mean to say that the story of the Jews, their history and culture, and the Jews themselves as people, are so rich in the ingredients of drama, so fruitful as a source of image, idea and symbol, that I feel I can at present more fully, even more easily, achieve my purpose as an American writer by writing of them.

What are the advantages inherent in a knowledge of what may be called "the Jewish experience"?

First of all, the psychological advantage of having a vantage point or frame of reference ("the second culture," Trilling calls it in his essay on Freud) as a means of judging the achievement and culture of one's society. To have understood one culture excites the appreciation of, and helps the judgment of the other. With the values of the Jew it is possible to judge and affirm the values of the American; with the values of the American it is possible to judge and affirm the values of the Jew. Both create the values of the individual. Hence it is possible to write about America while writing about the Jews. In this respect judgment can be a source of enrichment of understanding rather than a cause of alienation of one body of experience from the other. Alienation occurs when there is no true understanding of the meaning of either culture.

Looking at the matter from another point of view one may say that Jewish history is a compassable subject—that is, one which after thousands of years reveals what we may call an observable pattern, though there are some historians who deny that history reveals patterns. However, in the larger sense (perhaps symbolically) experience takes form, and Jewish experience reveals itself to us as a rich and tragic drama of the self-realization of a people. The Americans are also concerned with self-realization, especially in these times under circumstances as dramatic as those the Jews faced in the past and presently face in Israel. It is obvious that in its few hundred years of history America has made only a beginning of its unfolding, the long journey towards maturity, and we can better measure our progress as Americans, or partial progress, or failure to progress by viewing our history in the light of Jewish history.

One might argue at this point that any student of the history of any civilization can judge the progress of American life by comparing it with that of any other western civilization; indeed, this is the purpose of the study of history, to give the insider a perspective of his society; the sort of thing that has been done for us as Americans from the time of Tocqueville.

That is, of course, true, but the writer is as a rule not a professional student of history (too great an immersion in it seemed not to have helped Mark Twain), and since history abstracts from experience, his problem is to find one he can really respond to emotionally as well as intellectually—one, in a sense, he may be said to have lived in, where he can derive the fullest data of life. Therefore he is fortunate to have been exposed to a second culture, to have become familiar with its past and present, and thus to have acquired an almost immediate basis of comparison of one environment with another: this is what I mean by "vantage point."

Another advantage inherent in a knowledge of what may be called "the Jewish experience" is, as I said before, that it provides subject matter, a rich body of drama, offering uncommon combinations of act, event, conflict, background, point of view, idea, possibility that may be said to assist the working of the imagination. Everyone has a heritage, but the Jews because of their everlasting struggle to maintain theirs, are especially conscious of it. This consciousness may be limited to family, religious holidays and ceremonials, Biblical tales, or to the fear of anti-Semitism; or it may extend beyond these things to an awareness of and knowledge of Jewish history, theology, ideals, civilization. It is impossible for me to enumerate everything in Jewish experience that may appeal to the writer's imagination. However, some knowledge of these things I have mentioned gives me, as writer, a wider range than is ordinary, of sheer association when I have to select a fact or symbol or theme or character to work with in a story. Some may say that all knowledge, all experience is grist for the writer's mill, and that is true, but it is also true that we write best about what we know best, in the sense of having learned about a people, about their lives and beliefs and history by having lived among them. Therefore it is easier for me to write about a Jew as an immigrant than about a Negro as an immigrant, although I believe that a good writer will test his strength by essaying also an imaginative recreation of the Negro's or the Italian's or anyone else's immigrant experience, based on his knowledge of that of the Jews. A good writer will.

When I think of the history of the Jews, of which they are understandably so conscious, I think of the triumph of insight and value that makes their lives so basically rich (in a sense, life made rich by what they give it) although the primal knowledge is that life is tragic, no matter how sweet or apparently full. In other words, they know that despite life's tragic quality (a never-ending shipwreck, Ortega y Gassett calls it) the rewards of life, if not in sheer being (a miracle too often forgotten nowadays) are centered about the development of a spirituality that raises man to his highest being.

There are, we know, two acts to this drama: the tragedy centers around that which is given. The highest gift is given, and to affirm its endless value, it is taken. Or to put it another way, because the gift is pure and man is not, the gift, paradoxically, is a punishment; yet the punishment renews the extraordinary value of the gift. Though they came overnight to their concept of one God, and from that to spirituality, to the Prophetic Way of Gentleness, the Jews have spent the millennia afterward in an oftentimes agonizing defense and almost unconscious renewal for the insight that came to them so quickly and completely, originally.

Continuing in terms of drama, there is, in the first act, the moral compact with God and the Jews' ineluctable betrayal of Him. Hence the Destruction and Exile (as if it were foreordained that the truest learning must be of suffering, because in suffering the self is contemplated as it has never before been contemplated, and it is the self that is at fault— we may call it—for not being the God-self); and after the Exile, the period of expiation through cleansing of the self, the Restoration. There is then a time of renewed spirituality, followed by a weakening of ideals, temptation, and the inevitable renewal of Sin. Just as inevitably come the Destruction and Exile.

The second act is the diaspora, which like the first, retains a quality of inevitability, of event determined by character, yet less so, since the antagonist seems no longer to be God but history; and there is in history the possibility of a diminution, even end, to tragedy, in that man— not only the Jews—will become aware of that in themselves which prolongs and intensifies the tragedy, and who in so doing, will create the conditions which may bring the tragedy to a close. The end may never be reached, never fulfilled, but the drama, in human terms, is made more poignant because it offers this possibility. Although there are many who do not believe that it exists, still, it exists as a possibility, and possibility is necessary to man. Without it he is, of course, less than man; just as art is less than the greatest art without it.

This may be called the symbolic drama of Jewish experience, of which all historical events are individual scenes, and the writer keeps the pattern of the whole in mind to give scope, enlargement, to his imaginings; just as he will keep in mind, I may say, parenthetically, certain individual scenes from recent history, especially the memory of those poor Jews who were murdered in droves by barbarians and tossed into unmarked mass graves. In remembering them, the artist awakens in himself compassion for their memory as well as for all suffering humanity; and in doing so affirms the value of the individual human life. He will not, as an artist, preach this, but he will not permit his readers to forget it.

And if the part may symbolize the whole (torn from the whole the symbol is whole), mayn't it therefore be said that Jewish history—suffering, expiation, renewal—in essence portrays the experience of man and therefore may be said, in one form or another, to prefigure the American experience in one form or another. If a man realizes what this experience means, if he is not a Jew, he cannot help, at the very least, to wish the Jews well; and at the most, at the height of his understanding, he may discover that he is, symbolically, one of them. That is what I mean when I say that there are more Jews around than one sees or knows of. And because I think this is so I have defined a Jew as a person who wants to be one.

History is swallowed into the past; it is the past yet lives in us now; as an antique spirituality and an antique morality of surpassing beauty and importance, because it is a tie to God himself, lives in the Jews. Some of my knowledge of the Jewish past came to me, of course, through the immigrant Jews of New York City, those who visited our house to sit and talk, or came to my father's place of business to sell him something and talk; and those whom I saw on the streets and in the trolley cars, often not comfortable with them until I taught myself to understand their lives. Since I tend, to some degree, to idealize them, let me say at this point, that I am not unaware of the less attractive among them, the meager, dishonest, selfish, distorted people—those ashamed of themselves and their backgrounds, men and women who would be sickly and lost in any society. I haven't forgotten them, nor do I desire to. I can explain them to myself, observe how often a broken character lies upon a broken life—but the point is they were much in the minority, and the others I talk of were those who, in one way or another, taught me to respect people, so it is easier to remember them.

I remember especially the poor immigrant of thirty-five years ago: his concern with getting settled, often landing up among others so concerned; the long, hard seeking of *pernusseh*, starting with nothing and living on it for a long time, poverty the prevailing condition so it brought no shame, the drudgery of labor; the drama of the small storekeeper entombed in his store, and of his opposite number, the *luftmensch*, the man nobody could catch, whose materialism (whether or not he achieved "success"), his undying concern with goods and money, was perhaps an attempt to pick up more than he had lost in flight; also the constant concern with matters of health; the man broke down away from home; the woman waited until she got back to the house to be sick; the problems of citizenship—how much of being a Jew did you give up to be an American?; the *kinder*, to give them the absolute best, yet afraid once the opportunity came to do so, of giving more than one should, giving to the point of eliminating the necessity of struggle, and thus depriving the children of the means to protect themselves in the future; then the problem of religious training, the fears of assimilation (betrayal), and, eternally, of violent anti-Semitism. If for two thousand years, why not once more? If elsewhere, why not here? Yet though the anxieties never ended, they lived in life. It may be my imagination but I saw less real neurosis among them than I do among us.

I remember those through whom I became aware (as I was to again among the Italians in Italy last year) of what personality means: a full commitment of one's self to the events of daily living. This is especially important to comprehend at a time of evaporating personality, when there is such a strange movement among us for everyone to be like everyone else. They were true individuals, who unconsciously understood the value of their uniqueness as persons. From their vivid selves emerged the image of the man or woman so deeply engaged with life that he could not fail to offer it anything less than the fullest selfhood. If they were in any way reticent about themselves it was done with mirrors. They spoke then without voices, with their hands, eyes, even with inert bodies. If you were alive, could you hide it? They couldn't.

I remember them as an emotional people, giving quickly of their generosity and compassion. Many had a special kind of gentleness that was old in their culture. It was rooted in the teaching of the Prophets, in a miraculous transfiguration of the bitter experiences of the past, that they could go through what they had and live without rancor to man, in gentleness and love, especially for children. To learn, from love of one's own, to love other children is not as easy as it sounds. It was a magical experience to come into their homes and be loved.

What they wanted from life they hoped to find in America. Sometimes it was hard to find, they strayed, sometimes they forgot what they wanted. They tried different ways: business, socialism, wealth, communism, among others; but mostly they tried to find what they hoped for in the American promise, in democracy, which they came to as if they had known of it for ages. In speaking of their ideals, I can no longer strictly separate what I learned from them and what I later read about them, but the lessons themselves are clear: the importance of the human being; the importance of that society which places man close to its center; the strict necessity of morality, the Law; the importance of a mature liberalism to help people improve their condition, to help them create their small measure of contentment and peace, inspire them in the everlasting seeking of life's best values, and the wisdom to live by them.

In his Nobel Prize acceptance speech, Albert Camus has this to say about the writer's art: "It is a means of stirring the greatest number of men by providing them with a privileged image of our common joys and woes." The writer, says Camus, must accept "as completely as possible the two trusts that constitute the nobility of this calling: the service of truth and the service of freedom." Later in this speech he says that the purpose of his generation in art "consists in keeping the world from destroying itself." Therefore "it ought to reestablish among nations a peace not based on slavery, to reconcile labor and culture again, and to reconstruct with all men an Ark of the Covenant."

I think that a knowledge of Jewish experience through the ages affirms these purposes that Camus enumerates. It teaches us that although the task seems insuperable, we must continue to seek its achievement, that we have the possibility to do so, and that even when possibility is narrowed, as it is in these times, we still have courage, will, faith in the future: they have been strengthened in us by what we know of the past.

However, Camus warns the writer "that he may not, in his art, be a preacher of virtue." This is a fair warning, for no art can stand the burden of preachment and still be art. If art is trivial without morality (which creates man's value among men) the artist must create the morality into the art. The reader, in comprehending the art frees the meaning, which in its totality contains the moral. To free it he must respond to the art with his deepest emotions; and to do so spontaneously and fully he must understand what is valuable in human experience. Knowing, he will not be able to resist the emotion that unlocks the expected yet ever surprising meaning, surprising because we cannot know human experience fully and for all time. In literature, therefore, it may be said that morality becomes esthetic. It becomes—is—beauty; and that suggests the highest purpose of the writer: to create beauty indivisible from morality.

You know now what I meant when I said before that a knowledge of Jewish experience extends the power of the imagination. Speaking as an American writer, for myself only, I say that the wonder of that experience is that it inspires me in my attempts to fulfill the artistic ideal.

23

◆

A criticism one hears of the contemporary novel is that it is too often concerned with the merely personal, the "mystery of personality," the self and search for self, to the neglect of a serious examination of the social structure and certain significant ideas and issues of our times. Alfred Kazin, a perceptive and interesting critic, in an essay on Dreiser, puts it this way: "More and more the contemporary novel is stocked with individuals who have nothing to think about except themselves, and who in their dullness justify the mechanical psychology with which they are conceived." He also says, "The concern with outward reality is one that contemporary novelists often reject in an age when the novel may seem as abstract as today's all-powerful science of physics." Physics is neither abstract nor all-powerful, but we get the point. And Kazin speaks elsewhere of "our new writers who have a society but don't believe in it enough to describe it—to deal with it not merely as it is but as something that is." And almost as a corollary of that, he dislikes in our present writing, as though it evades the concerns of society, "the tyranny of symbolism," although he would like the writer to "identify with a social force to which he can give symbolic significance." In sum, he would like writers "to let their experience alone, to describe it as something that may be valued for its own sake." He longs for the writer, someone like Dreiser, perhaps, with a touch more of the artist in him, who is concerned with "life in its beautiful materiality." This is a bare statement of the argument.

His argument has an understandable value, though it is important to say at the outset that I doubt one is able to write about people—those "who have nothing to think about except themselves" are pathological—without involving them directly or indirectly in society, though not necessarily in consciousness of society. It can be argued, I think, that once a writer describes the kind of human beings one encounters in certain societies that he is, to some extent, describing those societies. However, there is a subject matter that may properly fall within the province of the social novel. Although this subject matter is not granted to all writers of fiction, there is a value to being concerned with society. Yet each writer must make his own emphasis: he may be greatly conscious or partly conscious of society, and he may thickly or thinly describe it. I think it's understood that even in the work of the social realists the amount of social fact one garners and depicts in a novel will differ from writer to writer, and it doesn't at all follow that the writer who depicts society most fully or realistically is necessarily the most effective writer.

Nor should it be assumed that if a writer is concerned with portraying a certain society or social milieu he must therefore kiss goodbye to the inventive or richly imagined, or to any particular methodology or technique of fiction: symbolism, myth, fantasy, the impersonal narrator, or anything else. Since Joyce, Kafka, Lawrence, and others, the novel has achieved new resources, new possibilities, and if, in the social novel, you don't want O'Hara all over again, you will have to make use of the devices and techniques experimental writers of the twentieth century have put at our disposal. These, it seems to me, are being used on the continent, in works like Günter Grass's *The Tin Drum*, more than among the new British social realists, who are saying it pretty much in the same old way.

Speaking for myself, who am not without concern for society and the ideas and events that improve or disturb it, I'd like to spend a minute saying why I think, for the novelist, continued concern with self—is the novel ever not concerned with the self's comprehension of itself?— whether lightly or heavily within the context of the social milieu, is necessary and profitable. I mean conscious concern in the sense of seeking one's personal meaning as it has been sought in literature from *Oedipus Rex* to *Henderson the Rain King*. I write about that particular search because it continues to be, religiously speaking, man's central drama— I know of no better way than the classic search for self to perfect an instrument that can recognize truth and live by it—and also because it

presents a challenge to the writer at a time when increased psychological knowledge coupled with increased irrational social behavior (from
Hitler's Germany to the age of possible nuclear destruction) once more
indicates the intricate and mysterious nature of man. He is yet to be
"explained" and if literature stops attempting it, nothing will succeed.
But I agree with Kazin that in portraying a human being successfully in
fiction we must dispense with mechanical psychological machinery. The
novelist nowadays must learn to use the illuminations of Freud without
dragging his machinery through the pages of his fiction. His most
important task is still to create believable human beings, hopefully as
interesting as some of the great fictional characters of the past, without
fear that he is violating psychological rules, and without citing them to
prove he isn't. In other words, among his tasks the present-day novelist
has to recapture his characters for the uses of his imagination, and one
way to go about it is to send them seeking themselves, their identities
and meaning, wherever they must—in the desert, industrial society, or
outer space makes no difference. Literature is concerned with man, with
what is human, and why, and how to create his humanity.

Another problem of the self becoming aware of itself that interests
me is the relation of personal morality to social morality. How much
selfishness and self-deception, for instance, does a man have to flush
down the drain to become an effective defender of the rights of Negroes?
What is the source of morality, and how is it discovered, of those few
Germans who hid a handful of Jews away from the ovens of the concentration camps? How much regret for Hiroshima must a man induce in
himself to commit a single good deed in this world? Though these questions as literary subject matter may seem to some as close to the province
of the social novelist, I will argue they are anyone's who deals with the
self. I doubt I'd be betraying the novel's best interests if I treat this subject matter as basically personal yet endow it, if I feel the necessity, with
a mythic quality to show how men and societies repeat their ideals and
errors. Again the search, the seeking, is for what being human is, what
its interests and obligations are; one might argue that this is the most
important subject of our time. The true tragedy of our time is the degra-
dation of the human being.

One additional word about method. I deny Kazin's remark that society is taken so much for granted in the contemporary novel that it can
no longer be seen. It can no longer be seen in the way Sinclair Lewis or
Arnold Bennett saw it. Society is much more complicated than our fore-
fathers, or Karl Marx, or perhaps even Freud—though he was closer to

it—imagined. Nowadays we are more greatly aware of the massive iner-
tia and irrationality of societies, of the sheer evil inherent in them. The
writer who is concerned with society must use every means at his command to portray it in its many-layered, ambivalent, cross-purposed, cre-
ative-destructive complexity. This calls for more than the merely realistic in fiction; it calls for the use of every imaginative resource at the
writer's command. The critic who feels that the salvation of the novel,
which is a continuous process and realization through time and the best
talent, is a matter of a return to "life as it is," "in its beautiful materiality," to "outward reality," pictured realistically is evading esthetic
opportunity, if not an understanding of reality itself. And may I suggest,
though there are some who deny this, that the novel as a work of art is
an objective thing in a real-enough world and often changes lives and
sometimes societies.

An argument related to Kazin's was made by Steven Marcus in an
essay in the *Partisan Review* last year. Marcus states that the contemporary novel is "deteriorating" because too many of our better writers are
writing the poetic novel, one result of which is—given its formal quality—that "not an idea violates it." He defines the poetic novel as one
"now being written according to what we can describe as a poetic conception both of experience and of the shape which experience must
take"; it is described as well-wrought, all ends neatly tucked in—practitioners in the past as diverse as Flaubert, James, Kafka, Virginia
Woolf—and characterized nowadays by too much uncertain suspension
in space and time, universality, symbolism, surrealism, fantasy, abstrac-
tion—though the last, apparently, is the result of a "disciplined effort of
dramatic rendering of theme through form." One gathers there are better ways of rendering theme through form.

The contemporary practitioners in America of this poetic novel are
Saul Bellow, at least in *Seize the Day*, and, I would imagine, *Henderson*;
Flannery O'Connor in practically all of her work; Marcus doesn't name
John Updike, but no doubt he would fit—and so do I, though Marcus
has some abstracting of his own to do to squeeze my work into his mold.
He thinks we are all working "in a minor mode" because we do not
explicitly deal with the larger social ideas and issues of our day. The essay
is an interesting speculation but reductive in that it does not first
attempt to assess what poetry is permissible in a novel—as, for example,
the poetry in Henry James's *Portrait of a Lady*; nor does it attempt to
weigh the novelistic virtues of the varieties of so-called poetic novels. In
more than one case the novels Marcus categorizes as poetic, contain a

proper novelistic poetry and have other novelistic qualities which he neglects to name. I sometimes think that what he really has in mind are books like Donn Byrne's *Messer Marco Polo*; and Thornton Wilder's *Woman of Andros*. I shall omit some of the details of his argument to get at his suggestions for handling ideas—increasing their use, one might say—in the present-day novel, a development of certain comments made by Lionel Trilling in his essay, "Art and Fortune."

"One thing that is clear," Marcus writes, "is that the novel has nearly ceased to give us what we need: an adequate notion of what it is like to [live] today, why we are the way we are, and what might be done to remedy our situation." Setting aside the thought that the best thinkers in our society can't give us the answers to these questions in some easily applicable way, I agree that the novel should attempt to formulate and answer questions of this kind, as Marcus says, "not merely [in] the embodiment of ideas in character and dramatic action, but [with] ideas as themselves, ideas represented in discourse as ideas." This is as Trilling meant it in his prognostic remark, sixteen years ago, that the novel of the future would explicitly deal with ideas. And Marcus advises us not to worry if the explication of these ideas disregards or loosens finely wrought form, nor if the ideas under discussion are topical and ephemeral; these qualities make for involvement in the fiction. He observes that "the novel can often be seen to gain as a work of art to the extent that it loses its connections with immediate topical experience." To put it another way: Let's not worry about the form of the novel; the genre is historically the least "artistic" of sovereign art forms and a little less art to get in a few good ideas won't hurt anyone. An excessive reliance on form—here is Trilling again—makes for limitation in fiction. Note the word is "excessive reliance"; there can not be, I should imagine, excessive form, though Marcus worries about finely wrought form.

Trilling's prognosis that the novel of the future would be concerned more explicitly with ideas was apparently wrong. In fact, says Marcus, things went quite the other way and not an idea violates the contemporary novel, especially the so-called poetic. I think the prognosis failed because it is impossible to change the nature of fiction. The subject of ideas in fiction has been much discussed by critics but no one, I think, has managed to come up with a successful method of expressing ideas with total force as drama than through the fiction, through character and events; nor, may I say in passing, has anyone come up with a way to induce worthwhile discussion of ideas explicitly in the work of any writer whose talent it is to create significant drama in some nondiscursively ideational way: for instance, Hemingway and Faulkner. Ideas, even in Stendhal, are best embodied in character and events; and when there is explicit discourse, as in the work of many great writers, the genius of each writer modifies the discourse (perhaps even the factual truth of the discourse) to suit the conditions of the fiction; sometimes the truth of the book is camouflaged or denied by the explicit argument; nor can the whole truth be told in fiction as in a nonfictional work, although the wholeness of the truth may be implied, perhaps metaphorically, in the total fiction. What would Marcus have advised Hemingway, for instance, who didn't discuss ideas explicitly, for whatever reason, in his early poetic novels? Trilling wrote in 1949 that Hemingway's and Faulkner's fiction, though indifferent "to the conscious intellectual tradition of our time" seemed in their fiction to possess ideas, or achieved the effect of ideas. "What comes into being," he wrote, "when two contradictory emotions are made to confront each other and are required to have a relationship with each other . . . is quite properly called an idea." An idea is an idea, explicit or embedded in drama. The writer with an idea in his mind as he conceives a scene has always thought so, although his reader may be entertained without perceiving it. Still, it is there and can be important, more important, possibly, than some of the explicit ideas in Sartre. Trilling says that this effect as of ideas comes through the "activity" and "cogency" of Hemingway's or Faulkner's narrative, through their qualities of "wisdom and humility," and through "negative capability"—of not explaining the meaning of every possible action, every possible speech, of permitting mystery to reside in their work. And one might add to Trilling's list the quality of art achieved—the form—that releases the meaning of the fiction. If Hemingway had tried handling ideas as explicit discourses on topical and ephemeral material, he might have had to invent Lanny Budd. And what, one might ask at this point, of the topical works written immediately after the death of Sacco and Vanzetti, or since then? Is there one work of art among them? Ideas in literature are effective as drama when they are ignited in a way that reveals a man's soul, as Ivan Karamazov's is revealed in his dialogue with the devil during his delirium; rather than, shall we say, as in Tolstoy's chapters on determinism in history, placed between the narrative sections of *War and Peace*. Can't it be said that Tolstoy was a great writer despite some of his ideas? Who would want *What Is Art* written into *Anna Karenina*?

As for the answers to the serious questions Marcus asks: Who am I? Why am I? What to do about our bad situation? Aren't these questions that literature always tries to answer, with or without long discursive disquisitions? If by "bad situation" is meant the present-day Soviet American, nuclear-powered-and-weaponed world, the world of the cold war, of course we, even in the so-called poetic novel, are concerned with that, whether there are topical discussions or not, whenever we assert in the meaning of the drama, the necessity of morality, the value of the human being, the holy worth of life. We demand better terms, better conditions from society for the human being by saying what it means to be human. Without discussing the bomb we say what we must say about it, though we do not deny other writers the right to quote statistics or embark upon long arguments for its destruction. We say it as best we can and we will probably say it differently with each book we write. My books, to suit my needs, are tending to more society rather than less, but I also look upon this as esthetic opportunity.

As for the matter of loosening form to introduce the "extra-artistic" through topicality and ephemerality, which, Marcus says, induces "immediacy, involvement and appeal," what does the "extra-artistic" translate into other than non-art, or less than art? "Let your experience alone," as Kazin puts it, translates into either documentary autobiography, or let art alone. "The form of the drama," Trilling writes, "is its idea, and its idea is its form." Therefore what is best for the idea is that it have the best form. Not "less" form or "excessive" form but the best form. That form which most fully realizes the truth and beauty of the idea. If the critic means, when he depreciates the "well" or "finely wrought," that he is tired of beautifully formed ivory miniatures, I admit the value of his criticism, but all you can advise the artist or the writer is to enlarge his view, if he can; try to encompass a larger idea within the precincts of his work. Can a work of art, truly fulfilled, formed and meaningful, ever fail us?

What bothers me, I have tried to say, in criticism of the contemporary novel is the insistence by some critics, although it is not always stated in just this way—that there is an idea-technique either-or. That is to say, that technique counts much less than ideas, or technique spoils ideas. That may be true in individual cases but it is not true as a principle. The idea cannot be the idea without its form. The attack on the author's methodology becomes an attack on the content of the work. For instance, Mr. Wayne Booth's *Rhetoric of Fiction* attacks the morality of certain contemporary fiction through a criticism, apparently, of its rhetoric. Steven Marcus, who dislikes the "poetic" novel, depreciates the accomplishments of novels he defines as such. Alfred Kazin, though he does not worship realism or social realism, tends to undervalue contemporary symbolic fiction. The truth of the matter is, there is no single "correct" esthetic approach to any content. And a good writer knows there is more than content to communicate to the reader. Part of the pleasure a fiction affords is the pleasure of being affected by the admittedly imagined, what some call illusion in fiction, and I like to call the visible fiction. Some very good writers give that pleasure, not quite drawing attention to the illusion but fabricating it in such a way that the reader responds to it as though it were music, and perhaps it is. On the other hand, there are writers (just as there are readers of fiction) who will have no part of this if they can help it. There are readers who go through their lives avoiding fantasy, as though it were a threat to their existence.

The artist who paints a picture is not arguing you don't know it's a picture, not only the abstract expressionistic forms but also the realistic figures, though they are, so to speak, trumped up; and in the later statuary of Michelangelo, which some art historians call "unfinished" and others argue no—though of course it makes no difference—the figure barely steps out of the stone, and the sense of stone is part of the agonizing drama, the miracle of the "real" and imagined in one; and there is no reason why the contemporary writer of fiction should not give his readers the same conscious double pleasure. For this reason he will use any technique at his command, including the symbolic, not only to suggest the oneness of disparate things, but as a fabrication of language through which one may respond to the fiction; he will abstract to heighten certain effects, by simplifying, highlighting, clarifying; and he will fantasy, when he feels the necessity, to show the reader what "reality" consists in and is capable of; to surprise and excite the mind, to light the imagination. What the writer ultimately does with method and technique depends, of course, on his talent and intellect, not on method per se.

I sometimes think of Abram Tertz, the pseudonymous Soviet writer who sent out of Russia, or managed to have taken out for him, a short novel, *The Trial Begins*, a book of fantastic short stories, and an already famous essay, "On Socialist Realism." It is from the essay that I would now like to quote a short passage. Speaking about Soviet literature he says:

> Let us hope . . . that our need for truth will not interfere with the work of thought and imagination. [I think you understand that "truth" means "socialist truth."] Right now I put my hope in a phantasmagoric art, with hypotheses instead of a purpose, an art in which the grotesque will replace realist descriptions of ordinary life. Such an art would correspond best to the

spirit of our time. May the fantastic imagery of Hoffmann and Dostoevski, of Goya, Chagall and Mayakovski . . . and of many other realists and non-realists teach us how to be truthful with the aid of the absurd an the fantastic.

We don't know where to go; but, realizing that there is nothing to be done about it, we start to think, to set riddles, to make assumptions. May we thus invent something marvelous? Perhaps; but it will no longer be socialist realism.

An artist can tell the truth in any language and by any means. He can tell the truth realistically, naturalistically, fantastically, poetically, in comedy or tragedy. He tells the truth in the fiction methodology he is most effective with. He tells it with an effaced narrator, or an omniscient narrator, with a moral narrator or the immoral narrator. He may tell it in "No in thunder" or "Yes in Blood"; but he cannot tell it by fiat or dogma. He must avoid the prohibitions of the dogmatists who would rob him of the variety of his means of expression and thereby hurt the quality of his art. His business is to stay free, and through art, create freedom.

24

THE WRITER IN THE

MODERN WORLD

◆

The writer's world, limiting it to what we call the outer, differs from the average person's not in kind but in degree. That is to say, the writer, by inclination and training, and because of the very nature of his work, as a rule senses more in, and reacts more deeply to life, by which of course we mean the world of living with his fellow men, than the ordinary man does. The sense of things is stronger in him, Lionel Trilling says. I think there is little doubt that the writer's greater awareness of the world tends to disturb him more than it does the average person, because he is more thoroughly cognizant of one of the central phenomena of our times: the slow shrinkage of liberty for the individual—this strikes him to the heart, for freedom is the true condition of the creation of great works of art (think of the meagerness of the arts under fascism and communism). He knows that as a result of this loss of freedom—for reasons that I shall attempt to make clear—he has suffered a loss of wholeness in outlook and living, and therefore his power as an artist is diminished. It may not always be a rule to go by (one wonders at the productivity of the Russian novelists under the Czars, but there the censorship was not as all-embracing as it is in the Soviet Union today), but I find a correlation between the free, whole man—the humanist—and the great writer; and between a free age and the proportion of great works produced in it.

I do not, in this lecture, intend to characterize the entire production of our modern writers as inferior in art quality and meaning—far from it—but I do believe, despite some individual instances of very fine work, that the main body of the writing of the last thirty or so years—what I call my own generation—taken collectively, is perhaps more negative, fragmented, and monotonous than it need be, and that the writer of this time, particularly the contemporary writer, is less successful in what he attempts to do in art than he would be if he were less the victim of his world, less afraid of it, or to put it another way, freer in it. I should, however, like to qualify this last statement by limiting it to the novelist, and at that the American novelist, though I suspect the same would probably hold true for some of our poets and dramatists. To understand the American novelist and his works of this period, we must of course understand his world. I shall not try your patience with an extended description of it, but there are some salient facts which must be mentioned.

Let me say beforehand that a clear knowledge of the nature of the conditions of human existence, as philosophy and science have revealed them to us, need not necessarily be a burden to man, once he has brought himself to accept the cosmological facts of life yet gives himself to searching for and extending the boundaries of his freedom. Just as happiness lies in its pursuit, so does freedom, for the very nature of pursuit implies the preconditions for pursuing. But apparently it is only the rare man who will kick determinism in the teeth and see how far he can run without being caught. Most of us, and this holds true for too many writers of our time, who confront the egg that science has laid around us, tend to be somewhat depressed by the fact of its existence, which represents, on paper at least, a loss of a certain quantity of freedom of will and choice. I say on paper because the knowledge of the workings of fate, time, history and death need not cut down the domain of our immediate freedom (here the ignorant benefit), yet there are many thoughtful people, who, instead of taking stock of all they have left, are troubled by man's philosophical plight and find that the heritage of our knowledge, which describes the slow closure of necessity over our heads, to be all but unbearable. This, interestingly enough, happens to be especially true if they are unhappy in their personal lives, perhaps immature or given too much to self pity, or neurotic without any insight into their neuroticism.

However, sometimes the surprising forms that determinism takes— like marble masks out of our dreams—and the sudden, almost rude thrust of these forms upon our consciousness makes it, if we are not subjective idealists, legitimately impossible for us to break through the iron bars of our knowledge and o'erleap the wall. So much change of our cherished concepts is demanded of us, sometimes within the short while of a single generation, so much destruction of old assumptions, let us say of the perfectibility of man and the everlasting progress of civilization, compelling a further delimitation of areas of retained freedom, with the result that we resignedly accept the "human condition" without trying it for "give." It takes a long while to become truly objective, and I may say brave, about data (brandished like spears in our faces) that make us question the truth of ideas previously basic to our security. Some of the concepts of late nineteenth- and twentieth-century science, are still too close for perfect perspective: the new physics, for instance, has toppled absolutes—not for all, it should be said—and mixed good and evil in the jelly of relativity; evolution has forever destroyed man's favored position over the beasts; and psychoanalysis discovered the most fearful beast to be in our souls. We were, moreover, shown this image of the demonic in ourselves at the very moment of our discovery of a greater source of physical power than the world has heretofore known, the power to destroy ourselves if we lost our vigilance but for a moment.

Another subtle effect of science upon us, an effect upon which Lewis Mumford lays the blame for some extremes of modern art, is that although essentially neutral in itself, science becomes evil in man's neglect to fit it to the best needs and uses of the human personality. Science made less of our humanness because it led us to value the machine over the human being, the objective over the subjective, material things rather than spiritual. It left us with a greater knowledge of our world, but through our own error less suited to live in it.

Science [Mumford says] has not merely eliminated a thousand irrelevant fantasies and wishful projections that had kept man from understanding the nature of the physical world; but it also had undermined man himself, and all but eliminated from every department of life the essential concepts of purpose, value and quality. Man's autonomous inner world, the impulses and urges he projects and realizes in the forms of art, were foreign to science and irrelevant to its aims. In the ideal world that the scientist was creating, machines increasingly took the place of men, and men were tolerated only to the extent they took on the attributes of machines. . . . Since man is himself part of the order of nature, he learned much about his own nature and his circumstances from this new method of thought; but at the same time he forgot many truths about his constitution and aptitudes that religion and art had abundantly recognized. Only in the final stages of mechanization, the stage we are now entering, could the essential nature of what went before be fully discerned; and it was not until our day that the artist surrendered to forces that, in the end, were to overwhelm the human personality.

I, for one, see more good in modern art than Mr. Mumford does, and I will deny any mass surrender of our artists to forces that overwhelm the human personality, though I wish they would deal with the human personality more fully than they do; but I think Mr. Mumford's thesis helps explain another aspect of the writer's loss of freedom in modern times: in the sense that it represents a loss of interest in the human.

Now let us for a moment review a bit of contemporary history. Has there ever before, in the short interval of thirty-odd years, been such a headlong, mad rush of events?—in so short a time such a great loss of personal peace and shrinking of free ground? Consider, if you will, what a man has had to live through in half an average lifetime. I was born during the First World War, a war, you will remember, to make the world safe for the democracy it finds so difficult to stomach, when our soldiers in leggings were pelted with flowers—a colleague reminds me—as they marched to the ships, and crowds lining the streets cheered their glory, all unaware that these same soldiers, marching home, would lose in the flow of time their dearly bought victory and emerge in the end with little more than nothing for their efforts (the secret of all wars, a fact we seem never able to learn). It was this disillusionment that helped set the mood and tone of Hemingway's novels for the next two decades.

Came the twenties, ten years of ponderous peace conferences and piled high scraps of paper, of material prosperity for us in America, and with it, its inevitable concomitant of false values, "the dazzle and fever and ruin"—a nation seduced to the worship of the money ideal—the escape from things of the spirit into the glitter and blare of the jazz age, which consumed the talent of one of our most gifted novelists, F. Scott Fitzgerald, unseeing, yet wise. As night follows day followed the Great Depression, still too familiar to us to need description. Although characterized by privation and sadness it was somehow a spiritually healthy time, because it brought us back to fundamentals. Steinbeck sensed them, while Dos Passos was crying down with the society that breeds such horror, and Thomas Wolfe was engaged in the many-volumed bray proclaiming the presence of the gargantuan self. There was more to these times than our writers, understandably enough, told us of, but at the very end of the thirties Hemingway, tired of "nada," affirmed that there *were* things worth fighting for.

The effect of the Depression upon us was mild compared to the emotions we were to experience after the Nazis rose to power and restored torture and slavery as a way of dealing with the human spirit. Without any apparent sense of guilt among them, and with surprisingly little anguish on our part, they destroyed the lives of some six or seven million human beings. And though for a long time we wanted not to be, we were, inevitably, embroiled in a new war, a war that had, I agree, to be fought, though the imperative is surely a mark of man's basic weakness. This was the war to end all wars, or at least to bring peace in our time, and not unexpectedly it did neither.

It seems to be an axiom that every time we fight anew war we do so with new weapons, and it is of course necessary to test them, as we did at Hiroshima and Nagasaki. Therefore it is not without irony that we now fear the same weapon in the hands of former allies, but we are at least engaged in perfecting a more powerful weapon to use against them if we should have to. As if the fates were writing history, the hot war was followed by a cold war against an enemy by proxy, who having never known freedom, was of an easy mind in denying it to others. Followed hard upon the cold, the Korean war, or the unpopular or half-forgotten war, as much ours, and not Mr. Truman's, as one's right arm is his own, though it be roasting in the oven as he munches popcorn and stares at the television screen. (At about this time, William Faulkner was recognized as the creator of a great moral drama and universal tragedy and was awarded the Nobel Prize for Literature. This may have been a good sign whose significance we are still unable to measure.)

The moment, then, finds us in Korea, with inflation rising on the home front, a bickering, not very bright Congress, doing little about it, and a spate of congressional committees punishing a somewhat utopian, somewhat purblind generation for the sins of its youth, by hacking suicidally away at the civil rights guaranteed us in the Constitution, our greatest weapon against communism. Moreover, we are in the best sense of the word, leaderless, by which I mean that the great minds and spirits that rise to our aid in times of calamity are nowhere, at the moment, visible. Where leaders are concerned, we have an unfortunate talent for underselling ourselves.

Now it is obvious what is lost under such conditions as these. Nothing definite, some may say, but it is definite enough to one of the writer's outlook and temperament, though these qualities are hardly alike in all artists. The writer, or would-be writer, misses the freedom to make casual personal decisions about what to do or not to do next, especially, let us say, if he is subject to the call of his draft board, or an atomic war threatens; just as he misses the freedom to travel at will from country to country if he has the urge to do so and the means to accomplish it. True, one does not *have* to travel in the Orient, presently aflame, or among the dark shadows of the Iron Curtain countries, or in fascist Spain, to be a writer, but it somehow affects one not to be able to; and that brings us to the loss of perhaps the most crucial freedom, the freedom to feel free, so necessary to imaginative creation. How can one feel free, snarled in a tangle of violent events, when warnings and *verbotens* descend from the sky like a shower of rocks?

Luckily for us life has ways of demanding our attention, drawing it from the contemplation of our limitations to the necessity of living. Whether it hails or snows we go about the making or buying of bread, and indeed the eating of it; and it is, naturally, good for us that we do, without pausing too long to listen to the creaking of the universe. Thus to some degree, we become free of our knowledge of what is going on. Freedom, it should be pointed out, is a subjective quality, for some men feel free even in prison. It would seem to depend on what a man is used to, on the strength of his ideals, or conscience, or nervous system, or perhaps his powers of forgetting. This last does not mean a hardboiled who-the-hell-cares attitude, or necessarily an escapist's act, excluding by some delightful enticement what is not too pleasant to contemplate. The quite simple fact is that it is sometimes necessary to bury one's head in the sand of one's own little affairs. Our nervous system can take just so much voltage; a little more and you may blow a fuse: heart attacks are a statistically popular way of dying, and schizophrenia is on the increase. Therefore it pays, whenever possible, to keep fingers crossed, hope for the best, and with one ear half-cocked for unpleasant sounds in the distance, to go on working. To be able to do so speaks well for man's desire to lead a sane and normal existence. To be sure, there are writers who keep themselves at work in the very teeth of bad times, some seeming to flourish when conditions are at their worst, like well-built bottoms riding the crashing waves during a storm. To these artists bad times mean having at hand a certain quantity of recalcitrant stuff out of which to hew some decently formed art object. So doing, the artist feels himself to be in control of his destiny, which is one reason why men strive to be artists. But men like these are rare; and many good artists, afflicted by times such as ours, ultimately abandon their art.

Yes, some writers write, but we must consider that in writing an artist has to face the world on two fronts: the reality it mirrors for him, and the reality he conceives. In his conception he is once again open to the onslaughts of the times, even though he has barred his window against them for the peace to create. The conceived world is of course a different world, as I have said, because the writer contains it, and will make of it what he will, subject to certain inevitable laws, rather than that it make out of him what it will, as sometimes the outside world does. The writer then learns, if he does not already know it, that there is, by and large, no escape from the outside. Oh, it is true that some do create private worlds, and find therein a dubious sanity, but your workaday artist would rather live where everyone else does, or at least deal with people who do. This being so, he is consciously brought back to affairs as they are, and has of necessity to deal with the reality he finds so disappointing and irritating, and which often fills him with confusion and doubt.

He will struggle to keep his vision clear so that he can instill meaning—while he gropes for it—to its fullest, as the work evolves from his pen; and at the same time as he upholds the vision that teaches him to externalize his conception, at the same moment as he is also endowing it with soul, he must, like a man in quicksand making sand castles, retain the objectivity and critical vision that informs him he has or has not succeeded in fulfilling his purpose.

At this moment, in this act of creation and constant judgment of it as he is creating, like a blind man slowly evolving sight and insight into sight, or like someone trying to measure a dream with a dissolving ruler, the writer cannot amid his creative striving refrain from asking himself—however softly—some agonizing questions:

- How did I get here and what am I doing? What can I possibly say that will be of use or interest to anyone in this wide, wide world?
- How can I continue to remain chained, day after day and far into the night, to this chair in a little room at a time when civilization threatens to destroy itself? How can one live his young life at the same time he has imprisoned it to write?
- How can I even remotely begin to invent a drama that will concern us all, in a world that shrieks with drama and tragedy? How can I compete with life for emotion?
- How shall I keep hysteria our of my voice, when "no thought is permissible," a critic writes, "except an extreme thought . . . emblematic . . . of concentration camps, alienation, madness, hell, history and God?"
- Why am I writing? Whose salvation or damnation am I creating if not my own?
- Is there *anything* positive to say?
- Will I complete this or die first? Who, besides me, cares?

Hysteria, or the new failure of nerve? Hardly: the normal process of creation in abnormal times. One of the triumphs of the contemporary writer, it seems to me, is that he does continue to produce. Ultimately to complete one's work under present conditions is a triumph of imagination and will over matter, over reality; but oftentimes the expenditure of energy needed to triumph is enough to make a young man old. No wonder so many of our young writers, having got out one decent book, are too exhausted or depleted to produce another.

Our times are, in a sense, the precipitate of their philosophy and history. Naturally they contain other elements, forces, or "worlds" that condition the fate and freedom, therefore the domain of the serious writer. Of the greatest importance to him, of course, is country (as *patria*), its culture, and—although this is saying practically the same thing—the people whom he is writing for. It goes without saying that the writer cannot function continually and prolifically, granted he is able to, if he does not succeed in pleasing his audience. Their response determines his publisher's reception of him. Their acceptance always "makes" him, and their neglect, though not always, usually "breaks" him.

To understand why America treats its artists as it does (I am characterizing the reaction of the dominant majority) we must first comprehend that ours is a country incorporating in our national life a strange and serious cleavage, a cleavage between what we believe we ought to do and what we finally do; between the idea and the institution we make of it. This is evidenced in our almost sentimental respect for moral idealism while we practice a way of life popularly called materialism. It is a quality so characteristic of us that we are almost all aware of it, yet we bristle when it is called to our attention. As a people we pay homage to the "way things ought to be," yet frequently, especially when our own interests are concerned, work for the opposite. Our Constitution, for example, is our most revered historical document, yet we cannot, at present, conceive enough ways to circumvent its intention. We pretend to a great respect for education but spend more on whiskey. We eat too much and think too little. We pay lip service to "values" then proceed to define them as business values. Among us the spirit is too often mortified between the press of silver dollars.

One should note, however, that the condition I have just described has provided some of our writers with their best material: Sinclair Lewis's *Babbit* and *Main Street*, John Dos Passos's *U.S.A.* trilogy, and John Steinbeck's *The Grapes of Wrath*—novels which paradoxically are popular sellers in the United States, because, as I have pointed out, our idealistic strain is strong; we love to have our wounds probed although we will allow them to fester long past the danger point. On the other hand, many an artist feels like an alien among us, and many of them—including some very fine writers—have flocked away from our shores—the expatriates of every decade, happier where they are respected. For the simple fact is that the cleavage I spoke of is manifested also in the contempt the so-called man of action (by which is sometimes meant a man without any inner life) has taught himself to feel for the intellectual—the artist as well as the professional thinker. With an occasional exception, our popular conception of the professor is a semi-comic one, and our artists (though never forget we very secretly respect them) are bohemians, longhairs and oddballs. Martin Turnell points out that the writer suffers a loss of popular esteem because of his often uncomfortable discoveries about human nature, because he will not subordinate his interests to those of his own class, because he is committed to development and change; in a word, because he dares be independent. He so often feels isolated, not necessarily (as Stephen Spender seems to think) because there are no other artists around, but essentially because the public is uncomfortable with him. He often feels he has no one to write for.

I am of course speaking of the American audience in general. I know that there are among us many cultivated appreciators of all that is good in our writing and thinking, but they amount to too minute a fraction of our population of one hundred fifty-five million. They do much to generate interest in classical music, ballet and opera performances, little theaters and art galleries, but even among them it is difficult to scrape up seven thousand purchasers of a good first novel, that number of copies being about the break-even point for the publisher. The price of books is comparatively high now and there are many activities and entertainments to take up one's time, but does it take anything more than a mild act of will to buy a good novel and read it? Jacques Barzun asserts that the problem of appreciation of art is intertwined with that of the large numbers of people in this country, and that it is not a question of the decadence of the public. Never before has there been so large a mass of people to contend with in our society, he says, and it is that overwhelming number of people (whom we are compelled to initiate, in new groups, to the meaning and uses of the arts) who thus keep the level of our popular culture low. Whether it is the mass age that accounts for a deplorable situation, or because a great number of individuals who ought to, are too lazy to use their wills to become, or remain, oriented in a culturally positive direction, we are reading fewer books, and fewer good books, than ever before in our history. Never forget that *Forever Amber*, the story of the life and loves of a Restoration trollop, was the popular best-seller during the tragic years of World War II.

There can be little doubt that the publisher nowadays reflects and represents public taste. Even so short a time as two generations ago, he felt it his responsibility to uplift that taste. He was not ashamed to be something of an educator. And if by chance one or two of the first-rate books on his list did not sell, he shrugged off the loss, because it was his duty to put out high quality books, and the loss would be made up by the profit on the popular things he printed. Not every book was expected to make money. A good book was its own reason for being. In fairness to the publisher of today, one ought to say that he too is on the lookout for the best books he can find, *but they must sell*. He daren't attempt to educate, to experiment, to encourage. He leaves that sort of thing to the very small houses like New Directions. He himself is admittedly engaged in Big Business. Costs are high; he has an enormous overhead and many economic headaches. As a result he tends to be concerned with business first and the quality of literature afterward. A book equals a product, like shoes or Wheaties. Either you sell it or you don't, and if you don't you junk it, which means he will not take chances.

Fifty years ago novelists made money. Fiction, good and bad, sold eight to one over nonfiction. Now the opposite is true by about the same ratio; therefore the publisher buys less fiction. He is no longer in love with the well-written literary first novel, because the first novel almost always loses money. Before the Second World War he could afford to gamble with it, because the break-even point was then roughly twenty-five hundred copies; now, as I have said, it is about seven thousand, and therefore the publisher is wary of buying a first novel unless it has movie possibilities. He splits with the author on the movie price of the book, so it is not strange that he sometimes encourages an author to write according to the movie formula. And there are other subsidiary sources the publisher would like to sell to: the book clubs, which have their own way of stereotyping public taste, the magazine digests, which often distort the intent of a novel, and the twenty-five-cent reprint houses, who ask openly for a sufficient quantity of sex and violence. Let me quote an item which recently appeared in the book review section of the *New York Times*: "We don't want any subtle character studies," wrote the editor of one eminently successful reprint house to a publisher. "The story should be hard-hitting and socially realistic with elements of sex and violence."

For such novels he offered an advance on royalties of from ten to fifteen thousand dollars. What effect will this offer, and many others like it, have upon what the publisher will accept for publication? What effect can it have on the writer of a "subtle character study," slaving away in his room, unaware that he is slowly being squeezed to death by sales statistics? Where now is the writer's freedom to write what he best can?

These are some elementary facts of the economics of present-day publishing. How does this picture affect the working conditions and life of our writer? Since the average writer cannot live on his earnings from writing (the average annual earnings of the majority of American writers is estimated at less than three thousand dollars), and since starving in a garret is no longer fashionable, the writer who *will* write may have to make one of the following choices:

1. Pare his personal needs to the bone, which means sacrificing the possibility of a family of his own and consequently the growth and richness that come from family life, and allow himself to continue to be housed and fed by and with his parents, and work there, as ever the child in the house. Or he may marry and permit his wife to support him, with all the disadvantages and friction that sort of arrangement is sure to generate, no matter how benevolent or generous the wife.

2. Find himself a nonwriting, part-time job and live and write in a furnished room. Some writers have done quite well under such circumstances but not for too long. An extended dose of such an existence may lead to neuroticism or nervous collapse, especially if the book that is born under these conditions cannot find a publisher.

3. Hunt out some freelance jobs and knock out journalistic pieces, while he is engaged on his novel. As a rule the market pays little for this sort of work, or for book reviews or critical articles. And too much of Grub Street may debase the quality of one's style. Stephen Spender, the British poet, points out that the freelance situation is better in England. There the writer may add to his income by doing high quality radio scripts for the BBC's Third Program, or he may work as a publisher's editor or reader. In America, professionals do most of this sort of work, and there are few secondary outlets where the writer can earn some money yet retain his self-respect.

4. Forget all about self-respect and turn out the sort of books reprint houses are clamoring for. Or he can take the long ride to Hollywood, and granted he is hired, manufacture the kind of swill

they want, or do the same for radio and television. "All that is needed," Graham Greene says, "is the dried imagination and the dead pen."

5. About the best compromise I know is that the writer find a job in a university, preferably as a teacher of writing. Thus he will have a regular salary and a quite respectable job, and even some free time in which to do his writing. The last is the rub: at best he is a half-time writer. And if, as a teacher, he is moved to augment his income by getting out a textbook or two, he may before long give up creative writing altogether and head into criticism.

I wish I knew some sure way out of this dilemma, but there is none at present. There is much talk now of subsidizing the writer, and I would be for a subsidy if it were provided by the writer's community, or by the universities, or by our publishing houses; but I am against the federal government's doing so. The dangers are apparent. Yet, often, the economic problem is in essence a social one. That is to say, if we were able to create the conditions of a true appreciation of art in America—which would naturally mean a great change in values for our people—the economic problem would solve itself. I like to think that in talking of the possibility of this solution to the artist's problem that I am not being utopian, but I am afraid I am—at least for the present.

Now as I come to the last part of this paper, let me review briefly what I have been saying about the writer's sense of his freedom in these times. I doubt that scientific determinism alone sets the mood for an age if events themselves leave us feeling free and easy and gay, but I do think that our present conception of the nature of the universe does intensify an unhappy mood, when unhappiness already hangs upon the air. As for the argument that science hurts our freedom by dehumanizing us, I will qualify Lewis Mumford's thesis and say that science sometimes does forget that the source of its power is man, and not the other way around; but when it forgets that, it is our own fault for letting it forget. As for contemporary history, it hardly leaves us feeling free and gay. Rather, it impels us to believe that our spirits have been imprisoned. We feel this because we have no control of events, hence little over our lives. We are aware our age is one of suffering and terror, and *that* frequently disgusts us. You will find expressions of that disgust and other reactions like it, or just a desire to escape from life, in the works of just about every one of our modern novelists. Moreover, our cultural situation and a diminishing audience of understanding readers leaves the writer with a diminishing sense of purpose. As for the economic dilemma, the sheer difficulty of being able to write steadily for any extended length of time, and after that, of being published—well, I have just gone into that.

I don't pretend that these facts alone explain the outlook and accomplishment, or lack of it, of our modern writers, but I do believe that this sense of loss of our freedom in this world certainly does seriously condition the writer's choice of subject matter and his method of handling it.

Of course, writing in this country in our time has a good deal to be proud of: certain books by William Faulkner, Ernest Hemingway, Scott Fitzgerald, John Steinbeck, and others; also works of such minor writers as Robert Penn Warren, Jean Stafford, and James Gould Cozzens. And the wonderful short stories of Eudora Welty, Katherine Ann Porter, and J. F. Powers. Moreover the recent revival of interest in the works of Henry James, E. M. Forster, Joseph Conrad, Fitzgerald, and others reveals that both the readers and the writer still have not forgotten the meaning of quality in literature.

But, as I said at the beginning of this talk, when it comes to an evaluation of the total accomplishment of our modern novelists, we sense a lack. Our literature is poorer, more negative, more immature than it should be (many of our writers are so appalled by the facts of our lives that they use them like firecrackers instead of clay). The modern novel tends to shock, rather than move the reader. It lacks wholeness and humanness, true depth and vision. It sees man as a broken fragmented creature, instead of exploring the conditions and possibilities of his wholeness.

These criticisms hold true especially for our newest novelists, as John Aldridge points out in *After the Lost Generation*. For them modern life is basically purposeless; its condition doubt, hopeless confusion, and fear. Having, they think, nothing to affirm, possessing no true insight into the nature of drama, they seek out explosive subject matter and handle it journalistically. They know what is bad in us, and it is bad enough, but they are hardly concerned with the good. Many of them are still too closely bound to the early Hemingway, aping the superficial things about his writing: the flat, enigmatic declarative sentences, the adolescent sex, the secretive emotion of his heroes, and their hard suffering without catharsis; these young writers would do better to learn from Hemingway's extraordinary craftsmanship and then go on to make meanings of their own. Poor Hemingway is taking a bitter beating over the head these days for the errors of his disciples. He wrote as he saw the world, and he writes well. Those who are the victims still of his enormous impact have only themselves to blame for not having disengaged their talent from his view of life. They have not learned the best lessons Hemingway teaches: integrity, honesty to self, and the taking of infinite pains.

Their own craftsmanship is not secure: they are impatient with careful construction, architecture, true style. And if they happen to have mastered something of a technique, they often use it to hide themselves from others; to escape into private worlds, particularly that of childhood. Sometimes they can't read their own symbolism. (Let not this be understood as an attack upon the use of symbolism in the novel. Symbolism makes the complex simple while it preserves the richness of experience, but symbolism for its own sake does not make good writing. Nor shall I decry the literary experiments, no matter how abstruse, of the avant-gardists. If these experiments had not been made for us, we should have had to make them ourselves. The novelist cannot afford to neglect any new knowledge of men or their ways of art. I think that the writers of the future will benefit immeasurably from what Joyce, Proust, Faulkner, and others have done, provided that they remember that these writers had rich bodies of subject matter, and did not use their technique as an end in itself.) Many of our younger writers take the trimmings but omit the meat. Many of them, like birds wounded by secret arrows, seem to be falling in the beginning of their flight. It is far too early to be writing off Mailer, Vidal, Burns, Capote, especially Buechner, and other present-day novelists, but they are in trouble now because they cannot see man steadily nor see him whole. Many of them have yet to learn, despite psychoanalysis, that man's personality and life are essentially mysteries. Those who dare explore these mysteries have made rich discoveries and written wonderful books. The more wonderful the book, the more depth, scope, feeling, the more human possibilities the people in the book contain. This is one secret of good writing I should not like to forget.

American life in these times, says William Barrett, "tends away from the emotion and organic depths out of which the greatest literature has sprung." He states, "We can hardly expect a Tolstoy or a Dostoyevsky in America when the deepest experience of our writers [those I have just spoken of] is not an organic or recognized part of American life; our extrovert civilization has developed other means of adjusting to life without their [Tolstoy's and Dostoyevsky's] spiritual struggles. We have the crack-up and breakdown, neuroses and maladjustment, but we have not their tragic sense of life."

There, in a word, we have why the American writer of today so often fails: he lacks the tragic sense of life, that sense of life that comes from suffering and learning from the suffering of others the necessity of identifying himself with them. Instead, he attempts in deadpan fashion to absolve himself from pain, and by locking himself within the self, refuses to be engaged in the needs of others, or their pain. He too is a victim of our values, and therefore without "the emotion and organic depths out of which the greatest literature has sprung." Thus he is unwilling to learn what he must learn: to think and work himself towards freedom. "He simply follows the data of acceptance that seem to be opening out before him," says Jacques Barzun. "Being a good fellow, blithely uneducated, a democrat at heart, he is neither wild enough nor self-controlled enough to forge and temper his soul; and at the first strain it cracks."

Without this tempering of soul through knowledge and self-discipline, without this tragic sense of life he does not develop compassion for the human person, nor understanding that freedom grows from the human spirit; that society's freedom arises from man's inner depths. He cannot successfully substitute a cynical or hardboiled attitude toward life for will and discipline, qualities that invite self-knowledge, which teaches the self's surprising contradictions yet how to win unity for it; that teaches the freedom that lies in love, not our superficial conception of it, but the love that is a way of life, which, considering our natures, we must ever struggle to attain. We must sacrifice in order to love, and I doubt it has ever been or can ever be otherwise; but the sacrifice is good to make because it is only a sacrifice of egoism and pride; and to sacrifice that is no sacrifice at all. The conditions of our existence are such that if we do not embark upon this difficult way of love, we may in the future be unable to do so.

In freeing ourselves to love we broaden the freedom of others, and create the conditions of living together that we call morality, which is a further means of making us free and thus releasing in ourselves, instead of anxiety and fear, the creative power to live meaningfully.

Under this freedom the imagination of the writer wings aloft; emotion leads man to man, the writer to a subject worthy of his art, and therefore to the creation of the conditions of his own acceptance in our culture. It will be his task to scout the area of hope, explore possibility, and in so doing, create a vision of life, so dignified, whole, and lovely that it will lead humanity to a changed conception of itself. This I conceive to be the true function of the writer and his art.

25

National Book Award Address,
March 3, 1959

Ladies and gentlemen: thank you for the honor.

A small miracle has come to pass, and I am grateful to the judges, among other things for their courage. I hope the choice of a non-best-selling short-story collection sets a precedent for more of the same. The short story, as you know, is strong and accomplished in American fiction, and I hope that some of its expert practitioners, especially those who come rarely if ever to the novel, will be recognized by you in the future, and their work, valuable for us all, brought emphatically to public attention.

May I say a word about an idea that animates my writing?

To put it simply, I am tired of the colossally deceitful devaluation of man in this day, for whatever explanation: that life is cheap amid a prevalence or wars; or because we are drugged by totalitarian successes into a sneaking belief in their dehumanizing propaganda; or tricked beyond self-respect by the values of the creators of our own thing-ridden society; as when demography counting two where there was one, by the law of supply and demand cheapens all; or because, having invented the means of his extinction, man values himself less for it and lives in daily dread that he will—in a fit of passion, pique, or absentmindedness—achieve his end. Whatever the reason, his fall from grace in his eyes is betrayed in the words he has invented to describe himself as he is now: fragmented, abbreviated, other-directed, organizational, anonymous man, a victim, in the words that are used to describe him of a kind of synechdochic irony, the part for the whole. The devaluation exists because he accepts it without protest.

However, the writer dare not accept it; he *must* not, or his art, too, will suffer grave loss, just as it suffers when he depicts man according to the tenets of economic or psychological theories that only partly explain him, that in the end abstract from who he is or may be. Theory is fine to awaken insight or institute therapy, but, as Freud and others well knew, it is no substitute for art; if theory is substituted for the necessary probings, the impassioned explorations of art, it maims a complex infinitude—man with the sky in his head—by crippling the writer's imagination and distorting his vision. If the writer does not stay clear of these false restrictions upon his writing, no matter what he may achieve thus restricted, there can be no triumph of character, of person, of *human* being. It seems to me that his most important task, no matter *what* the current theory of man, or his prevailing mood, is to recapture his image as *human* being as each of us in his secret heart knows it to be, and as history and literature have from the beginning revealed it. At the same time the writer must imagine a better world for men the while he shows us, in all its ugliness and beauty, the possibilities of this. In recreating the humanity of man, in reality his greatness, he will, among other things, hold up the mirror to the mystery of him, in which poetry and possibility live, though he has endlessly betrayed them. In a sense, the writer in his art, without directly stating it (though *he* may preach, his *work* must not) must remind man that he has, in his human striving, invented nothing less than freedom; and if he will devoutly remember this, he will understand the best way to preserve it and his own highest value.

Ladies and gentlemen: I've had something such as this in mind, as I wrote, however imperfectly, my sad and comic tales.

Thank you.

26

A MIGHTY THEME

◆

National Book Award Address, 1967

One thinks a good deal about
the subject matter of his fiction: What can he write about that will,
almost of itself, contribute to his book's originality, strength, distinction? Melville, who journeyed from *Typee* to *Moby Dick*, stated it, you
will remember, in these terms: "To produce a mighty book you must
choose a mighty theme." His corollary was that one couldn't write a
great and enduring book about the life of a flea. I'm not so sure about
that—it seems to me that a writer with a profusion of metaphor like
Barth might make a go of it. However, it's obvious that a mighty theme
doesn't necessarily guarantee a mighty book. Some writers may chance
upon one and don't know that they have it. And some who recognize
such themes—indeed, keep lists of them in their billfolds—once they
try to make use of them, beat a hollow drum. They may attempt to work
with a fine theme but it doesn't evoke anything in their nature, or excite
their experience, or speak to their talent. A god or hero appears on paper,
but the visage is Rock Hudson's and the voice is the voice of Bob Dylan.
What the matter boils down to, I think, is that a mighty theme is useful only when it inspires a good writer to a symphonic response. When
it proliferates possibilities in every thought. If one is, as an individual,
moved by themes that could be called "mighty," obviously it will pay
him to seek them out, a task that isn't so simple, because the mighty
themes have been used again and again, and one must discover how they
can be presented in such a way as to seem new. On the other hand, no
subject or theme is *verboten*, and any theme, however slight, may in the

right hands be embodied in a work of art, though the danger is that at best it may be the work of a miniaturist. Of course there is scope, depth, breadth in the novel, and these qualities are not only the province of genius; the writer who makes the effort to educate himself may find his way to them.

Theme has an almost tangible quality—it has texture, visibility, flavor, but these differ from book to book and, of course, from writer to writer. Think, for example, of Melville himself, Mark Twain, Cervantes, E. M. Forster, Hemingway, Faulkner, Tolstoy. Sometimes theme seems surface deep, almost touchable; sometimes it lies hidden in dusk or a deeper dark and may reveal itself as light long after the book has been read, in sudden insight; and sometimes it invisibly transfigures the very experience it seems to be not present in. It is, of course, not an intrusion in art; it is an effect of imagination. It has as much value in the art of fiction as anything else in fiction provided that (whatever its effect on the reader) it has become an aspect of the book's form. By drawing the action close to its ultimate elucidation it helps create the artwork of the novel, just as plot, characterization may help, and that which we call style. To achieve style the writer must envision the essence of the work; and it is envisioned partly with a plan, partly without, in the act of writing as possibilities occur, and the book as a form emerges. Theme which may also be discovered in the writing—one doesn't clip it out and paste it on the page—may lead to understanding essence, hence to style and form. If the theme, unimaginatively handled, hardens to exoskeleton, or drips like printer's ink from the center of the fiction, then the failure is of the art and not of the worth of the theme. The existence of theme, contrary to the thinking of some, does not contaminate the work. It achieves the formal value in art that only an artist can give it. Theme comes from understanding, knowledge, though it may pretend to show neither. History can be shaped to contain theme, but then it is no longer history. It becomes, when the form of the work is right, fiction partly through the effect of crystallization in time, as Stendhal's branch is crystallized.

But theme, according to the latest in criticism, is meaning, "signification," imposed by interpretation; therefore content in fiction, and content interferes with the ascendancy of form. To subordinate content to the highest concerns of art—to art as pure esthetic—new forms, different forms from those in traditional use—the argument goes—must be conceived. The traditional novel, though it may run in a path "parallel" to the "new novel," is burdened by narrative, characterization ("Our world . . . has renounced the omnipotence of the person"), and an anthropomorphic view of experience; therefore it ought to be replaced by a novel whose content is the form of form. The purpose of the new novel, according to Robbe-Grillet, is "to construct a world more solid and more immediate" rather than "a universe of signification"—to present, in other words, what is there; hence a seeking of new forms "capable of expressing (or of creating) new relations between man and the world." As a writer, I would most gladly welcome the invention of new forms that may bring the novel to greater power, but I cannot welcome a theory of the novel that will ultimately diminish the value of a writer's experience, historical and personal, by limiting its use in fiction. I was born just before the profuse bloodletting of the First World War, as massive armies assaulted each other over the scarred, corpse-strewn fields of France. I have not forgotten the bleak, hungry depression that for years corroded the American land. Nor how Stalin's Moscow Trials were passionately defended by men of goodwill. Then Adolph Hitler, a fanatic with a soul that stank, came to power in Germany. A line of Jews more than a thousand miles long, one by one stepped into gas chambers to breathe in their extermination. The Second World War, begun in a graveyard of sinking ships, ended with atomic bombs destroying Hiroshima and Nagasaki, bombs that should never have been dropped. The Cold War spawned, among other things, Senator McCarthy, who turned men into cowards the length and breadth of this nation. Overnight a new war flamed in Korea. A young American president had the back of his head shot off into the hands of his wife. In Vietnam, a small, gentle-faced people, caught between two armies, have become living torches.

How can one think of diminishing, underplaying, or giving up content in fiction if he has been moved by these events and attempts to understand them? What moves me moves me to art. What moves me to art I may deal with in any of a hundred ways. To say that this is the world and it is there is hardly satisfying or sufficient. I must as a writer say what I think of the world.

Since time is short let me limit myself to a few related observations:

1. A new novel will not come as the result of a theory or program in essence reductive, incomplete, proclaiming the part for the whole. Like everything else in the world the novel is changing but a new novel will, in all probability, appear when a single master of fiction

sits down and writes it. What one gives to fiction is what he has to give, not what is prescribed. One gives as much as he can; he limits as art demands, not definition.

2. I welcome, as I said before, the seeking for new forms of fiction. However, no form dies; they are all (traditional or not yet traditional) eternally available to the artist to use in a manner original to him. He reinvents them as he uses them. A nineteenth-century form used by a twentieth-century novelist becomes a twentieth-century form. Nothing is outdated if it works. The best form for an artist is that which uses his greatest strength.

3. That the world is present is only a small portion of the truth available to art. In the novel the world appears in language, itself a form of interpretation; therefore why should it not be further valued, judged, explained? One cannot sit on language; it moves beyond the presence of things into the absence of things, the illusion of things. Art must interpret or it is mindless. Mindlessness is not mystery, it is the absence of mystery. Content cannot be disinvented. Description of the world is not enough when it may be necessary to proscribe it.

4. If the world, as some say, is an esthetic phenomenon, so, too, in its way, is humanity. One might argue that there is such a thing as an esthetic of behavior. Wasn't it Santayana who said that the purpose of love is to increase beauty? Morality may have more than one source in beauty. Art is, moreover, the invention of the human artist, not an act of God or nature. To preserve itself it must, in a variety of subtle ways, conserve the artist through sanctifying life and human freedom.

5. If one is moved by the mighty theme he had better go find it.

Ladies and Gentlemen, I thank you.